Land Warfare: Brassey's New Battlefield
Weapons Systems & Technology Series

Volume 5

Communications and Information Systems for Battlefield Command and Control

Land Warfare: Brassey's New Battlefield Weapons Systems and Technology Series

---

Executive Editor: COLONEL R. G. LEE OBE, former Military Director of Studies, Royal Military College of Science, Shrivenham, UK

Editor-in-Chief: PROFESSOR FRANK HARTLEY, Principal and Dean, Royal Military College of Science, Shrivenham, UK

The success of the first series on Battlefield Weapons Systems and Technology and the pace of advances in military technology has prompted Brassey's to produce a new Land Warfare series. This series updates subjects covered in the original series and also covers completely new areas. The books are written for military men who wish to advance their professional knowledge. In addition, they are intended to aid anyone who is interested in the design, development and production of military equipment.

Volume 1   Guided Weapons R. G. LEE *et al*

Volume 2   Explosives, Propellants and Pyrotechnics A. BAILEY AND S. G. MURRAY

Volume 3   Noise in the Military Environment R. F. POWELL AND M. R. FORREST

Volume 4   Ammunition E. ARCHER AND P. R. COURTNEY-GREEN

Volume 6   Military Helicopters E. J. EVERETT-HEATH *et al*

Other titles of interest by Brassey's

PERKINS   Brassey's Weapons and Warfare

SHAKER & WISE   War without Men

SLOAN   Mine Warfare on Land

Other series published by Brassey's

Brassey's Sea Power: Naval Vessels, Weapons Systems and Technology Series
General Editor: DR G. TILL

Brassey's Air Power: Aircraft, Weapons Systems and Technology Series
General Editor: AIR VICE MARSHAL R. A. MASON

Communications and Information Systems for Battlefield Command and Control

M. A. Rice and A. J. Sammes
Royal Military College of Science, Shrivenham, UK

Brassey's (UK)
(Member of the Maxwell Pergamon Publishing Corporation)

LONDON · OXFORD · WASHINGTON · NEW YORK · BEIJING
FRANKFURT · SÃO PAULO · SYDNEY · TOKYO · TORONTO

UK (Editorial)	Brassey's (UK) Ltd., 24 Gray's Inn Road, London WC1X 8HR, England
(Orders, all except North America)	Brassey's (UK) Ltd., Headington Hill Hall, Oxford OX3 0BW, England
USA (Editorial)	Brassey's (US) Inc., 8000 Westpark Drive, Fourth Floor, McLean, Virginia 22102, USA
(Orders, North America)	Brassey's (US) Inc., Front and Brown Streets, Riverside, New Jersey 08075, USA Tel (toll free): 800 257 5755
PEOPLE'S REPUBLIC OF CHINA	Pergamon Press, Room 4037, Qianmen Hotel, Beijing, People's Republic of China
FEDERAL REPUBLIC OF GERMANY	Pergamon Press GmbH, Hammerweg 6, D-6242 Kronberg, Federal Republic of Germany
BRAZIL	Pergamon Editora Ltda, Rua Eça de Queiros, 346, CEP 04011, Paraiso, São Paulo, Brazil
AUSTRALIA	Brassey's Australia Pty Ltd., P.O. Box 544, Potts Point, N.S.W. 2011, Australia
JAPAN	Pergamon Press, 5th Floor, Matsuoka Central Building, 1-7-1 Nishishinjuku, Shinjuku-ku, Tokyo 160, Japan
CANADA	Pergamon Press Canada Ltd., Suite No. 271, 253 College Street, Toronto, Ontario, Canada M5T 1R5

Copyright © 1989 Brassey's (UK)

First edition 1989

Library of Congress Cataloging in Publication Data
M.A. Rice.
Communications and information systems for battlefield command and control/Rice, M.A. and Sammes A.J. — 1st ed.
p. cm. — (Land warfare; v. 5)
1. Command and control systems. I. Sammes, A.J.
II. Title   III. Series.
UB212.R53   1989   355.3'3041—dc20   89–9900

British Library Cataloguing in Publication Data
M.A. Rice
Communications and information systems for battlefield command and control.
1. Military communications equipment
I. Title   II. A.J. Sammes   III. Series
623.7.3

ISBN 0–08–036266 4 Hardcover
ISBN 0–08–036267 2 Flexicover

Cover photographs: *Top left*—M239 Smoke Grenade Launcher (*US Army photograph*); *Bottom left*—MLRS (*US Army photograph*); *Right*—Headquarters Operating Environment (© *M. Rice*).

Printed in Great Britain by BPCC Wheatons Ltd., Exeter

To Anna and Joan

Preface

This Series

This series of books is written for those who wish to improve their knowledge of military weapons and equipment. It is equally relevant to professional soldiers, those involved in developing or producing military weapons or indeed anyone interested in the art of modern warfare.

All the texts are written in a way which assumes no mathematical knowledge and no more technical depth than would be gleaned by any person who keeps himself or herself informed of developments in the modern world. It is intended that the books should be of particular interest to officers in the Armed Services wishing to further their professional knowledge as well as anyone involved in research, development, production, testing and maintenance of defence equipments.

The principal authors of the books are all members of the staff of the Royal Military College of Science, Shrivenham, which is composed of a unique blend of academic and military experts. They are not only leaders in the technology of their subjects, but are aware of what the military practitioner needs to know. It is difficult to imagine any group of persons more fitted to write about the application of technology to the battlefield.

This Volume

For the first time since the advent of the blitzkreig, Information Technology promises to allow the commander of a force to keep abreast with what is happening on the battlefield. Field Marshal Rommel failed to solve the problem with the rudimentary technology available to him in the desert. Consequently he was frequently to be lost to his headquarters, trying to find out for himself what was happening to the troops in combat. A modern commander, with a far more complex battle pattern, should now be able to maintain contact with his command system and have the filtered mass of information from the battle produced for him in the form of intelligence. He should then be able to act decisively and in a timely manner to influence the outcome of the battle.

August, 1989   FRANK HARTLEY
Shrivenham   GEOFFREY LEE

Foreword

by LIEUTENANT GENERAL SIR DAVID RAMSBOTHAM, KCB, CBE

The Information Technology revolution promises to change our lives even more than its agricultural and industrial predecessors. It is a curious phenomenon, because, while practically everyone can appreciate that this will be so, few know enough about how the technology can be harnessed to help them in their particular employment, and ensure that man remains its master rather than becomes its slave.

For no profession is this more true than the Armed Forces, for whom information becomes a force multiplier if properly harnessed. Ideally this harnessing should be done by those who have particular operational responsibilities or functions to perform, who are therefore in the best position to be able to decide which operational procedures would benefit from being automated. The problem is that very few of today's commanders know enough about what technology can do for them, or are able to advise a developer about what they actually want. This will, it is to be hoped, not apply to tomorrow's generation, which, having been brought up with the technology, will not only understand it—and not be frightened of it—but will know how to use it. But it is up to today's to prepare for tomorrow's.

The problem here is that there are few sources on which those with current responsibilities can draw. I therefore welcome Lieutenant Colonel Rice and Professor Sammes's book, which will do much to redress that situation. It is a particular honour and pleasure for me to be invited to write this foreword because, having been thrown into the IT deep end as a complete and utter ignoramus, I was rescued by being given Professor—or Colonel as he then was—Sammes as my technical guide and mentor for a study. This was a priceless advantage, and I can testify from firsthand experience that there is no one better qualified to explain the role of CIS on the battlefield to those who have to introduce or use it, now or in the future.

Professor Sammes had the foresight to realise the potential importance of CIS as a young officer. This is not the place to catalogue his unique career, but, on his own initiative, he became a pioneer in the field of harnessing Information Technology to the needs of the military commanders, in the United Kingdom, the United States and NATO, where he is held in high regard. Tomorrow's generation is fortunate that it will not labour under the disadvantages of today's, because it will have been taught by him at the Royal Military College of Science.

Lieutenant Colonel Rice is also a member of the College staff and a graduate of its Design of Information Systems MSc course. In co-authoring this book he has drawn on experience gained in a variety of appointments in both the communications and the information systems field.

I am delighted that Professor Sammes and Lieutenant Colonel Rice have committed their wisdom to print, so that those of us with immediate responsibilities for ensuring that our successors will have a battlefield CIS that they can exploit and develop, may have our direction sharpened and refined. I wish the book well, and hope that it will be read widely and with advantage.

Acknowledgements

The authors would like to express their thanks to all those who have helped with the production of this book:

General Sir Martin Farndale, KCB, for giving a fascinating insight into the nature of command, based on his experience of field command at every level up to and including Army Group;

Brigadier Sam Cowan, for his views on the command and control process, based on his experience as a senior CIS 'provider';

Mr David Thorpe of Dicoll Electronics Ltd, Basingstoke, for his help with the section on the ruggedisation of equipment;

All the providers of photographs and other illustrations, who are individually acknowledged where their contributions appear in the book.

Colleagues past and present of Computing Science Group at the Royal Military College of Science Shrivenham, and, in particular, Professor Ken Hunt, Dr George Bate, Mr John Hunter, Ms Morfydd Edwards and Mr Martin Lee for their helpful views, comments and discussions;

Colleagues of Planning Wing at the School of Signals, Blandford, for providing a fertile background of ideas, comments, criticisms and discussion.

MSDOS is a trademark of the MicroSoft Corporation.
UNIX is a trademark of AT & T.
VAX is a trademark of the Digital Equipment Corporation.
Occam is a trademark of Inmos Ltd.

Contents

Contents

List of Illustrations

List of Illustrations

List of Tables

Authors' Introduction

Other books in this series tell us how modern weapons systems and other battle-field equipment are being developed and improved in capability through ever-increasing technological complexity. None of these systems could be used to their full effectiveness, and most of them would be hardly of any use at all, without the means to direct and control their employment. The basic requirement for command and control communications and information systems (CIS) has always existed, but the scale and complexity of that requirement has had to increase to match the increased capabilities in speed of reaction and range of coverage of modern weapon systems.

The relationship of CIS to the command function is a central theme of this book, which introduces the reader to the principles and practice of modern CIS. After defining and describing the key principles and terminology in the CIS field, the book identifies and describes CIS components with reference to a model of the command and control process. The first part of the book is devoted to an account of the 'enabling technologies' of computer hardware, software and communications.

Having dealt in the earlier chapters with the basic 'nuts and bolts' of CIS hardware and software design, the book turns to examine the specific problems of designing systems which can survive on the battlefield. The requirement for, and the difficulties of, interoperability, both between national systems and those of our allies, are discussed, and the book includes a comprehensive account of the vital topic of information security. The penultimate chapter is devoted to an account of the expected impact of CIS on the Army's organisation and concept of operations in the near to medium term. The claim that CIS can, or should, act as a 'force multiplier' is examined. Finally, the book looks further into the future and considers the ways in which CIS technology might be expected to develop.

1.

Introduction

Introduction

Information has always been the commander's most important resource. Without timely and accurate details of the enemy's location, strength and intentions, and of the deployment and preparedness of his own forces, the commander's ability to fight the battle would be severely limited, no matter how effective his weapon systems may be, nor how well trained his troops. Communication has been recognised since ancient times as a distinct branch of the military profession, but it is only in the last couple of decades that the whole subject of information systems to support the command and control process, which, of course, includes communications, has been studied in a systematic way and treated as a topic in its own right. It would help to put the rest of this book into context if we take a little time to consider why this should be so.

There is no need to go right back to ancient times to find a suitable example of the way land warfare used to be; the battle of Waterloo, fought less than two centuries ago, will do as well as any. It would seem to be highly unlikely that either of the famous protagonists at Waterloo could have gained much benefit from the sort of automated support available to the modern commander. During the battle, in which Wellington deployed a force of 70,000 men in an area about the same as that occupied today by a mechanised company group, either commander could (provided he stayed alive) remain in personal contact with his subordinates and see for himself how the battle was progressing. All he needed to apply his tactical skill and leadership was his spyglass, a good horse, a supply of messengers, a lot of courage and a fair measure of luck.

To say that things are different today is something of an understatement, but it is worth examining the key areas of difference. First, the commander's area of interest has been increased by several orders of magnitude by the development of longer range weapons and sensors, and the increased mobility of the deployed forces. Equate Wellington to an Army commander and compare his area of interest with that of, say, Commander Northern Army Group in NATO's Central Region in the late 1980s! Second, speed of movement on the battlefield has increased enormously. Forces may be deployed by helicopter within minutes over terrain which would take foot soldiers many hours or even days to cover, and the threat posed to ground forces by fighter ground-attack aircraft may materialise with devastating suddenness. Finally, an overwhelming need for flexibility of response and the need to make the most effective use of numerically inferior forces are inherent features of the NATO defence strategy. To have any chance at all of coping effectively with the complexity of command and control on the battlefield of the late 20th century the commander must have the support of automated communications and information systems. It should also be mentioned that the size of the commander's supporting staff has grown over the years to keep pace with the increased complexity and span of command.

It would be wrong, however, to argue that Command and Control Communications and Information Systems (CIS) are being developed purely as a timely response to changing requirements. The requirements existed long before the technology was available to satisfy them. An armoured formation commander of the Second World War would recognise much in the equipment and procedures used by a modern armoured brigade, but he would not be accustomed to any communications support beyond single-channel voice radio backed up by morse, nor any information recording and display system more complex than map and chinagraph. The two technologies which have contributed most to the information systems revolution are the development of digital techniques for the representation and processing of information, and microelectronics. CIS, based on these two technologies, may provide the means for commanders to cope with the increased range and mobility of weapon systems and satisfy the need for flexibility, but in so doing they have the potential to go well beyond that. The synergistic effect of CIS will create a new area of capability, which will bring about radical changes in battlefield organisation and procedures. Current CIS development is at about the same stage as that of the tank when it was first introduced on the Western Front in the First World War. Most people can understand the obvious potential and look forward to its realisation, but the systems are neither fully deployed nor totally reliable, and some of the more conservative, potential users have yet to be convinced of their worth. It is a theme explored later in this book that, once CIS have progressed beyond the stage of getting bogged down rather too frequently in metaphorical ditches, their impact will far exceed that of the armoured fighting vehicle.

Terms and Definitions

The Need

The medium which is all too likely to bog down the student of Command and Control Communications and Information Systems is the mass of acronyms and abbreviations which abounds in this field. Most articles on the subject in the defence literature are sprinkled with terms made up of a number of Cs (anything from 1 to 5 nowadays) combined with I and sometimes S, e.g. C^{3}I, CCIS, C^{2}IS, and CIS. Although there is a full glossary of terms at the end of the book, which has included where possible the NATO agreed definitions, it is important at this stage to define and explain some of the more commonly used titles and expressions which are used in this book.

CIS

We have already used the abbreviation CIS in this chapter, without formal explanation or definition. It is important that the abbreviation be explained and defined without further delay. Although CIS is a widely used abbreviation, there is some divergence of opinion over both what the letters stand for and the scope of what is described by them. The abbreviation CIS as used here is taken to stand for Command and Control Communications and Information Systems. We are therefore dealing with the communications and information systems (assumed to be based on digital microelectronics) used to support the command and control process. To put CIS into its correct context it is therefore necessary to look more closely at the whole command and control process, and the role played by communications and information systems.

Command and Control

Command and Control is perhaps the most obvious of the terms we have to define. All commanders and staffs have their own interpretation of its meaning, which is probably one of the reasons why it currently has no officially accepted definition within NATO. Command as a concept is straightforward enough, although if we are looking for a definition of it the one given by the Roman centurion quoted in the New Testament is as succinct as any:

> For I am a man under authority, having soldiers under me: and I say to this man, go, and he goeth; and to another, come, and he cometh . . .
> [Matthew, c. 8, v. 9]

This definition brings out both the function of command, that is, the giving of orders to subordinates, and the fact that the authority to do so is derived from above. At the simplest level both command and control are exercised by a single person. It could be argued that the centurion is exercising command, when, having regard to the authority vested in him by his superiors, he deems it necessary for the achievement of his mission that man A should go and man B should come. In actually telling them to do so he is exercising control. Thus within a headquarters which is made up of a commander and his staff, we may say that the commander commands by taking the major decisions, and his staff control by turning those decisions into detailed orders and issuing them for execution. If we need a definition of command and control taken together, the following is offered:

> The process of directing and coordinating military forces in the execution of the commander's will, and the exercising of his authority over all or part of the activities of subordinate organisations.

Communication

Communication may be defined as the process of transferring or conveying information from one place to another, or the means for so doing. In the term Communication System, the word 'system' implies that there is more involved than a simple one-to-one link; communication is being provided by an ordered assembly of co-operating elements, i.e. a system.

Information System

Information is defined in the *Oxford English Dictionary* as 'items of knowledge', which is a satisfactory definition for our purposes. An 'information system' there-fore is a system which handles information, and 'handles' may include any or all of processing, storage or communication. It is normally assumed that the system being described is a computer-based system, that is, one which handles infor-mation in a digital electronic form, under the control of a digital computer or processor. From the definition given here, it may be inferred that a communication system is a form of information system. Strictly speaking, therefore, in defining CIS as Command and Control Communications and Information Systems we are guilty of tautology. Our excuse is that it is necessary to stress that communication is an integral part of the subject, by making it explicit in the title.

Command and Control System

The term 'command and control system' describes the combination of infor-mation systems (including communications systems), procedures and personnel used to effect the command and control process. The term may be qualified, for example to indicate the operational environment, e.g. Air Command and Control System, or the level of command, e.g. Tactical Command and Control System. The term Total Command and Control System (TCCS), used to embrace the com-mand and control of forces in all environments at every level of command from the highest strategic to the lowest tactical level, is sometimes encountered. A 'family tree', breaking down the concept of a TCCS into its component parts, is shown in Figure 1.1. The diagram emphasises the Tactical, Battlefield branch of the tree, since that is the area of concern in this book. It recognises that, even under the overall heading of tactical battlefield command and control systems, there will be a number of different information systems. Those serving headquarters are identified as headquarters information processing systems. There has been a tend-ency within NATO armies to develop separate information systems to serve the needs of the different so-called battlefield functional areas (intelligence, manoeuvre control, fire support, etc.). These are shown as Specialist Information Systems. The key to the effective operation of the whole command and control system is the way in which these specialist systems can interoperate with each other and with the headquarters information processing system; for example, by sharing information of common interest. This topic is examined in detail in Chap-ter 9.

The Battlefield

We have used the term 'battlefield' in the title of the book, and for that reason alone the term deserves some definition. It is used to describe the fact that we are concerned with communications and information systems to control forces engaged in the land battle (or more completely, the land/air battle, therefore we must include the airspace over the battlefield in our definition of battlefield). Thus what we are dealing with is the 'tactical' level of command, and within NATO this has been regarded in recent years as Corps and below. Selecting Corps as the highest level of battlefield command, and defining the limit of the battlefield as the Corps Rear Boundary may have some advantages, but it is becoming increasingly out of line with the development of operational concepts within NATO. We have, therefore, chosen to define the battlefield for our purposes as the area of responsibility of an Army Group, viewing the Army Group Commander as the highest level of tactical command.

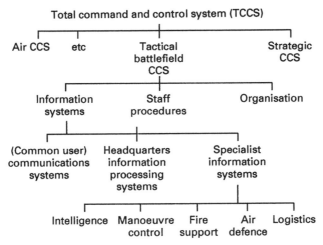

FIG. 1.1   The Total Command and Control System (TCCS)

The Nature of the Command and Control Process

The use of the term 'control' implies that the process under consideration may have something in common with control theory, or cybernetics. This last word is derived from the Greek word for a helmsman, and the word 'governor' has the same origins, which gives us a good clue as to the nature of the systems described. It would be instructive at this stage to examine a basic cybernetic or control system, and see how useful it is as a model for the study of military command and control systems. One of the simplest examples of such a system is illustrated in Figure 1.2.

The Simple Control System

The system illustrated is typical of those used to control the central heating in a house. The desired temperature is set by an external order, that is, by the user turning a control to the appropriate setting—in this case to 'maintain 65 degrees'. The temperature sensor produces monitoring information proportional to the ambient temperature, which is compared with the control setting. If the measured temperature, say 60 degrees, is lower than the desired temperature, a crude con-

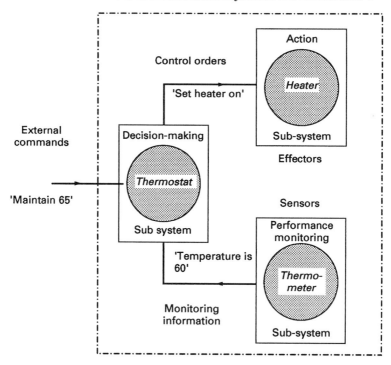

FIG. 1.2   Simple Control System

trol order (normally a simple on/off signal) is sent to the boiler system—the effector—telling it to generate more heat. Once the ambient temperature reaches the demanded setting the 'on' command is removed and the boiler system ceases to generate and circulate heat. Of course this is a very simple autonomous system; only one quantity is under control, and the 'decision making' element is a straightforward comparator. The only external input is the setting of the desired temperature; once set there is no further external interference. The value of the example is in identifying the basic components of a control system, for these same components are all present to some extent in the much more complex systems used for the control of forces on the battlefield. The basic components of the generalised control system are:

▶ The Decision-Making Sub-System
▶ The Performance Monitoring Sub-System
▶ The Action Sub-System

If we take the same approach to the simplest military command and control system, the result is as shown in Figure 1.3.

In this system, the external demand is the task or mission set by the superior headquarters; here shown as 'execute fireplan ALFA'. The three sub-systems are represented as follows:

Decision-Making Sub-System: In this example the decision-making sub-system

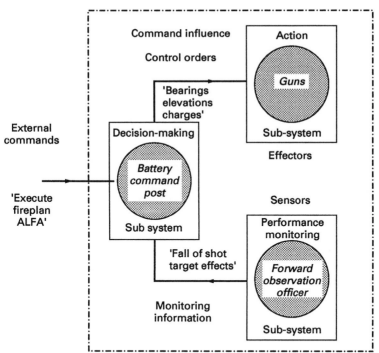

FIG. 1.3 Military Command and Control System

is very much more complex than the simple comparator used by the heating system. Not only are the quantities to be compared or assessed much more complicated, there is also an element of uncertainty involved. The battery commander must monitor the progress of his forces in the execution of his orders. If his view of that progress, which may be incomplete or uncertain, should indicate any divergence from the aim set, he may choose to issue further orders. He will also be required to report back to his superiors, thereby providing a higher level control system with one of its sources of control feedback or performance monitoring.

Performance Monitoring Sub-System: The decision maker will obtain information on which to base his decisions from all the sources available to him, including reports from the forces under command, sensor output and in some cases the evidence of his own eyes. We have shown in this example 'target effects' and 'fall of shot' reports coming from a Forward Observation Officer.

Action Sub-System: The action sub-system is represented by the gun detachments, which are given control orders in the form of 'bearings', 'timings', 'charges', and so forth.

An element which was taken for granted in the heating system example was communications, because the relatively short lengths of copper wire used to connect the elements of the system represent a virtually perfect communications system. This is not the case with the military command and control system, where communication must be considered as a sub-system in its own right. The system elements may be widely separated, and whatever form of communication is used it will be subject to constraints and vulnerable to enemy action, either physical or electronic or both. Imperfect communication channels contribute to the element of uncertainty in the battlefield command and control process.

These two examples serve to give some useful insight into the nature of the command and control process. The three sub-systems: performance monitoring, action and decision making, together with the interconnecting communications elements, form a closed-loop control system. External demands may be placed on this control system which may alter its internal aims, tasks and goals, and the system may be required to return external reports. From the viewpoint of some higher level authority, this control system may itself be seen as but one element of a higher level control system. To the extent that the command exercised by the lower level commander is a part of the overall process performed by that system, one could say that command at one level may be viewed as part of control at a higher level. This brings us back to the definitions of the terms command and control earlier in this chapter. The essential nature of command in the context of the examples we have been looking at here is that it represents the inclusion of man in the control loop.

So far in this discussion of the control model we have been looking at the system simply as a collection of sensors, effectors, communications links and information processors. Control systems that include man in the loop are much more complex than this. Each human element has an individual world view of his place in the system, of the goals of the organisation to which he belongs, of its achievements, of its culture and of its values; much of these we attempt to convey by the word 'ethos'. It is this that a good commander uses to develop within his command a synergism that welds together an effective team out of a number of separate individuals, striving to establish that most vital of all team characteristics: high morale. For this to succeed the personality of the commander must come through the system and he must be perceived to be in complete command.

All this has important implications for command and control systems, which must therefore be capable of conveying the presence and personality of the commander and of transmitting his intentions to his subordinates on those occasions when he has to be remote geographically from his command. We have shown this on the simple model by the phrase 'command influence'.

It is also important for the system to be able to adapt itself to different 'styles of command'. It has already been mentioned that command is a personal thing; whilst there are obvious basic principles which every commander must adhere to, there is a lot of scope for differences in individual styles, and any automated system which seriously diminishes or constrains that scope does so at some risk to its overall effectiveness.

A More Complex Military Command and Control System

We have already recognised in the previous description of the simple military command and control system that the control cycle or loop described operates at every level of command. Thus if we are to take a complete view of the command and control system operating at, say, divisional level, our system must include the control loops of all the formations subordinate to the division, and recognise that the division's control system is part of the control loop of its superior head-quarters, i.e. Corps Headquarters. This situation is illustrated in Figure 1.4.

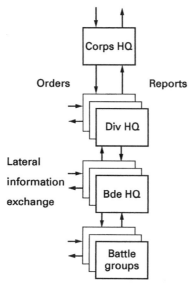

FIG. 1.4   Divisional Command and Control System

Having used the cybernetic model to identify the component elements of the command and control system, we will make no further attempt at this stage to apply it rigorously to the analysis of military command and control systems. Some authors do take the analysis much further; for example, the system dynamics technique for the modelling of command and control systems is essentially a cybernetic approach in which the interactions of the various elements of the system upon each other are quantified, in order to create a mathematical model of the system. This is a difficult and subjective area; we will accept for the present that military command and control systems behave approximately like control systems, without attempting to define the relationships with mathematical rigour. It will serve our purposes better to concentrate for the moment on the nature of the tasks which must be performed by the command and control system.

Command and Control Processes

The obvious starting point for an analysis of the tasks to be performed by CIS is the cybernetic model described earlier in the chapter. You will recall that this model breaks the system down into three sub-systems: the performance monitoring, the decision making and the action sub-system. We can afford to use the simple, single loop view of the process in this case, recognising that the functions identified on the way will be represented at different levels in the command hierarchy.

The Performance Monitoring Sub-System

This function represents the activity of gathering all the information needed by the decision-making sub-system. In a battlefield CIS this will include intelligence, that is, information concerning the enemy, his strength, disposition and intentions; information concerning the deployment and state of readiness of our own forces; and 'neutral' information, such as details of the terrain and the prevailing weather conditions. All these classes of information are present in the simple example used in Figure 1.3, based on a gunnery system. The intelligence required is a description of the target; where it is, what it is, what it is doing and what is to be done to it. Own forces information needed in this case would include the location and status of our own gun batteries, in order to assess which (if any) is best placed to engage the target; and weather information is a vital factor in the ballistic calculations to be performed in order to land the rounds accurately on the target.

The functions to be performed to support the performance monitoring sub-system are mainly concerned with information capture. This is an aspect covered in detail in Chapter 5, which is concerned with the man–machine interface (MMI). It is a cardinal rule of system design that the method chosen must be matched as closely as possible to the circumstances of whoever is putting the information in. A system which required an observer in a position very close to the enemy to go through a laborious keyboard dialogue in order to call for fire on a target would not find much favour with its users, and, as a result, would probably not perform very well.

The Decision-Making Sub-System

This is the area where the majority of CIS processing functions are to be found. To carry out its task the decision-making sub-system must:

- ▶ Assemble all the available information from the performance monitoring sub-system
- ▶ Analyse and assess the information in order to determine what is happening (or about to happen)
- ▶ Determine how the results of the above analysis affect the current mission; in other words, compare what is apparently happening with what is meant to be happening
- ▶ On the basis of the determination above, identify options for further action (or possibly, inaction)
- ▶ Decide on the course to follow
- ▶ Prepare and issue orders to the action sub-system

These decision-making sub-system functions may be supported by the following classes of CIS process:

Presentation

The system must present information to its users in the way which is best suited to their needs. For instance, a graphical display of unit locations on an electronic map is much more useful than a table of unit titles and locations in the form of numerical grid references displayed on a visual display unit (VDU). Information overload is a serious risk, especially as the capabilities of the performance monitoring sub-system increase, with the introduction of more sensor systems and improved communications. Although by itself it will probably not be enough to solve the problem, well-designed information presentation is a key factor in the prevention of overload.

Collation

This term is used in its most general sense to imply that information from a number of different sources must be assembled together to provide the best possible description of the true situation. As we saw at the start of this chapter, the information system contains a model of that section of the 'real world' which is of interest to the system's users. It will differ from an exact representation of the real world because the information on which the model is based will inevitably be incomplete, of different time origins, inconsistent between different sources, and distorted by 'noise' on the communications channels. In the present generation of military CIS, the evaluation of the information and the decision as to which items of information relate to which events in the real world are functions carried out by humans. The system merely presents the information to the user, collated in accordance with specified criteria, such as time and place, and the user interprets the information according to what is presented and his own knowledge both of the immediate situation and the 'patterns' which are likely to be presented by given activities. For example, an intelligence officer will look at contact reports, input from remote surveillance devices and all other available information relating to a specific area of the battlefield during a specific time period. From this information and his own knowledge of the enemy's basic organisation and normal operational methods, he will interpret the information to suggest what is happening, and, more importantly, what might be about to happen.

Fusion

The use of the term 'fusion' in the CIS context implies that some degree of evaluation is performed by the system. Items of information which are judged by the system to relate to the same event are flagged as such. Inferences are drawn by the system to suggest the meaning and significance of the fused data. This is an example of the knowledge-based system approach, which is described in more detail in Chapter 12. Suffice it to say at this stage that the technique is based on the embodiment in the system of some of the expert knowledge of the intelligence officer as described above. The system will hold details of enemy organisations and patterns of activity, and a mechanism or set of rules for assessing the input information to see if it fits any of the patterns.

Calculation

Much of the information handled by the system will be numerical, dealing particularly with numbers or quantities of men, vehicles, equipments, fuel, ammunition, etc. Thus the simplest type of calculation to be performed by the information system is the arithmetic manipulation of these items of numerical information to produce sums, averages and other statistical operations. More complex numerical calculations are called for in weapon systems, where the combination of target and gun locations, weapon characteristics and meteorological conditions must be transformed into firing instructions for the guns in the form of bearing and elevation. In air-defence artillery systems, the need to engage fast moving targets increases both the complexity and the required speed of calculation.

Modelling

The view of the information system as containing a model of that portion of the real world which is of interest to the system users has already been introduced above. This idea may be taken further, if the users have the ability to create a separate, hypothetical model which is used to determine the outcome of different options—the so-called 'what if?' type of analysis.

Decision Support

The term 'decision support' is commonly used to describe systems which analyse the situation described by all the available information, and produce suggested options for action. This is a new area of development and is related to the same Expert System type of approach that was introduced above under the heading of 'fusion'. Essentially it demands that the system should embody the knowledge of experienced commanders in the form of empirical rules. This type of processing is described here for the sake of completeness; it has not yet been employed in a battlefield CIS; some of the issues surrounding its possible use in the future are described in Chapter 12.

Formulation and Dissemination of Orders

The system should assist the staff to translate the commander's decisions into detailed orders for issue to the subordinate units or formations. It is normal for the commander to state the Aim of a particular operation, and to outline the Execution, and for the staff to generate the details, following the standing operating procedures (SOPs) of the formation concerned. Many of the details of an operation order (OpO) will be standard, or will at least follow a standard layout. The production of the OpO is an area where the now familiar word-processing functions, used to manipulate text, can help. Presentation is as important in the formulation of orders as it is in the display of information in the decision-making process, and the straightforward textual OpO is frequently not the most effective way to disseminate orders. The overlay OpO, consisting of textual information superimposed on a map, has found favour with many commanders and staffs. The production of overlay OpOs by the information system calls for the means to generate and display—possibly in hard copy form—the necessary graphics.

Action Sub-System

The action sub-system is essentially a receiver and implementor of orders. In most cases the orders are presented via a human interface, hence presentation is an important function. Some systems, particularly weapon systems, have a direct interface between the IS and the weapon; for example, to set the fuses in a gunnery system or to fire the weapon in the case of an anti-aircraft missile system, where human reaction is not fast enough.

The Structure of the Book

In keeping with the definition given earlier of the term Command and Control System, what we have described in Figure 1.4 includes the men and the procedures involved in exercising command and control over the division, as well as the information systems. In this book, although we cannot ignore the role played by men in the command and control process, or the need for procedures, we are primarily interested in the information systems. The scope of the book's subject matter lies within the boundary shown in Figure 1.5.

The Enabling Technologies

It goes without saying that CIS is a 'high technology' subject. Whilst no one would argue that CIS users should be experts on the detailed technical workings of the components of their system, an understanding of the technical strengths and weaknesses is necessary if the system is to be used to best advantage. Throughout Chapters 2—6, a 'bottom up' approach is taken, starting with the lowest level concepts and building up to a description of how they are applied and exploited in real systems. Chapter 2 introduces the fundamental concepts of information processing, especially the representation of information within the system. Chapter 3 takes this concept further and introduces the concepts of computer programming and the hardware of the processor. Chapter 4 is concerned with storage techniques, and covers this topic all the way from the low-level hardware devices to the concepts of database management systems. In Chapter 5 the design of the man-machine interface (MMI) is considered, by examining the characteristics of the individual input and output devices, and describing how they may be used to implement an efficient and effective MMI for the CIS user. Chapter 6 is devoted to the problems of communication data beyond the immediate confines of the system. It covers such aspects as error detection and correction, security, addressing and switching.

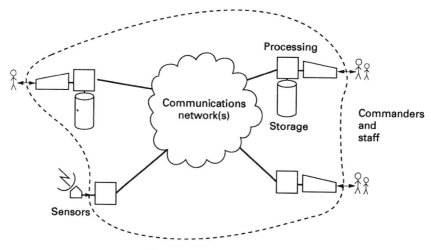

FIG. 1.5   Scope of the Book

System Implementation

Chapter 7 considers the problem of design for the battlefield environment, at the component, the individual equipment and the whole system level. A harsh environment imposes severe constraints upon hardware design, and some of the techniques employed to ensure the system's survival are described. In Chapter 8 attention turns to the most difficult element of the system to implement: the software. Software design for large systems, which CIS almost invariably are, is a process which is not yet developed to anything like the same extent as hardware design and manufacture. The chapter considers some of the reasons for this situation, which it terms the 'software crisis', and puts forward some possible remedies.

The next two chapters are concerned with specific aspects of CIS development. In Chapter 9 the question of interoperability between different systems is covered. Interoperability, through the introduction of a set of common standards for the wide interconnection of systems and the exchange of information and services between them, must be achieved if CIS are to function right across and beyond the battlefield rather than operating in isolated compartments. There is a serious potential conflict between this requirement and that for the maintenance of an adequate level of security. Systems must be able to protect the information they hold, in accordance with the mandatory security rules imposed by government, as well as being able to apply so-called discretionary security barriers between different 'need to know' categories of information. Chapter 10 is devoted to an account of the system security problem and some of the methods used to overcome it.

Impact of the System on the Organisation

We made the claim earlier in the chapter that a mature, effective CIS will have a profound impact on the nature of the organisation it serves. Chapter 11 examines this claim in some detail. In so doing it inevitably looks beyond the immediate generation of CIS, and considers how the organisation is likely to evolve as systems become more widespread and more indispensable. The chapter is also concerned with the organisation and resources needed for the provision of CIS, in the form of system management and support.

The Future

In its examination of the way in which the organisation will change in response to evolving CIS, Chapter 11 starts to look into the future. This look beyond today's systems is taken further in Chapter 12, which explores some of the likely technological developments and their potential impact on CIS. Topics covered include artificial intelligence (AI) techniques and parallel processing.

2.

Principles of Information Processing

Introduction

The Information Revolution

It is perhaps not inappropriate to start our brief examination of information and the principles which underlie its processing by first taking note of the factors that are bringing it into such current prominence. There are many who would claim that we are even now living through a new industrial revolution; a revolution that has been brought about in the first instance by an apparent need to manage and control ever larger quantities of time-critical information, and in the second by the very rapid technological developments that are providing us with the means to do so.

Dr Edith Martin, Vice President of the Boeing Aircraft Corporation, in a keynote lecture to the MILCOMP Conference in 1985, gave a graphic illustration of this view in the following words:

> In just this last 30-year period, something like 90 per cent of all scientific knowledge has been generated. This pool will double again in the next 10 to 15 years. Ninety per cent of all scientists who have ever lived are now living and working; and they will double again in that period.

The Japanese were perhaps the first as a nation to realise in any practical sense the significance and potential of this information revolution. Having taken the view that information may be looked upon as a resource, and having observed that the explosive growth of available information can make a timely précis of facts a very valuable commodity, then it would seem to follow that a profitable, inter-national information market could well be waiting for those able to seize the intiative.

The Japanese conclusion was that such a market could indeed be developed given the appropriate technology, and thus were sown the seeds of the Japanese Fifth Generation Project. This nationally funded programme, started in 1981 and planned to extend into the early 1990s, has acted as a stimulus spurring on others to invest in their own national information-technology programmes; Alvey and Esprit being the UK and the European response respectively to the Japanese initiative.

However, this perceived need for the management of time-critical information is not confined to the business and commercial worlds. In the military field of command and control, one area in particular is causing concern: that of data fusion. Information technology, as applied to command and control, is used to try to access ever more information about the combat situation, process it ever more rapidly and accurately, manage and distribute it ever more efficiently and thus provide to the commander a clearer and more timely picture on which to base command decision making. So much progress has been made in improved sensor devices that a flood of raw information is now becoming available that cannot sensibly be processed, merged and correlated quickly enough by the more traditional staffing means. The agencies concerned are fast becoming swamped by excessive data rates, and information technology is increasingly being seen as an essential aid in the data-fusion process.

Having acknowledged the need that is stimulating the information revolution, let us now look, in principle, at the technological means that can satisfy that need. To do this, we shall first consider what it is that we understand by the term information and from this attempt to develop an information-processing model. The manner in which this model may be used to represent and manipulate information and how the model relates to current technology then form the main two themes of this chapter.

The Nature of Information

A Working Definition

Attempts to define the term information are fraught with difficulty. Although we have used the dictionary definition elsewhere as 'items of knowledge' and this definition is entirely satisfactory for general use, it does not help us in our understanding of what information is nor of how information-processing models might work.

In an information-processing model of any kind we are concerned with the use of symbols which represent real world objects or ideas, and we are concerned with those symbols being manipulated in ways that are consistent with preserving the linkages with what the symbols represent; consistent, in other words, with preserving their real world meaning. Such information preserving transformations are sometimes referred to as isomorphisms. So, perhaps the physical realisation of a piece of information, in an information-processing model, might thus be defined as a pattern of symbols that has some real world meaning.

Patterns of Symbols

To illustrate this idea, consider one being shown an apparently arbitrary pattern of symbols and being asked to determine its meaning (Figure 2.1). The natural reaction to this, which itself provides an interesting insight into the nature of

FIG. 2.1   A Pattern of Symbols

information, is that one cannot possibly abstract any meaning from such an arbitrary pattern because one does not know how to interpret the symbols; that is, one does not know what they are intended to represent in the real world.

If visual clues to the representations are now given, by setting the pattern in some form of pictorial context, for example, abstraction of the intended meaning becomes trivial. This is because the pictorial context provides us with information about the set of interpreting rules that we need to apply to the symbols in order to evaluate their meaning (Figure 2.2).

Perhaps of much greater significance, however, is the fact that if we change the rules of interpretation then we can completely change the meaning. In Figure 2.3 a different set of visual clues suggests that an entirely different interpretation be placed on the same pattern of symbols.

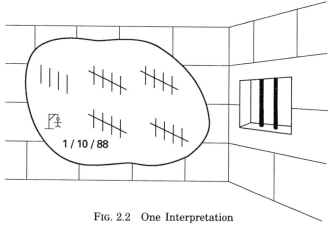

FIG. 2.2   One Interpretation

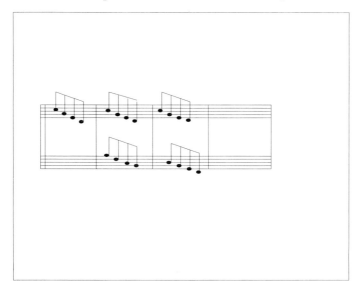

FIG. 2.3   A Different Interpretation

Clearly then, identical patterns of symbols can be used to represent quite different things by using different rules of interpretation. Equally then, can entirely different patterns represent the same things? Figure 2.4 demonstrates that, of course, they can. Here we see a different pattern of symbols representing precisely the same data as that suggested by Figure 2.2.

Now we all understand these ideas perfectly well intuitively; it is simply that in everyday life we tend not to think about them explicitly. The meaning that we ascribe to a pattern of symbols is clearly dependent upon two factors: the way in which the pattern is formed, that is, the particular symbols that are used and their conjunction with one another; and the way in which the pattern is to be interpreted, that is, the rules of analysis that are to be applied to the pattern by some interpreting system.

1988		October			1988	
Sun	Mon	Tue	Wed	Thu	Fri	Sat
						1
2	3	4	5	6	7	8
9	10	11	12	13	14	15
16	17	18	19	20	21	22
23	24	(25)	26	27	28	29
30	31					

FIG. 2.4   Another Representation of FIG. 2.2

Given that, it is perhaps instructive to ask ourselves whether any meaning can be ascribed to any pattern?

> *'When I use a word', Humpty Dumpty said, in a rather scornful tone, 'it means just what I choose it to mean—neither more nor less.'*
>
> *'The question is', said Alice, 'whether you can make words mean so many different things.'*
>
> Lewis Carroll

Clearly, the answer to Alice's question is yes; we can indeed ascribe any meaning that we choose to any pattern. However, if we wish that meaning to be retrieved later or to be communicated to someone else then we must be sure that we are thoroughly consistent and repeatable in the rules that we use both to generate and interpret the patterns.

Errors

This has an interesting consequence in relation to the concept of errors. We tend to be very conscious of the need to ensure the integrity of a pattern of symbols when we transmit it from one point to another. Indeed, we have developed comprehensive error detecting and correcting systems which aim to achieve just this. We are far less conscious, perhaps, of the need to ensure that the interpreting rules applied to the pattern when it is received are consonant with the rules that have been used to synthesise it. The meaning equally gets 'lost' if the two sets of rules are inconsistent in some way, as if the pattern has been damaged in transit.

The Car Park Story

The information-systems lecturer, in trying to convey the significance of these ideas to his audience, places five one pound coins, in a neat row on the top of the overhead projector and starts to tell the 'car park' story.

'It is 1430 on a fine Wednesday afternoon', he intones, 'and should you be looking out from the upper windows of Senate House over towards the campus playing fields you would see, parked in the VIP car park below you, five vehicles of various descriptions. This one', he points to the leftmost coin, 'is the Vice Chancellor's official car, and this', the second coin along, 'is the Dean's private vehicle. 'Here', the third coin, 'we have the Chief Executive's car, and there', the fourth coin, 'the car belonging to the Head of Finance and Administration, and this', the rightmost coin, 'this, is Professor Smith's bicycle'. (Figure 2.5.)

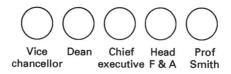

| Vice chancellor | Dean | Chief executive | Head F & A | Prof Smith |

FIG. 2.5   The Five Coins

'Now at approximately 2.30 on this fine Wednesday afternoon you note an interesting little incident taking place . . .' Here, the lecturer places his finger on the centre coin and swings it in a wide arc, down, round and up to the right until it crashes into the rightmost coin, causing the latter to fly off the overhead projector and onto the floor. 'Now, would anyone like to explain what it is that we have just seen take place?' he invites.

Invariably, of course, if the story has been properly told and appropriately embellished, reactions from the audience tend to centre on the Chief Executive leaving somewhat early for a game of golf and backing his car rather too enthusiastically into Professor Smith's bicycle.

At this point, the lecturer pounces, 'What complete and utter nonsense', he says, 'we saw nothing of the sort. What actually happened was that one of five similar coins lying on top of this overhead projector was deliberately pushed into another one causing it to fall onto the floor. Isn't that the case?'

And this, of course, is the whole point of the story. Particular and well-defined meanings have been ascribed to the five coins and their environment by the telling of the story; they represent something other than themselves. What at first sight might appear to be no more than a trivial manipulation of two coins does, in fact, represent a non-trivial piece of 'information processing' in the real world. The coins are acting simply as symbols for some other set of objects and the manipulation of those symbols can be directly linked to a related manipulation of the objects themselves.

Such an approach is no cause for surprise. Any pattern can mean any thing that we choose it to mean. Any set of objects arranged in patterns can be ascribed any meanings that we like simply by choosing and applying appropriate sets of manipulative and interpretative rules to the objects as symbols. Humankind has been using models of this nature since the first cave man scratched marks in the sand to describe some distant event to his fellows. We are continually using similar models in our everyday lives. The ideas are not new; they are as old as man himself. It is the way in which the ideas have been put to use by modern technology that has created the information revolution.

An Information Store

Two States

The design of a simple, home weather-station, for the enthusiastic hobbyist gardener who has everything, might start with a photoelectric cell in the garden wired to an indicating lamp in the front room. When sunlight falls on the photo cell, the lamp in the front room lights; and when there is no sunlight on the cell, the lamp extinguishes. In one sense, therefore, it can be said that the 'meaning' of the lamp being on is 'the sun is shining' and the 'meaning' of the lamp being off is that 'the sun is not shining'. From an information-processing viewpoint, the symbol is, in this case, the lamp: either on or off; and the rules of interpretation which permit us to extract the meaning come about from our knowledge of the

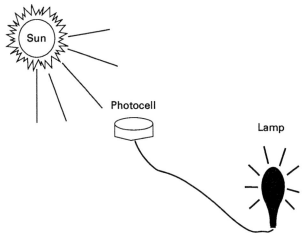

FIG. 2.6   The Sun is Shining

way in which the devices work and are connected together (Figure 2.6).

This idea of signalling a complex 'meaning' by way of a simple lamp is not unfamiliar. A red lamp on the dash board of a car might well 'mean' that the oil pressure is too low or that the alternator is not charging. Similarly a blue lamp could well 'mean' that the main beam headlamps are lit. It is clearly possible, therefore, to use simple symbols to convey arbitrarily complex ideas; this being achieved by effectively shifting the complexity from out of the symbol structure

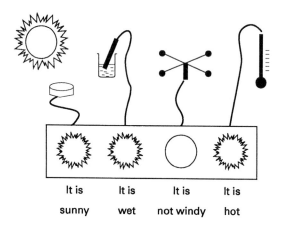

FIG. 2.7   The Simple Weather Station

and into the rules of interpretation. Simple symbols can be defined to have complex meanings.

Further development of the weather station might see the addition of three more units: a water detector connected to a second lamp; an anemometer connected to a third lamp; and a maximum registering thermometer connected to a fourth lamp (Figure 2.7). The pattern that is now shown on this bank of four lamps, some of which are on and some off, has a specific meaning. The pattern: on, on, off, on, can literally be taken to mean: 'it is sunny, it is wet, it is not windy, it is hot'. The rules for this interpretation come about, as before, from our knowledge of the ways in which the devices behave and are connected to one another.

However, let us now assume that our enthusiastic hobbyist, in addition to being able to see the current situation, would like also to have recorded the weather state as it was at some fixed time earlier, say noon. This is not at all difficult to achieve. We simply arrange for a time clock to operate, at the appropriate moment, causing the pattern then set on the lamps to be 'latched' into four relay switches. That is, the four relays are set: closed where the equivalent lamp is on, open where the equivalent lamp is off; and locked with the pattern that existed on the lamps at noon. The pattern: on, on, off, on would result in relay settings of: closed, closed, open, closed (Figure 2.8).

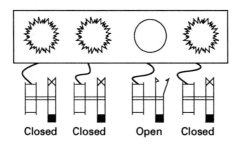

Closed   Closed   Open   Closed

FIG. 2.8 Relays as Memory

Latched Relays and Other Stores

Of course, that pattern of relay settings, were we to observe it, can be just as easily interpreted as were the lamp settings. We can read it as: 'it is sunny, it is wet, it is not windy, it is hot'. That is what the pattern 'means'; but now there is an important addition. That pattern, and thus its meaning, has been stored by the system. The information about the weather state at noon has been saved in the settings of the relays and it can be consulted again at some time in the future. We now have the concept of a store that can hold information for future use. Equally, we can store this pattern, and thus its meaning under this interpretation, in any four devices which have two distinct states, for example: on or off, open or closed.

Now it becomes clear where all of this is beginning to lead. The two-state devices could be pieces of magnetic material: individual beads or perhaps strips of tape or discs that can be magnetised with one of two polarities, North or South; or they could be semiconductor transistor switches that can be set either on or off; or they could be electrical pulses that can be either present or absent in a circuit at a particular place and time; or they could be the more familiar switches, relays and lamps that we have talked about so far. All of these devices can thus be used for 'storing' information in this manner.

Binary Patterns

Throughout this discussion we have concentrated solely on devices which have two distinct states, as, for example, on and off. It might be thought that this restriction is unnecessarily limiting. Clearly, devices which have more than two states could equally well be used to store information in similar ways, but modern technology tends exclusively to use two-state or binary devices. The reason for this is simply that two states are the cheapest and the easiest to realise using electronic devices. Since we have already noted that any patterns, including two-state patterns, can mean whatever we choose them to mean, then we might just as well select a form of representation that is the most economical to manufacture and best suited to keeping the electronics simple.

However, in order to continue sensibly with this discussion, we need to dispense with the artifice of drawing pictures of relays and lamps whenever we wish to refer to a binary pattern which we are using to represent some piece of information. Again, noting that any pattern can mean whatever we choose it to mean, including, of course, representing some other pattern, we may choose, in future, always to represent the separate states of any two state device by the numbers 0 and 1. Let us then define that 0 is 'off' or 'open' and that 1 is 'on' or 'closed', and that the presence of a device is always indicated by one of these two numbers, the value of which identifies its current state. The previous two sketches of lamps and relays may now be represented perfectly well by the pattern of 1s and 0s shown in Figure

On	On	Off	On
Closed	Closed	Open	Closed
1	1	0	1
It is sunny	It is wet	It is not windy	It is hot

FIG. 2.9   Binary Patterns

2.9. This pattern itself, of course, also represents the information: 'it is sunny, it is wet, it is not windy, it is hot'.

Now the pattern '1 1 0 1' may easily be mistaken for a binary number. That is not, in this example, what it was set up to represent. It was set up to represent the piece of information: 'it is sunny, it is wet, it is not windy, it is hot'. It could, indeed, be interpreted as a binary number by applying an entirely different set of interpreting rules. We are so conditioned to this particular way of looking at binary patterns that we tend to think of them all only as binary numbers. This, in turn, may lead to the false premise that digital computers are basically 'number-crunchers' that can only manipulate information in the form of binary numbers. This is not the case. Digital computers manipulate sets of binary elements and the binary patterns that result can, as we have seen, represent any kind of information that we wish, providing that the rules of manipulation and the rules of interpretation for those patterns are suitably chosen and are consistent with one another. The class of binary numbers is but one such class of information that we might choose to have represented; the scope for representing other classes of information appears to be, for all practical purposes, unlimited.

An Information Processor

Having formed a view of what it is that we mean by the term 'information' in this particular context and how we can represent real world objects and ideas, we are now able to determine what it is that we need, in abstract terms, to build an 'information processor'.

Clearly we must start with a set of elements that act as our symbols, and permit us to represent the real world information that we wish to have manipulated. We also require a mechanism to manipulate those symbols, in ways consistent with the real world objects that they represent, and in accordance with some set of given rules.

A Black Box View

We can draw a 'black box' diagram of this requirement as shown in Figure 2.10. One box holds the elements that act as the symbols representing the 'information',

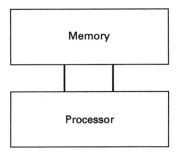

FIG. 2.10   Memory and Processor

and we call this box, not unreasonably, the memory or store, and the second box contains the mechanism which manipulates the symbols in accordance with the given rules, and we call this box the processor.

In the car park story, the memory was the overhead projector with its five coins; each coin being one element of the memory and acting as a symbol representing one of the vehicles. The processor was, of course, the lecturer who manipulated the coins according to a set of rules which were made explicit by means of the story.

Practical Considerations

If we relate this black box version of an information processor to the current technology, we find that the most likely candidate for the memory element is, as we have suggested earlier, the electronic transistor switch, implemented by means of the silicon chip. Not, however, just a handful of memory elements, as was the case with the coins on the overhead projector, but millions upon millions of transistor switches, each one being a memory element, and each one capable of being used as a symbol within the system.

Furthermore, we find that the processor, also implemented in the form of a silicon chip, is capable of manipulating those memory elements at speeds of the order of many millions of operations per second. It is interesting to contrast this figure with the moving of the coins on the overhead projector at something less than one operation per second.

A modern digital computer thus provides us with the two fundamental information processing facilities that we need: a means to represent and store a set of patterns; and a means to manipulate those patterns according to some set of given rules. What is so very different about the digital computer of today compared with earlier modelling systems is that the size of its pattern-holding capacity is incredibly large and that the speed of its pattern-manipulating facility is unbelievably fast. The information revolution is coming about, not because of any fundamental change in concepts, but because of the very high speed and very high capacity of the increasingly affordable, mass produced, information-processing microchip.

A photograph of a typical microprocessor, in silicon-chip form, is shown in Figure 2.11. The dimensions of the chip itself are approximately a quarter of an inch square, the size of a little finger nail. In that same space we can today expect memory chips in production that contain up to one million elements, and research indicates that future chips will hold considerably more.

The technology of the hardware is advancing at a rate that is far outstripping our ability to exploit it fully; the numbers, in terms of capacity and speed, are becoming too large for us sensibly to comprehend their true significance.

Bits and Bytes

Let us consider now the memory or store of a computer into which we can put representations of any information that we wish. For electronic convenience, it will probably be implemented as a very large number of transistor switches, of the order, perhaps, of several millions. Each switch can take up one of two states: either on or off electronically and, as we saw earlier, we can represent these binary switches and their states by a sequence of 1s and 0s, typically as shown in Figure 2.12.

In order to be useful, however, we need to be able to refer to patterns of memory elements that are of manageable size. Figure 2.12 shows some of the groupings which are used to permit this. A single element is called a *binary digit* or *bit* for short; four consecutive elements are called a *nibble* and eight consecutive elements are called a *byte*.

Addressing

A careful examination of Figure 2.12 will establish that the memory states shown there include the sequence '1 1 0 1' which is perhaps where the information

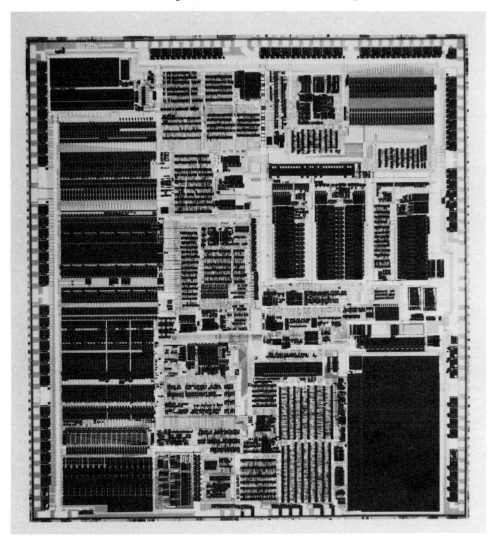

FIG. 2.11   A Typical Microprocessor (*INTEL Corporation UK Ltd*)

| 1 | 0   0   1 | 1   0   0   0 | 1   1   0   1   0   1 | Millions more |

▲ Bit ▲

▲   Nibble   ▲

▲   Byte   ▲

FIG. 2.12   Bits and Bytes

'it is sunny, it is wet, it is not windy, it is hot' has been stored. Clearly, in order to distinguish a particular sequence of bits representing a particular piece of information from the millions of other bits in the store we must have a means of accessing uniquely any sequence that we require. The mechanism used to achieve this is known as *addressing*.

Each eight-bit grouping, or byte, within the store is assigned a unique numeric address; rather similar in principle to the numeric address that might be assigned to each house in a street of identical houses. Using this address we can then consistently and repeatably identify any particular group of switches that we require. Having placed a piece of information in some particular place in the store, that is, by setting the respective switches to an appropriate sequence of states, we can then reliably retrieve a copy of the information again and again by reading back the states of those specific switches.

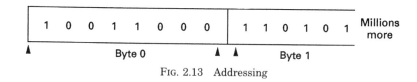

FIG. 2.13   Addressing

As Figure 2.13 demonstrates, we are able to access the information about the weather situation by reading back and interpreting the states of the first four switches addressed by byte 1, that is, the first four bits (or the first nibble) of byte 1. We often refer, in such circumstances, to the contents of the byte, reinforcing the idea that each byte is 'storing' or 'holding' information.

Because the computer is designed to use two-state devices throughout, it turns out to be convenient from the viewpoint of the electronics to arrange for the total number of addressable storage elements (and an addressable storage element is invariably the byte in the current range of computers) to be a power of two and for the address counting to start from zero. Since most modern computers are likely to have many thousands or even millions of bytes in their memories, it is normal to refer to memory size using some multiplying factor; and for this purpose the nearest powers of two to one thousand and one million are employed. A kilobyte of store, sometimes written Kbyte or just K, is thus 1,024 bytes and a megabyte or Mbyte is 1,048,576 bytes.

Typical memory sizes for production systems are rapidly changing upwards; at the time of writing, home microcomputers are likely to have between 64K and 512K of immediate access store; small business machines up to a few megabytes and minicomputers as high as 64 Mbytes. In terms of information storage capacity, it is interesting to consider just what these sizes really mean. In the weather state example only four bits were used to represent all the information, and even a 64K home microcomputer can hold 131,072 times that number of patterns. However, it is important also to note that we have not yet discussed how the rules of interpretation and manipulation get implemented and, as we shall see, memory capacity is needed for that purpose as well.

Interpretation of Binary Patterns by the Computer

We have stressed several times now that two-state memory patterns can be used to represent anything that we wish them to represent, and we shall discuss shortly how this can be effected in a quite general way. As part of the necessary mechanisms, most computer systems have permanently built into their electronics (the so-called hardware) at least three distinct sets of rules for the manipulation and interpretation of binary patterns. These enable the machine to interpret binary patterns either as numbers, characters or as instructions, depending upon which set of hardware rules is applied to the pattern. A brief examination of these processes provides valuable insight into how an information processor, implemented as an electronic digital computer, really does function, and how instructions can be used to make up any sets of rules that we wish.

Binary Numbers

As suggested earlier, many people tend automatically to associate patterns of 1s and 0s with numbers and, in particular, with binary numbers. The reason for this is largely historical and stems from the early mathematical uses to which computers were put. In an information-processing context, this view is far too narrow; binary numbers are but one representation in what seems to be an unlimited set of possibilities. Nevertheless, all such machines do include at least one number representation in their repertoire of hardware rules and most use binary arithmetic in order to simplify the electronics.

In the thoroughly familiar decimal system of numbers we use a positional notation approach with rules of interpretation which assign to each digit position a multiplying factor that is ten times that of the neighbouring digit position to its right. We further define that each digit position may contain one of 10 different digit symbols (0 to 9 inclusive). Thus the pattern 384 is easily interpreted, through long familiarity, as 'three hundred and eighty four' $(3 \times 10 \times 10 + 8 \times 10 + 4 \times 1)$.

In a similar way, the binary system of numbers uses a positional notation approach with rules of interpretation which assign to each digit position a multiplying factor that is two times that of the neighbouring digit position to its right. We further define that each digit position may contain one of two different digit symbols (0 or 1). Thus the pattern 1101 is interpreted as one eight and one four no twos and one one $(1 \times 2 \times 2 \times 2 + 1 \times 2 \times 2 + 0 \times 2 + 1 \times 1)$ which, in decimal notation may be written as 13 or thirteen. In passing we may note that this pattern '1101' is the same pattern that we were earlier interpreting as 'it is sunny, it is wet, it is not windy, it is hot'. The same pattern, of course, can mean whatever we choose it to mean depending upon the rules of interpretation that we apply.

Using this binary system representation we can clearly store and manipulate binary patterns that are to represent numbers. With our basic unit of addressable storage as the byte, it is convenient to be able to evaluate the equivalent decimal number for any given eight-bit pattern. This may be achieved, as shown in Figure 2.14, by applying the appropriate multiplying factor to the 0 or 1 value in each

```
 0  +  64  +  0  +  16  +  8  +  0  +  2  +  0      = 90
```

FIG. 2.14   Whole Numbers

column and summing the results. In the case of Figure 2.14, for example, this evaluates to the decimal equivalent of 90.

From the same diagram it is also clear that the range of whole numbers that we can store in a single byte runs from 0 (when all the bits are set to zero) to 255 (when all the bits are set to 1). It may be thought, with some justification, that this range of numbers is simply too small to be useful in any practical application. However, the problem can be easily overcome by using more than one byte in sequence to represent a single whole number (Figure 2.15).

```
8 4 2 1 5 2 1 6 3 1 8 4 2 1 5 2 1 6 3 1 8 4 2 1
3 1 0 0 2 6 3 5 2 6 1 0 0 0 1 5 2 4 2 6
8 9 9 4 4 2 1 5 7 3 9 9 4 2 2 6 8
8 4 7 8 2 1 0 3 6 8 2 6 8 4
6 3 1 5 8 4 7 6 8 4
0 0 5 7 8 4 2
8 4 2 6
```

```
0 1 0 1 0 0 1 0 | 0 1 0 0 0 1 0 1 | 0 1 0 0 0 1 0 0
```

FIG. 2.15   Increasing the Range

Figure 2.15 shows the effect of using two or three bytes in sequence. Using two bytes, the range becomes 0 to 65535 and using three it becomes 0 to 16,777,215. Negative numbers may also be represented by defining one of the bits in one of the bytes, most usually the leftmost byte, to represent a sign. If the bit is set to 1 then the number is negative, if the bit is set to 0 then the number is positive. In practice, a slightly more complex representation is adopted for negative numbers called twos complement in order, again, to simplify the electronics of the hardware. Number representations of this kind are known as fixed point and may be used for signed fractions and signed mixed numbers as well as signed whole numbers, provided that care is taken over interpreting the position of the binary point; this being to binary numbers what the decimal point is to decimal numbers.

The hardware of most machines will include sets of rules to interpret single and, in some cases, double byte patterns as signed, fixed point binary numbers, and to manipulate those patterns in accordance with the rules for arithmetic addition and subtraction. More complex arithmetic operations, such as multiplication, division and extraction of square roots, are only likely to be available as hardware sets of rules on the larger machines, as are the interpreting and manipulating sets of rules for other, more complex number representations such as floating point. This representation provides a method of storing numbers in the form that is sometimes known as 'scientific notation'. Many of the smaller systems that are not equipped with the requisite hardware will, nevertheless, provide the more complex arithmetic sets of rules implemented in software; that is, by having the rules made available in the form of computer programs.

Characters

Returning once more to the theme that we can make patterns represent anything that we wish them to, we now suggest that the eight-bit pattern in a single byte of memory be used to represent any one of the range of characters that we might wish to have placed on a page of typescript. If we count up the number of different characters that we might wish to represent we find, for the English language, that we will need: 26 upper case letters, 26 lower case letters, 10 numeric digits, perhaps some 30 punctuation characters and, say, some 8 or so page layout or 'white space' characters, such as space, carriage return, line feed and tabulate. In all, we are unlikely to need more than about 100 different patterns to be able to represent any character that we need and, since we have available in one byte 256 different patterns (the same as the range of different numbers), a single byte can easily be used to represent any one of the range of typescript characters that we wish.

Now we could, of course, assign particular patterns in a byte to represent particular printed characters on the page (or on the display screen) in a completely arbitrary way, but, as a result, we would then require very specific purpose printers and displays which had associated, built-in hardware rules of interpretation that exactly matched our arbitrary definitions. Far more useful, of course, would be to agree, internationally, a standard set of pattern definitions, the rules for which are then built in to all printers and displays. Whilst this desirable aim has not yet been entirely achieved, in practice a standard mapping of patterns to characters is in widespread use. The mapping is called the American Standard Code for Information Interchange of ASCII (pronounced 'askey'), and it defines the patterns for 128 different characters, some of which do not print but are used to pass control orders to printers, displays and communications equipment.

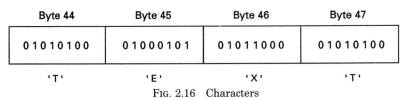

FIG. 2.16   Characters

Now if we can hold and store a representation of any individual typescript character that we wish in a single byte, then we can hold and store, in a sequence of bytes, representations of any pieces of text of documents that we wish. Further, by moving sequences of bytes around in memory, we are effectively moving pieces of text around in a document; in short, we have the ability to carry out the function of word-processing. If, for example, we wished to store the word 'TEXT' we can do this simply by storing the ASCII representations for the characters 'T' 'E' 'x' 'T' in four adjacent bytes in the memory; shown as bytes 44, 45, 46 and 47 in Figure 2.16.

In principle, of course, we can hold and store electronically the complete works of

William Shakespeare, the *Encyclopaedia Britannica*, even the entire literary works of man, by using this very simple approach. We are limited only by the practical considerations of how much memory store would be needed and how we might set about indexing and accessing in an acceptable time any particular part of such an enormous library.

Instructions

We have now seen how we can represent and manipulate numbers and how we can represent and manipulate characters and text. The last category that we need to look at carries with it perhaps the most important idea of all. If binary patterns in the memory can indeed be used to represent anything that we wish, should it not be possible to use them to represent the rules to which we have continually been referring throughout this discussion? Cannot patterns in the memory themselves be used to represent the rules of interpretation and manipulation that give specific meanings to other patterns within the memory?

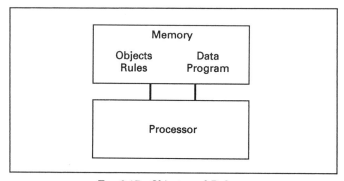

FIG. 2.17   Objects and Rules

Clearly this is indeed possible, and it is achieved by building into the hardware of the processor a mechanism that interprets binary patterns held in the memory as instructions or rules that are to be obeyed by the processor. A sequence of patterns stored in the memory can thus represent a sequence of orders to the machine; a set of rules which when obeyed by that machine causes it to perform a series of operations that gives meaning to some other patterns held elsewhere in the memory, and executes some information-processing task that we wish to have carried out. Such a sequence of rules is called a *program* and the idea itself is referred to as the stored program concept. We thus have the situation shown in Figure 2.17, where the memory contains not only patterns representing the objects to be manipulated (the data) but also patterns representing what is to be done and the interpretations that are to be made (the program).

The Processor Mechanism

The processor mechanism may be very rudimentary. All that is required is a small scratchpad memory, often referred to as the registers and a very simple, in-built procedure. One of the registers in the processor holds the address in main memory of where the next rule that the processor is to obey can be found. This register may be called the sequence control register or the program counter. The in-built procedure causes the processor to step through a small number of simple activities, repeating the same cycle continuously all the while that the processor is switched on.

In essence, the steps are as follows. The processor first of all looks up its program counter to find out where in main memory the next rule it is to obey can be found. It then obtains a copy of the pattern representing the next rule from memory and changes its program counter so that that is now referring to the rule that follows the current rule. The processor then interprets the current rule pattern to determine what action it is to take and then executes that action; possibly accessing and manipulating data patterns in the process. The cycle then repeats, this time, of course, with the program counter referring to the next rule in the sequence; and so the procedure continues, each time with the program counter being stepped to the next rule in the sequence. Modern processors may perform this cycle at speeds in excess of one million times per second. Indeed, a value in MIPS (millions of instructions per second) is often used to indicate the power of such a machine.

An Example Machine

Instruction Format

In order to explore these ideas further, consider an example machine where an instruction or rule is defined to be represented by the pattern in two consecutive bytes in memory, and that the interpretations to be placed on that pattern by the

FIG. 2.18 Format of a Simple Instruction

processor are as shown in Figure 2.18. We have decided here that the pattern in the first byte of the pair is to represent an imperative to the machine, DO THIS; the particular THIS being defined by the particular pattern, in this case: 00101010. We have also decided that the pattern in the second byte is to represent the object on which the imperative is to be carried out, in this case: 10110011. The whole is therefore to be interpreted as DO THIS (imperative 00101010) TO THIS (object 10110011).

Example Codes

In a practical machine, we would have a host of different imperatives available, known collectively as the order code for that machine, and these would relate specific patterns in the DO THIS byte to specific functions available in the hardware of the processor. Typical examples might be: ADD, SUBTRACT, MULTIPLY, DIVIDE, INPUT, OUTPUT, MOVE, COMPARE, and so forth. The range and functionality of the imperatives are thus defined by the hardware of the processor. For our purposes we need only consider three imperatives or orders: GET VALUE, PUT VALUE and ADD VALUE, and we shall define GET VALUE to have the pattern 00000001, PUT VALUE to have the pattern 00000010, and ADD VALUE to have the pattern 00000100.

An Example Sequence

The objects, as we have already seen, are specified by binary patterns in the memory and thus the TO THIS portion of the rule represents, in the majority of cases, the byte address where the object referred to is represented in the main

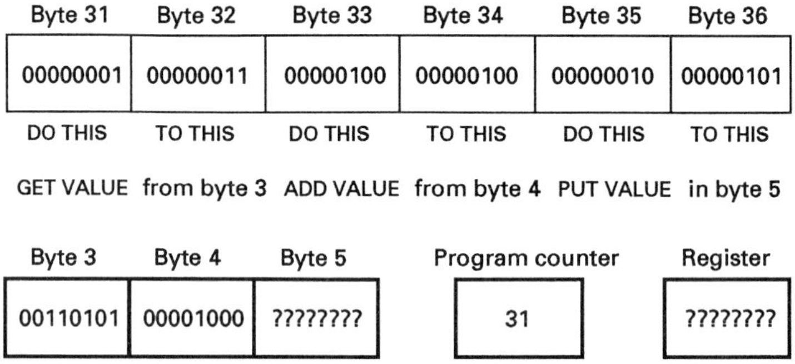

Byte 31	Byte 32	Byte 33	Byte 34	Byte 35	Byte 36
00000001	00000011	00000100	00000100	00000010	00000101
DO THIS	TO THIS	DO THIS	TO THIS	DO THIS	TO THIS

GET VALUE from byte 3   ADD VALUE from byte 4   PUT VALUE   in byte 5

Byte 3	Byte 4	Byte 5		Program counter		Register
00110101	00001000	????????		31		????????

FIG. 2.19   Example Machine: State 1

memory. Figure 2.19 shows a small portion of main memory from our example machine, with patterns of interest in the six consecutive bytes 31 to 36 and in the three bytes 3, 4 and 5.

Acting the part of the machine, having been directed by the setting in the program counter to interpret bytes 31 onwards as rules, it is not difficult to determine just how all the patterns would thus be interpreted.

Executing the Example Sequence

Bytes 31 and 32 would first of all be accessed and a copy of their pattern (00000001 00000011) taken to be interpreted as the first rule or instruction. The program counter would then be changed to 33, the byte address of where the pattern representing the next rule in sequence is stored. The first rule would then be interpreted: 00000001 in the DO THIS byte evaluates to 'GET VALUE', and 00000011 refers to the object in byte 3, so the rule becomes 'get the value from byte 3'. The processor would then execute the interpreted rule and in so doing would obtain a copy of the pattern 00110101 from byte 3 storing it away in one of its registers. At this stage, the result would be as shown in Figure 2.20.

The cycle would then repeat. This time the program counter holds 33 and the processor would access a copy of the pattern (00000100 00000100) from bytes 33 and 34 as the next rule. The program counter would be updated to 35 and the processor would then interpret this next rule as follows: 00000100 in the DO THIS byte evaluates to 'ADD VALUE' and 00000100 refers to the object in byte 4, so the rule becomes 'add the value from byte 4'. (Although both halves of this rule are

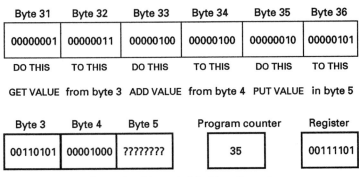

FIG. 2.20   Example Machine: State 2

represented by an identical pattern, they are interpreted quite differently: the first half is the imperative DO THIS and the second half refers to the object TO THIS.) On execution, the processor would access a copy of the pattern in byte 4 and add that pattern into the register containing the value previously obtained from byte

Byte 31	Byte 32	Byte 33	Byte 34	Byte 35	Byte 36
00000001	00000011	00000100	00000100	00000010	00000101
DO THIS	TO THIS	DO THIS	TO THIS	DO THIS	TO THIS

GET VALUE from byte 3   ADD VALUE from byte 4   PUT VALUE in byte 5

Byte 3	Byte 4	Byte 5	Program counter	Register
00110101	00001000	????????	35	00111101

FIG. 2.21   Example Machine: State 3

3. This result is shown in Figure 2.21. The cycle then again repeats. The program counter now holds 35 and thus the rule represented by the pattern (00000010 00000101) is the next to be executed. It is clear to see, when the cycle repeats, that this would result in the updating of the program counter to 37 and the execution of the rule 'put the value in byte 5'. A copy of the previously summed value in the processor's register would then be written into byte 5, replacing the previous contents (Figure 2.22).

In a real system, this entire process would have taken some three millionths of a second (or 3 microseconds). The processor would not stop after the third instruction, however, but would continue to interpret patterns as rules, taking them in sequence from bytes 37 onwards, and executing them continuously until it was switched off.

Program and Data

It is instructive to note how the various patterns in the memory have been interpreted. Patterns in bytes 31 to 36 have clearly been interpreted as instruc-

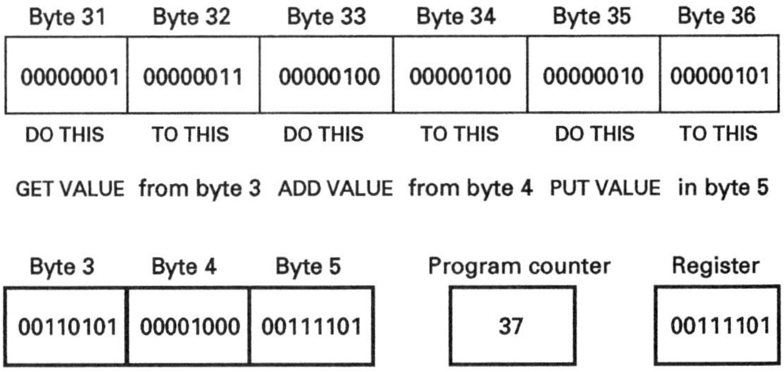

Byte 31	Byte 32	Byte 33	Byte 34	Byte 35	Byte 36
00000001	00000011	00000100	00000100	00000010	00000101
DO THIS	TO THIS	DO THIS	TO THIS	DO THIS	TO THIS

GET VALUE from byte 3 ADD VALUE from byte 4 PUT VALUE in byte 5

Byte 3	Byte 4	Byte 5		Program counter		Register
00110101	00001000	00111101		37		00111101

FIG. 2.22   Example Machine: State 4

tions or rules, and this interpretation has been dictated by the setting of the program counter. It is the program counter that defines what patterns are to be interpreted as rules. The patterns in bytes 3 to 5 have been interpreted as data, in particular as binary numbers; the evidence for this is that the pattern from byte 3 has been added, using the rules of binary arithmetic, to the pattern from byte 4 and the resulting sum has been placed in byte 5. This interpretation has come about through the execution by the processor of the patterns in bytes 31 to 36 as rules. The execution of one set of patterns as rules has given meaning to another set of patterns as data objects. Patterns can mean whatever we choose them to mean; the specific meaning being determined by the set of rules that is applied.

It would have been equally feasible for the program counter to have been set initially to 3, in which case the patterns in bytes 3 onwards would have been interpreted as rules. In one sense it could then have been said that the processor was extracting the 'wrong' meaning from the patterns; it would be executing patterns as rules that were perhaps intended by the designer to be interpreted as numbers. This is not an uncommon problem. The processor slavishly, and at very high speed, executes as rules whatever patterns it is directed to by its program counter, regardless of what the intentions of the programmer may have been. The stored program computer is completely general purpose and in most systems any part of the memory can be used for data or program, that is, for objects or rules, and it is the responsibility of the programmer to ensure that such use is consistent with the intended interpretations. In most modern machines he is assisted in this by hardware.

A Complete Information Processing System

Expanding on the 'black box' model of an information processor developed earlier (Figure 2.16), we now add a typewriter keyboard as a specimen input device and a visual display unit (VDU) or television screen as a specimen output device. To complete the basic model of an information-processing system, we need also to add what is sometimes called backing store or secondary storage, resulting in the arrangement shown in Figure 2.23. One important reason for this is that the main memory of the system is usually volatile, that is, all the existing patterns held in

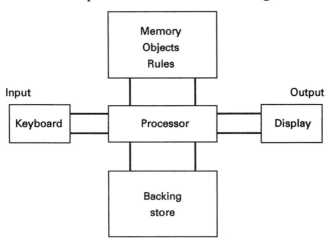

FIG. 2.23   Black Box Model

the memory are lost when the system is switched off and an undefined set of patterns takes their place when power is restored.

In principle, the operation of the backing store is simple. When it is required to retain a program or data held in main memory, a magnetic tape or a magnetic disc may be used to record a copy of the states of all the relevant transistor switches in that memory. When it is required to restore the program or data, then that piece of magnetic tape or disc may be played back, resetting all the relevant transistor switches to their original states and thus restoring the original rules and objects.

Summary

This chapter has discussed the nature of information and the fundamental principles underlying information processing by the use of the stored program digital computer. A black box information-processing model has been developed which forms the basis for all current information-processing systems. The next three chapters describe the elements of the model in more detail. Chapter 3 builds on the description of the basic processing concepts given in this chapter, Chapter 4 describes memory technologies and information storage techniques, and Chapter 5 covers input and output devices. In each chapter the approach is 'bottom-up'; the basic techniques down at the 'bit and byte' level are described first, and on this foundation is built the description of how the techniques are used to support the command and control functions. This chapter provides the foundation for a more complete understanding of what follows.

3.

Processing

Introduction

The previous chapter introduced the fundamental concepts of information processing with the digital computer. In this chapter we will build on this description of the basic concepts and see how they may be applied to processing of information in military command and control systems. The chapter is deliberately entitled 'Processing' rather than 'Processors', indicating that we are interested in the whole business of 'doing things' to stored information, and not simply the devices and mechanisms used for processing. The approach taken in this and the following chapters on information storage, and input/output devices is 'bottom-up', starting at the level of the manipulation of binary symbols, and describing the further techniques which are needed in order to harness the power of the low-level activities to the support of the highest level, user-visible functions. This approach may be viewed as a process of increasing abstraction in a series of layers, in which the complexities of a lower layer are summarised and exploited for the benefit of the next higher layer. A view of this process is given in Figure 3.1.

Figure 3.1, although helpful as a start, is hopelessly over-simplified as soon as one attempts to apply it to any real system. Figure 3.2 goes some way towards recognising the complexity of the true situation. Although it still contains the concept of layers of complexity, it recognises that the ultimate function for the user may be performed by entities at the different layers of complexity which co-operate with each other. It indicates that there may well be a number of different processors involved in a system, and, at the same time, that a number of different processes may be performed by the same processor. This introduces the concept of transparency; we say that the complex, interacting processes going on below the surface of what is visible to the user are 'transparent' to him, to indicate that he cannot see them, nor has he any need to be aware of them in order to use the system to support his own functions.

The last chapter introduced the concept that groups of electrical charges in the computer's memory may be interpreted in different ways, according to the rules being applied at any given instant. For example, the bit pattern 01000001 may be interpreted as a binary number, equivalent to decimal 65, it may be treated as representing, in the ASCII code, the letter 'A', or it may be an instruction to the computer to perform some processing task. At a higher level of abstraction, the

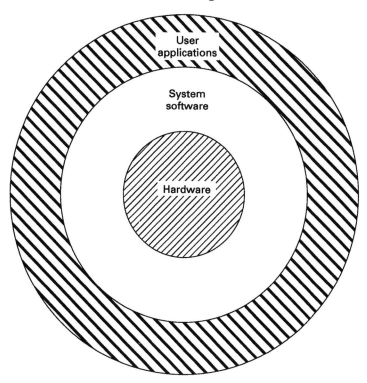

FIG. 3.1   Simple Processing System

whole body of data being processed by the computer and stored within the computer system is viewed as a model of that element of the real world in which the system user has an interest. It is possible to represent, using this essentially very crude means, concepts which are as complicated as man is capable of imagining and describing.

An Example: the Flight Simulator Program

A good example to illustrate this idea is a program with which readers with home computers may be familiar; the flight simulator. By using a microprocessor of modest power, with relatively little memory, with input from a keyboard and possibly a joystick, and output via a colour television screen and loudspeaker, it is possible to achieve a remarkably accurate simulation of the problems of flying and navigating a light aircraft. How is it possible to achieve such a realistic representation of a 'system' which costs tens of thousands of pounds, on a collection of items which can be bought for a few hundred pounds from any High Street electrical goods shop? Consider first that a clear boundary has been drawn around that portion of the real world which is to be represented. After all, you cannot actually go anywhere 'in' your home computer flight simulator. The 'functionality' of an aircraft as a means of transport is outside the boundaries of the model. All that is represented, and that in a limited way, is the interface between the machine and the pilot. There are 'controls' with which the pilot tells the machine to do

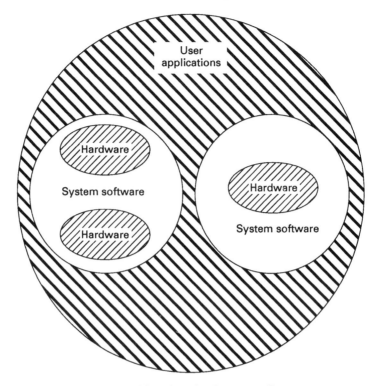

FIG. 3.2   A More Complex Processing System

things, and there are 'instruments', and an artificial view of the world outside the
aircraft to tell the pilot what the machine is doing. In between the two, inside the
computer, is a numerical description of the 'aircraft'. This is shown in Figure 3.3.

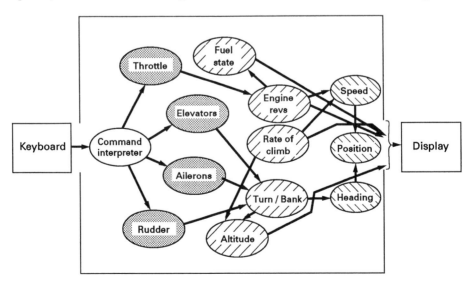

FIG. 3.3   The Flight Simulator Program

There will be numbers representing the aircraft's altitude and position relative to the ground, its speed, heading, attitude, and rate of climb. Other numbers will represent the rate at which the engine is operating, the amount of fuel remaining, and the position of the rudder, elevators and other control surfaces.

There will be a set of rules relating the quantities describing the aircraft to each other and to the demands set by the pilot. For example, there will be a relationship between the speed of the engine and rate of change of the level of fuel. A 'joystick forward' command will cause a change in the aircraft's attitude to make it 'nose down', which will lead to an increase in speed, and negative increase in the rate of climb. If not corrected, this combination of circumstances will eventually lead to a sudden reduction to zero of the aircraft's altitude, probably followed by a message of sympathy (or admonition) to the pilot and an invitation for him to have another go and do better next time. The only element of the whole system which in any way looks like an aircraft is the picture on the television screen of the instruments, and the view from the cockpit. Yet, thanks to the skill of the programmer in writing rules which describe the relationship between control movements and aircraft response as accurately as possible, the simple home-computer simulated aircraft can be as difficult to 'land' as the real thing. The pilot at the controls of his simulated craft may be exercising almost as much skill as one at the controls of a real aircraft, and may be just as absorbed in his task. The difference is that behind the controls and displays of the simulator, instead of a complex assembly of airframe, engine, controls and avionics there is just a collection of numbers, represented as bursts of energy on a silicon chip.

Programming Concepts

It has become clear that the first layer we have to add to the basic processor model built up in the last chapter is some means of programming it. We have seen how certain of the symbols stored in the memory may be treated as instructions to the computer to perform processes on other symbols. If we return to our original example machine of Chapter 2, with its program of rules held in bytes 31 to 36,

Byte 31	Byte 32	Byte 33	Byte 34	Byte 35	Byte 36
00000001	00000011	00000100	00000100	00000010	00000101
DO THIS	TO THIS	DO THIS	TO THIS	DO THIS	TO THIS

GET VALUE from byte 3   ADD VALUE from byte 4   PUT VALUE in byte 5

FIG. 3.4   Binary Program

we may ask ourselves how it is that those patterns came to be put there? (Figure 3.4.)

One possible answer would be for each bit of those six bytes to be implemented, not as an electronic transistor switch, but as a physical ON-OFF switch located on some control panel accessible to the user. Programming could then simply be achieved by setting up the switches appropriately: OFF OFF OFF OFF OFF OFF OFF ON, that completes byte 31; OFF OFF OFF OFF OFF OFF ON ON, that completes byte 32, and so forth. This could genuinely be called 'programming in binary' and some very early machines were indeed programmed in this way. However, it is such an error-prone and tiresome task that, had no alternative methods been identified, it is doubtful whether the modern digital computer would ever have come about.

A more useful approach recognises the full potential of the stored program computer concept. Here we have a machine which we wish to program so that we might represent, manipulate and interpret information about some real world problem. Our current difficulty is in placing into the memory of the machine the patterns that will represent the rules to solve that problem. However, is not the nature of the difficulty the same as the nature of the problem itself? Is not the nature of the difficulty concerned with representing, manipulating and interpreting information, in this case the information being the set of rules or program that we wish to place in memory to solve the problem?

There is, of course, no reason at all why we should not devise some other program (or, more probably, have it devised for us by the manufacturer of the machine) that is specifically designed to translate programs written in an external form convenient to us into the internal binary patterns that the machine itself requires. Such a program is called a *translator*. We thus have the interesting situation where the machine is used as an information processor to prepare programs for itself.

Byte 31	Byte 32	Byte 33	Byte 34	Byte 35	Byte 36
00000001	00000011	00000100	00000100	00000010	00000101
1	3	4	4	2	5

FIG. 3.5   Decimal Equivalents

The simplest form of external representation that we might use is to replace the pattern in each byte with its equivalent decimal number, as shown in Figure 3.5. We could then lay this sequence of numbers out on a piece of paper as shown at

Decimal machine code		Assembly language	
		Instruction	Remark
1	3	GET NETPAY	;Form net pay
4	4	ADD TAX	;plus tax giving
2	5	PUT GROSSPAY	;gross pay
(a)		(b)	

FIG. 3.6   Comparison of Decimal Machine Code and Assembly Language

(a) in Figure 3.6, or perhaps type it in to the translating program at a terminal. Each rule or instruction is here designated by a pair of decimal numbers: the first of which defines the imperative and the second the object for each rule. In this form the program statements would be known as decimal machine code.

There is no reason, however, why we should limit ourselves to a solely numeric external representation. We know that '1' as an imperative means 'GET VALUE', '4' means 'ADD VALUE' and '2' means 'PUT VALUE'. In addition, we could replace the object byte numbers 3, 4 and 5 by symbols chosen to represent the 'variables' of our program, giving us the form shown at (*b*) in Figure 3.6. This is slightly more readable than the previous version; with its accompanying 'remarks' which can be added by the programmer to the lines of assembly language code, it is quite easy to read and follow. Here we note that each rule is designated by a pair of character groupings: the first of which is a mnemonic name for the imperative and the second some relevant name for the object. In this form the program statements are known as *assembly language*, and the translating program that converts them from this representation to the required internal binary patterns is called an *assembler*. Assembly language programming is the lowest level at which practical programming on any serious scale is carried out.

Advantages and Disadvantages of Assembly Language Programming

Assembly language programming is the nearest to the hardware of the machine that a programmer will normally approach. It is not surprising, therefore, that effective assembly language programming demands a good understanding of the underlying hardware and of the way it works at the binary level. For very time-critical applications, and where computer memory is strictly limited, assembly language programming may be the most effective way to implement a solution. However, since processor speeds have increased considerably in recent years and memory is seldom a limiting factor with today's hardware, it is becoming harder to justify the use of assembly language programming against its drawbacks, which include:

▶ *Poor programmer productivity*. Assembly language programming is much more difficult and time consuming, and demands high skill levels.
▶ *Poor supportability*. Assembly language programs, especially when they have been written to meet tight time and memory constraints, can be very difficult to follow and understand, something which is a serious drawback when a program needs to be amended or modified at a later date. The technique lends itself to the use by clever programmers of ingenious and often idiosyncratic programming 'tricks', which even the original programmer has difficulty in understanding when he comes back to the program some time after its design.

High Order Languages

We have already seen that in assembly language programming the programmer is working right down at the hardware instruction set level, and even the simplest operation must be detailed precisely in terms of the instructions to be used and the actual memory locations to be accessed. A high order language adds another, and possibly several, layers of abstraction on to this primitive machine level. The language starts to approximate to the way in which the programmer might express the problem in human terms, although it is perhaps paradoxical that natural language turns out to be an unsuitable medium for programming. It is difficult to specify unambiguously the very formal and exact sets of rules that are needed to make up a computer program in such a rich and powerful language as English. For these reasons it is better to design a more limiting artificial language that does not permit ambiguity in its structures. In that way a programmer can be helped by the form and nature of the programming language itself. In a high order language the programmer does not deal directly with the contents of memory locations but with abstract, variable names which represent quantities and qualities which have a meaning in the real world. Compare the style of the short example below (Figure 3.7) of a section of a program written in BASIC with the earlier

```
10 REM program to calculate net pay
20 INPUT 'Enter Gross Pay'; gross
30 INPUT 'Enter Rate of Tax (percent)'; tax
40 net = gross - (gross * tax) / 100
50 PRINT 'Your Net Pay Is'; net
```

FIG. 3.7   Example of BASIC Code

example of an assembly language program. There are two main areas of difference: the commands, or instructions; and the representation of data.

Commands and Functions

In the high order language the commands are intended to provide a convenient way of instructing the computer to perform the sort of operations for which the particular language was designed. For example, one would expect a language designed for scientific applications, such as FORTRAN, to be rich in mathematical functions (e.g. the trigonometric functions sine or cosine) and so it is. A business-oriented language, such as COBOL, has features for handling large data files built into it, which makes it suitable for such applications as payroll processing and inventory accounting. A single function or command in a high order language will be implemented by a number of machine-level instructions. The more complex high order commands will be implemented by sections of machine code which are almost sub-programs in their own right. The process of converting high order language programs into machine code is covered later in this chapter.

Data Representation

In the assembly language program, the instructions operate directly on the contents of specified memory locations. It is up to the programmer to keep track of the relationship between the binary patterns stored in memory locations, and the 'real world' entities they represent. An important feature of high order languages is the concept of data variables; the data are handled by the program as named variables, and in most modern high order languages those variables can be given names which are meaningful to someone reading the high order language code. This point is illustrated in the BASIC program example given above. The programmer is no longer concerned with the exact location in the computer's memory of the items of data; the computer itself makes the necessary translation between, for example, the variable called 'net' and the value stored in a particular memory location.

Data Types

The concept of data types is an important feature of high order languages. Most high order languages allow variables to be declared as belonging to a specific type, or class, such as integers, 'real' numbers (numbers with a whole and a fractional part), or alphanumeric characters (so called 'string' variables) – these are the fundamental data representations introduced in Chapter 2. The main point of typing is that, having declared a variable to be of a particular type, the computer will treat it in the manner prescribed by the language definition for that type of variable. It will allocate the appropriate amount of storage space for the variable, and it will check when the variable is used in an operation that the type of the variable is appropriate to the operation. It would not be appropriate, for example, to multiply together two string variables, and any attempt to do so would result in the generation of an error message. Typing can provide a degree of validation on input; if the program is expecting a variable of a specified type to be input, it will reject any input which is of the wrong type. These aspects of typing offer a degree of protection against the effects of errors. Some languages, notably Ada and Pascal, allow the programmer to define his own types, thus extending the degree of protection. For example, in an Ada program one could define the type 'colour', and all the valid members of that type as Red, Orange, Yellow, Green, etc. Anything presented to the program which purports to be of type 'colour' but does not have one of the specified values would be rejected.

Compilation

For a program written in a high order language to run on a computer, it must first be translated into the machine code for that particular computer, normally via a process known as compilation. The compiler is itself a computer program, designed to perform the following tasks:

▶ Check that the high order language program submitted to it obeys the 'grammatical' rules, or syntax of the language. Any errors in the syntax will normally be reported by the compiler and will need to be corrected by the programmer and the program re-submitted to the compiler.

▶ Generate the appropriate machine code from the high order language statements. Normally this will be the machine code for the computer on which the compiler is running; but it is possible to cross-compile programs, that is, to generate machine code for a computer other than the one being used for the compilation. In this case the machine code will need to be output by the computer and transferred by some means to the target machine. The terms used to distinguish between what is submitted to the compiler and the code it produces are 'source code' to describe the high order language program, and 'object code' to describe the resultant machine code.

▶ Link into the generated machine code any library routines called for by the source program. These are standard routines which are part of the high order language, and which are called by name in the source code.

▶ Determine actual memory locations for the variables declared by name in the source code and for the program itself. It would also allocate working space in the computer's memory to be used by the program during its run.

Interpretation

An alternative to compilation is interpretation; in an interpreted language the high order language statements are translated and executed one at a time. No complete machine-code version of the source program is ever created. The most commonly encountered interpreted language is BASIC (Beginners' All-purpose Symbolic Instruction Code), which originated on multi-user, time sharing systems in teaching establishments. It was designed for interactive use, where speed of execution of a whole program is not significant compared with the speed of program preparation, development and modification. BASIC, in various forms, was adopted as the primary language for most home computers. Some readers would hesitate to call BASIC, in its original form at least, a high order language, although we have used it earlier as an example of such. We would defend this choice of example by pointing out that more recent versions of BASIC include all the expected program construction features such as WHILE-DO loops and CASE statements, and support block structuring through the use of procedures.

Operating Systems

The term 'operating system' is used to describe the programs which control the operation of a computer, manage its various resources of memory of different types, and the I/O devices which may be connected to it. The reader will recall from Chapter 2 that the simplest form of control program is one which loads the address of the first instruction to be obeyed into the sequence control register and then loads and executes instructions sequentially from subsequent memory locations until it runs out of instructions. At the other extreme the operating system for a large mainframe computer may occupy several megabytes of memory and contain a large range of capabilities. However, a requirement common to all computer systems is a simple program whose job it is to 'start up' the computer when it is first switched on.

The Bootstrap

At switch-on there are no 'meaningful' patterns in the volatile memory (none, that is, that represent intentional rules), so what is the processor doing? Clearly there is a need for some start-up mechanism whereby the processor at switch-on always commences by obeying some predefined set of rules that put the system into a fully specified state. This set of rules is known as the 'bootstrap', allegedly named after the phrase 'pulling oneself up by one's own bootstraps', and gives rise to such jargon as 'I must re-boot the machine'; that is, restart the system by causing the processor to re-execute the bootstrap instructions.

The bootstrap is normally provided by a special set of patterns that is permanently pre-programmed into the machine by means of a small segment of read-only memory (ROM). This set of patterns is usually located at the lowest address end of the main random access memory (RAM) and represents the first few rules that the processor is to execute immediately after switch-on. To achieve this, the program counter is preset by the hardware at switch-on to the first memory address of the pre-programmed ROM; often memory address zero.

Operating System Tasks

Some of the main tasks performed by the operating system are listed below:

▶ *Control of the Running of Programs*. This is a higher level task than the simple sequence control register operation described above. It will attend to the requirements of programs by allocating memory space for the program's variables and allocating workspace in memory. It may, in a multi-programming environment, have to control the activities of several programs running 'simultaneously' on behalf of a number of users. The term is used in quotation marks because in a single processor system true simultaneous processing is impossible by definition. Down at the hardware level, the machine can be obeying only one instruction at a time. The operating system, by sharing the time of the processor between a number of programs can create the illusion of simultaneous or concurrent activity. Complex rules are required to tell the operating system on what basis to allocate time to different programs, depending on such factors as the priority allocated to the program and the nature of the different tasks. Some tasks are relatively light users of the processor, whilst others, notably those involving many mathematical calculations (i.e. 'number crunching'), impose a heavy load on it. A system which must respond in real time to transient events in the outside world, such as a weapon control-system, must have a means of allowing the control of programs to be interrupted in order to attend to the demands of the outside stimulus.

▶ *Control of System Resources*. Resources include memory and input/output devices. Programs running 'under the control' of the operating system will make requests to the operating system when they need to use resources. The operating system will contain sections of program code known as 'handlers' for dealing with the different types of device which may be connected to the system. These will handle requests from programs for the services of the devices concerned, and pass them on to the device in a form which it can 'understand'.

▶ *File Management*. Most operating systems contain features for the management of information held by the system. This aspect is covered in Chapter 4.

▶ *Security*. The operating system may have security features built into it, such as a user password scheme which is used to control access to the system and its resources. This topic is returned to in Chapter 10.

Processor Hardware

We have managed to get this far without using a hardware model any more complicated than the rudimentary one introduced in Chapter 2. To complete this account of processing in support of CIS, it would be appropriate to drop down a couple of layers of detail and see how the processing functions are implemented by real hardware. The essential processor configuration is shown in Figure 3.8.

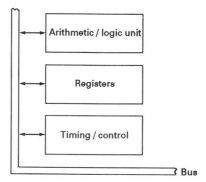

FIG. 3.8   General Microprocessor Architecture

Although it has to be admitted that there are processors in use in current CIS applications which are based on multi-component implementations of that basic architecture, the trend is for CIS to be based on processors which have all the elements of Figure 3.8 fabricated on a single silicon chip, i.e. on microprocessors. Such is the power of the modern, single-chip microprocessor that there are no applications in the CIS field which it would not be feasible to base on a system using microprocessors. This is not to say that inside the 'box' of a modern micro-computer there will be only one integrated circuit, or chip. Whilst the main central processing unit (CPU) will be on one chip, i.e. a microprocessor chip, there will be many other chips inside the box, mounted on printed circuit boards (PCBs). There will be a number of chips for the computer's memory, and the several forms this memory may take are described in the next chapter. There will be other chips doing such jobs as controlling access to the system's peripherals, such as mass storage devices, and yet other chips controlling input and output (I/O) devices, such as keyboards, displays, printers and communications channels to the outside world. Some of these auxiliary chips may be microprocessors in their own right, so that a box which purports to contain a single computer may, in fact, contain a number of microprocessors. In conventional computers, only one of these chips will be 'in charge', i.e. is the CPU of the computer, but as will be shown later on, a new architecture is appearing where computers are able to harness the power of several CPUs simultaneously.

To describe the increase in capabilities of microprocessors since their first appearance around 15 years ago as 'dramatic' would be an understatement. The first commercially available microprocessor, the Intel 4004, used a 4-bit word, that is, it could operate on only four bits at a time. The chip contained the equivalent of over 2,000 transistors,and could execute a simple instruction, such as adding two numbers, in about 11 microseconds. Compare that with the latest offering from the same manufacturer. The Intel 80386 is a 32-bit microprocessor, whose chip contains the equivalent of around 275,000 transistors. It can execute the simple 'add' instruction in a fraction of a microsecond.

The 4-bit devices were of little use in general purpose computing, but found application in programmable calculators, and a wide range of 'embedded' roles, where they took the place of 'hardwired' electronic logic. In the mid-1970s, the first 8-bit microprocessor chips, such as the Intel 8080 and the Zilog Z80 were marketed. Curiously, their main impact was in the home computing and 'hobby' area. Such machines as Sir Clive Sinclair's ZX80, ZX81 and ZX Spectrum, Acorn's BBC 'B' microcomputer and a range of offerings from firms such as Atari and Commodore, supplied a completely new computer market place. There were relatively few 'serious' computers based on 8-bit chips. Only one operating system, Digital Research's CP/M, has survived from the 8-bit era.

In the late 1970s, with the introduction of 16-bit microprocessor chips, such as the Intel 8086 and the Motorola 68000, microcomputers came of age and started to make a major impact on the business computing market. Without a doubt, the flagship of this movement was the IBM Personal Computer based on a variant of the Intel 8086. The architecture of this machine, and the accompanying MicroSoft Disc Operating System (MSDOS), have become *de facto* industry standards for 16-bit microcomputers. As with most 'standards', it may be argued that the IBM PC is not the most efficient design for a 16-bit microcomputer, nor is MSDOS an ideal operating system from a number of viewpoints. Their advantage lies in the vast numbers in which they (and the compatible devices or 'clones') have been sold, and therefore the enormous range of useful software which has been developed to run in this environment.

The advent of advanced 32-bit microprocessors like Intel's 80386 and Motorola's 68020 has brought us to something of a crossroads in microprocessor system architecture. The direct way ahead would seem to be the development of microprocessors with increasing complexity and power, but at least two other paths now seem to be available. One of these is the reduced instruction set computer (RISC) approach, and the other (which may itself be based on RISC microprocessors) is the development of parallel processing.

RISC

We have already introduced the concept that assembly language is the lowest level at which programming is normally carried out. The commands available for the assembly language programmer to use are generally those which form the instruction set of the processor concerned, and they are implemented in the hardware of the processor. Although, as we have seen, the program used to convert the mnemonic codes of the assembly language into the binary form understood by the hardware is itself a program, i.e. software (the 'assembler'), the instructions in their binary form are translated into the appropriate action by features of the processor's hardware. A major block of circuitry in the design of any processor is the instruction decoder. The trend in the design of processor chips until quite recently was to implement as many instructions as possible in hardware. For example, the Z80 8-bit microprocessor chip made by the Zilog company and found in an enormous range of applications has a very rich instruction set, with over 600 elements. Given that the Z80 is an 8-bit processor, and $2^8 = 256$, less than half the instructions can be held in a single byte. Many of them are therefore held in two bytes, and some in three. With instruction sets of this style, some very complicated operations indeed can be implemented using a few machine-code instructions. The Intel 80386 has an enormous range of capabilities built into the hardware. Its instruction set recognises the concept of data types, which was discussed earlier in this chapter as a feature of high level languages. On the 80386 chip is hardware to support a wide range of memory-management features, as well as multi-tasking (i.e. the support of a number of apparently concurrent activities).

The price to be paid for the flexibility of a processor with a very full instruction set lies in the complexity of its design and in its speed of operation. For many applications, quite a lot of the more 'exotic' features of the instruction set will never be used. Applications which do use these features are totally dependent on the hardware, and may be difficult to transfer to other hardware which does not support all the instructions of the original hardware. The current trend is towards processors with much smaller instruction sets, using the so called reduced instruction set computer (RISC) approach (the 'conventional' processors are known as complex instruction set computers—CISC—to distinguish them from RISC machines). An example of the RISC approach is the Acorn RISC machine (ARM), a 32-bit machine whose instruction set has been pared down to the bare minimum. The flexibility is restored by using instructions implemented in software, which, of course, are built out of basic instructions from the RISC set. One of the stimuli for the development of RISC architecture is the greatly increased density and reduced cost of memory. At the time the Z80 and other chips of its 'period' were being designed, 1 KByte was a lot of memory, and there were clear advantages in having a very capable processor which allowed compact code to be written. As we shall see in the next chapter, memories of several MBytes are now commonplace in microcomputers. Very high processing speeds are possible in RISC.

Parallel Processing

For the very highest processing power, the whole concept of the computer as we have seen it so far in this chapter must be challenged. When we spoke of 'multi-tasking', the apparent concurrency was just that—an appearance. Down at the machine level the processor, albeit very quickly, is obeying one instruction at a time. The only way around that bottleneck is to build systems with several processors in parallel. Parallel processing achieves true concurrency, but demands a whole new approach to the design of the software to take advantage of its power. One of the most exciting new developments in the processor field in recent years is the transputer. (TRANSistor-comPUTER: the name is chosen to imply that the transputer will be just as much of a 'building block' in future systems as the single transistor was in the past.) This takes the microprocessor concept a step further and puts a whole computer: processor, memory and input/output channels, on to a single chip. The computer is a RISC device; it is very fast and can be used singly to good effect, but its main strength lies in the capability to connect a number of devices in parallel. A transputer can be connected directly to four other transputers, using input/output channels built into the chip. Using this capability, arrays of transputers may be built, offering extremely high processing power. It is claimed by the manufacturer (Inmos) that the processing power available is directly proportional to the number of transputers in the array, regardless of its size. With conventional microprocessors, some increase in power can be achieved by connecting a number of them together in a network, but the relative increase drops off sharply as more devices are added, because of the computing power 'overhead' needed to manage their interaction.

The Architecture of a Typical Microprocessor

It would be inappropriate to finish this chapter without devoting a little time to looking in some detail at an actual microprocessor chip, to identify its component parts and compare its structure with that of the simplified processor models given thus far. The device chosen for this investigation is the Intel 8086, manufactured by the Intel Corporation. This chip is widely used in personal computers and a variant of it, the Intel 8088, is used in the ubiquitous IBM PC and its 'clones'.

Basic Structure

Figure 3.9 illustrates the internal architecture of the 8086 chip. All of the elements of the general processor model in Figure 3.9 can be identified, such as the registers and the arithmetic and logic unit (ALU). The buses are data 'highways' between the different elements of the CPU. They are 16 bits 'wide', that is, they can handle 16 bits in parallel. The registers are also 16 bits wide, but the machine's instructions are byte-oriented, that is, they are treated as being composed of a number of 8-bit bytes. It is the bus width that distinguishes the 8088 chip from the 8086. In the former the internal bus width is only 8 bits, although it has a 16-bit CPU identical to that of the 8086. In applications such as the personal computer, which are used largely for byte-oriented tasks like text processing, the use of a 'pseudo' 16-bit chip has not been found to be a significant drawback.

The CPU divides into two sub-systems. On the left of the dotted vertical line is the bus interface unit (BIU), whilst the area to the right of the line is the execution unit (EU). Access to the memory and all other resources in the world outside the chip is via the external bus and the BIU. Instructions are fetched from memory and 'queued' for the EU in the instruction queue. This queue is termed a 'prefetch queue' or 'instruction pipeline', and is used to speed up the operation of the CPU. By overlapping the time taken to execute instructions and the time to fetch the next instruction, the time wasted by the CPU in waiting for the next instruction is minimised. Of course, the 'prefetching' is done on a purely sequential basis, that is, instructions are fetched in the sequence in which they are stored in memory. When an instruction is encountered which breaks the sequence, such as a jump, the prefetch queue must be reset, and the prefetching carries on in sequence from the memory location to which program execution was transferred.

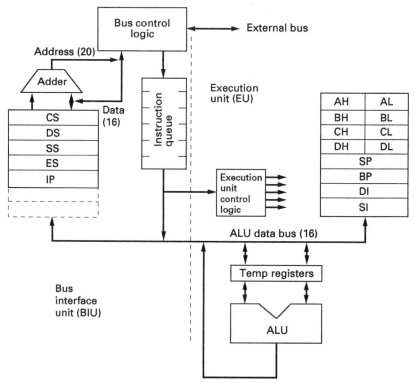

FIG. 3.9   Internal Architecture of 8086 Chip

Addressing Strategy

Although the CPU is a 16-bit device, it has a 20-bit addressing scheme. The adder in the BIU is used to add four zero bits to the low end of a 16-bit 'segment' address (where a segment is 64 Kbytes) to form a 20-bit word, and then to add to that another 16-bit word from one of the segment registers. Using the 20-bit address thus formed, the CPU can directly address 1 Mbyte of physical memory.

The Execution Unit

The EU operates independently of the BIU, fetching and executing instructions from the BIU instruction queue as required. If the instruction queue is empty, the EU will wait for the BIU to place another byte in it. The main components of the EU are the eight 16-bit general purpose registers, and the arithmetic and logic unit (ALU). The registers are arranged as four general purpose registers (grouped as eight 8-bit registers), and four special purpose registers used to support the addressing strategy. The general purpose registers may be used for such tasks as the storage of intermediate results from a calculation, or to hold data which is frequently used by a program. The ALU is organised to work on two 'operands' at a time, to perform arithmetic operations such as addition, multiplication or division, and logical operations such as AND, OR, Exclusive OR and inversion.

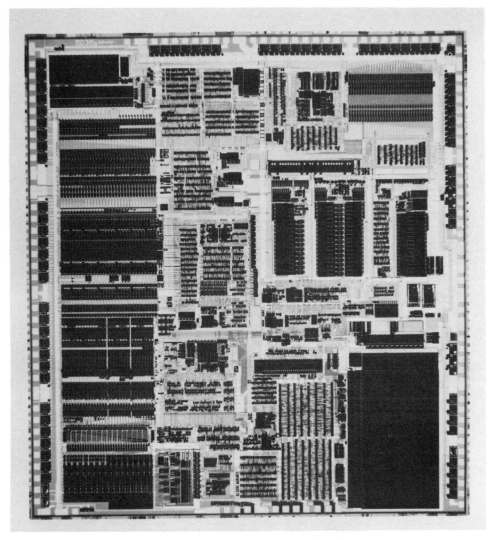

FIG. 3.10   Component Layout of Intel 80386 (*INTEL Corporation UK Ltd*)

Physical Construction

The whole of the device illustrated in Figure 3.9 is fabricated on to a single silicon chip. A greatly enlarged photograph of the more complex 80386 chip is shown in Figure 3.10. The same fabrication technique is used in the manufacture of processors, memories and other microelectronic devices. Using a series of photographic masks, the pattern of the microcircuit is transcribed on to the surface of a thin wafer of silicon, and the circuit is created through an etching process. The accuracy with which the pattern can be transferred on to the silicon surface is a key determinant of the component density of the chip. Using conventional photographic methods, 'feature sizes' (i.e. line widths) of 2 to 4 μm are possible. To achieve smaller feature sizes, down to and below 1 μm, techniques such as X-ray

Fig. 3.11   Sectioned View of Encapsulated Intel 80386 (*INTEL Corporation UK Ltd*)

or electron-beam lithography are called for. Through a process known as doping, measured amounts of impurities are introduced into the silicon in order to give it the required semiconductor properties. The most common variety of silicon microcircuit is that using the metal oxide semiconductor (MOS) technique, the title of which is a reference to the type of material used to create the circuit on the silicon surface.

The connections to the outside world are made via the pads around the perimeter of the chip. Wires are connected between these pads and the pins of the device, which provide mechanical support as well as electrical connections. This is shown in the sectioned view of the whole encapsulated device in Figure 3.11.

Summary

A large conceptual step has to be taken to get from the machine-level manipulation of simple symbols in Chapter 2 to the complex processing capabilities described in this chapter. In the flight simulator example used at the beginning of the chapter we attributed the success of that program to the skill of the designer in capturing the essential characteristics of the system to be simulated, and in representing them in a realistic way on a simple computer system. In CIS the problem is too complex and the conceptual step between the raw hardware of a digital computer and the processes required by the user is too great to be taken in one step. Between the design of the top level, user-visible functions and the basic hardware of the machines used lie several layers each of which summarises the complexities of the lower layers and harnesses their capabilities for the designers of functions in the higher layers. This approach is essential if we are to stand any chance at all of understanding CIS.

Imagine a complex system, more complex than the flight simulator model given earlier, which was described in one diagram down to the level of detail of the circuit diagrams of the individual microcircuits. The use of such a diagram as an aid to understanding the whole system would be about as sensible as using a 1:50,000 scale map to plan a journey from London to Karachi. The concept is much easier to describe than it is to implement reliably. The practical problems in the design and implementation of large scale CIS, of managing the levels of complexity, of co-ordinating the work of many people, and of selecting the right components and integrating them into a system are dealt with in Chapters 7 and 8.

4.

Storage

Introduction

We saw in Chapter 2 that the ability to store symbols, whether they represent information or instructions for processes to be performed on other symbols, is at the heart of the information processing concept. The point was made that any device which can be in one of two possible states can potentially be used as a 'store' for binary digits, or bits. Thus a mechanical switch, which can be in one of two possible positions, or a lamp which can be either on or off, are examples of devices which could in theory be used as digital storage devices. A variety of different physical devices are used to store information in practical computer systems. In the first part of this chapter, the characteristics and capabilities of these devices are examined. The chapter then goes on to show how, using the physical storage devices as a foundation, the storage of information may be organised to support the CIS processes.

Physical Storage Categories

The Classes of Information Storage

Although all the storage devices used by computer systems have in common the requirement to store information in a binary form, when one looks more closely at the details of the systems and the way they work, four different classes of information storage may be determined, and it would help our investigation of storage devices to examine them in these four groupings. They are shown below, listed in an increasing order of potential capacity and decreasing order of speed of access.

▶ Temporary storage for processors
▶ Processor main memory
▶ Mass storage, with direct access
▶ Auxiliary, archival or backing storage.

Temporary Storage for Processors

As seen in Chapter 2, processors use temporary areas of memory in the form of registers which are used to hold the data words being worked on by the processor at any given moment. Some processors use other small areas of memory to speed up their operation. Scratchpad memory is used to hold intermediate results of processes, in much the same way as one uses the memory function on a pocket calculator. Another way to speed up operation is to anticipate the order in which instructions will be executed and queue instructions for the processor via an instruction cache or pipeline, which is another form of temporary storage. An example of this was seen in the Intel 8086 chip described in the previous chapter. Temporary storage calls for the fastest possible access but small capacity; probably no more than a few thousand bits.

Processor Main Memory

The 'main memory' is that block of storage which is directly addressed by the processor, and referred to by the descriptions of memory locations or addresses which form part of the hardware level instructions of the machine. The term 'random access memory' (RAM) is frequently used, or rather misused, to describe this type of memory. Although RAM does indeed allow random access, in that the time to access any memory location is the same, the term is normally used to imply that the memory may be written to as well as read from, to distinguish it from read only memory (ROM), which is described a little further on. The amount of main memory which a particular machine can access depends upon the address structure used. For example, in a machine which is based on an 8-bit word, the amount of memory which can be directly addressed is 256 bits, since $2^8 = 256$. This is a very small amount of memory, and not enough for most practical purposes, so means have to be found of allowing the processor to address more. The most common technique in 8-bit processors is to use two words at a time, i.e. 16 bits to address the main memory, thereby allowing direct access to 65,536 memory locations, (or 64K). Even this is not a very large amount of memory by the standards of today's machines, so other techniques, such as bank switching, are employed to allow access for microprocessors with 16-bit addressing to many megabytes of main memory. In the case of more recent machines with full 32-bit addressing, such techniques are unnecessary, since with 32 bits one can theoretically address up to 2^{32} or about 4.3 thousand million memory locations (i.e. 4 gigabytes, assuming that each memory location contains one byte).

Main memory must be fast to keep up with modern fast processors. If the processor cannot access the memory within one of its operating cycles, it must wait for the memory; these so-called 'wait states' are a waste of processor time. Fortunately, the same technological advances which are making faster processor speeds possible are also responsible for decreasing memory access times, so 'zero wait state' operation is frequently possible.

High storage densities are necessary for main memory. Having said earlier that main memories of several megabytes are becoming commonplace, they have to be accommodated in a relatively small space. Memory density has increased dramatically in recent years, as the graph at Figure 4.1 shows.

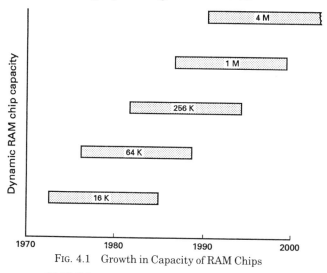

FIG. 4.1   Growth in Capacity of RAM Chips

Read only memory (ROM) has many characteristics in common with main memory, but the vital difference is that its contents may be read but not altered during normal operation. Some ROM is permanently fixed, i.e. once the bit pattern has been set it is there for the life of the device. This is the 'masked' ROM, so-called because the bit pattern the device is to hold is described by one of the photographic masks used to determine the pattern to be etched on to the surface of the silicon chip. In other types of ROM, the contents may be altered. The programmable ROM (PROM) can have its contents set by a special instrument in a process commonly referred to as PROM 'blowing'. Other varieties of the PROM include the EPROM (erasable PROM), whose contents can be erased prior to re-programming by exposure for a few seconds to intense ultraviolet light. The chip encapsulation has a quartz window set into it to allow this process to be performed. In the EAROM (electrically alterable ROM) the contents may be altered electrically without the need for UV erasure. The program code held in such devices is known as firmware; it is somewhere between hardware and software. In general, one will encounter masked ROM in applications with very stable code, that is, code which is not likely to be subject to change and fairly large production quantities. For applications involving small numbers of devices, or where changes are likely, one of the PROM devices will offer better economy. ROM needs to share many of the characteristics of the read/write random access memory (RAM) used for main memory. It must have low access times and a storage density comparable to that of RAM.

Storage of Data for On-Line Access

Mass store usually has a large capacity compared with main memory. It is commonly used for holding data files to be worked on by programs and elements of programs which are too large to fit into main memory all at once. When an element of a program is required to be run, it is copied into main memory from

FIG. 4.2 PROM Chip (*INTEL Corporation UK Ltd*)

mass storage, either into a vacant area of memory, or by overwriting an area of main memory which was occupied by an element of the program which is no longer required. Mass store is not directly addressed at the basic machine instruction level, but is accessed via a software routine or handler, which is part of the operating system of the machine. Mass store may be used in close conjunction with main memory, in what is known as a virtual memory system. The processor appears to be able to address much more main memory than is physically available, because the operating system allows it to view main memory and an element of mass storage as one address space. The operating system's memory management facility must control the exchange of data between main memory and mass storage. The combination of physical main memory size, virtual memory size and the size and characteristics of programs to be run by the system is critical. If the physical memory size is small relative to the size of the programs to be run (or the size of the segments into which the programs are divided), the system will run very inefficiently, spending an inordinate amount of time 'swapping' program segments in and out of main memory from mass storage.

Speed of access is not as critical a requirement for mass storage as it is for main memory, although for applications which make frequent use of mass store, such as data retrieval or a virtual memory system with a small physical memory, access to mass store may become a critical factor in system performance, as described above.

Mass storage may be fixed, that is, built into the machine, or exchangeable, in which case the storage medium is removable from the machine. With exchangeable store, though the amount of information actually present on the system ('mounted') is limited to the capacity of however many units of exchangeable store the system is equipped to have mounted at any one time, there is no limit to the number of units which may be off-line. This type of storage may also be used as a medium for the physical transfer of programs and data between computer systems, in which case common standards for data recording media are important.

It is normal for mass store to be non-volatile, that is, the contents of the memory are preserved when the power to the memory device is removed.

A form of read-only mass storage is being taken into use by systems with a requirement to have large amounts of fixed information on-line. An example of this type of information in a military system is digital terrain data, used as the basis of map displays.

Auxiliary Store

The fourth 'level' of storage is required mainly for the long-term storage of data. In systems served by fixed mass store there is a need for a storage medium which can be used to take archive copies of the contents of the mass store, and to provide a means of data transfer between installations. In systems with a need to be able to recover from failures with minimum loss of information, auxiliary store may be used in an on-line, archiving mode. As changes are made to the information held on mass storage, a copy is sent to the archive store. Following a system failure in which mass storage has been corrupted, the information may be restored by loading the last complete copy of the information from back-up dumps which have been made periodically (say daily), and updating this by applying to it the changes recorded on the on-line archive store. Auxiliary store is not required for on-line read access during normal system operation, hence 'random' or direct access is not a major requirement, nor is speed of access. The overriding need is for high storage density and low cost per bit.

In the table at Figure 4.3, the requirements and characteristics of the four levels of memory are compared. The table also shows the technology which is used to implement each memory type; the technologies are described below.

Storage Technologies

Semiconductor Memory

Semiconductor memory uses the same technology as the processor, that is, microcircuitry fabricated in the form of 'chips' of silicon and certain other materials. There is a range of different types, according to application. Semiconductor memory is essentially volatile (except ROM, of course), but in many applications memories are now built with battery back-up, so that they remain powered and retain stored data even when the main power to the installation is removed.

There are two basic varieties of semiconductor memory, regardless of the fabrication technique; that is, static and dynamic RAM. In static RAM the basic storage element is the transistor bistable circuit, or 'flip-flop', illustrated in Figure 4.4. The circuit design is such that if one transistor is switched on, i.e. is conducting current, then the other will be switched off. One state is used to represent the

Memory Category	Technology	Access Time	Capacity	Transfer Rate
Processor temporary storage	Static RAM	Under 30 ns	256 Kbit per chip	10 s of MBit/ s
Main memory	Dynamic RAM	Under 100 ns	1 MBit per chip	10 s of MBit/ s
Mass storage	(a) Hard disc (b) Floppy	15-25 ms 100 s of ms	Up to 1 Gbyte per disc Up to 1.44 MByte per disc	2-8 MBit/ s 100 s of KBit/ s
	(c) Bubble	10 s of ms	Up to 1 MBit per chip	100 s of KBit/ s
Auxiliary	Magnetic tape	Serial read	At least 40 MByte on 800 m reel	100 KBit/ s- 1 MBit/ s
Read only (or Write once, Read many - WORM)	(a) Optical disc	150 ms- 1.5 s	2 GByte per side 12" disc	0.4-4 MBit/ s
	(b) Optical tape	Serial read	1 TByte [1] on 800 m reel	expected to be 100s of KBit/s

[1] TByte = terobyte, or one million megabytes

FIG. 4.3   Memory Characteristics and Requirements

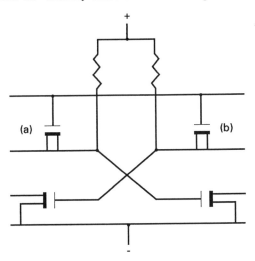

FIG. 4.4   Static RAM Circuit Element

binary '1' condition and the other binary '0'. Once the memory element has been set to one state or the other, it will remain that way until the power is removed from the circuit. The static RAM has the advantage of speed, but suffers from the disadvantage of size and hence reduced storage density, due to the relative complexity of the individual storage elements. Static RAM may be found in the first level of memory described earlier in the chapter. In the dynamic RAM the storage element is created by the inherent capacitance of single transistor circuit, as shown in Figure 4.5.

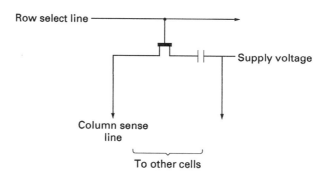

Fig. 4.5   Dynamic RAM Circuit Element

When the capacitor is charged, the '1' state is represented, and when it is discharged, the '0'. The snag is that, because of the leakage resistance of the circuit, once set to the '1' state, the capacitor's charge takes about a millisecond to drain away down to the '0' state. To prevent this from happening, a periodic refresh signal is required, to top up all those cells which have been set to '1', in order to keep them that way indefinitely. It is from this refreshing action that the term 'dynamic' is derived. The refreshing must not interfere with the processes of reading and writing, so these activities must be interleaved with each other in time. The simplified block diagram of a dynamic RAM chip at Figure 4.6 shows the mechanism required to control access to the memory and the refresh cycle.

The example shown is a 4-KBit dynamic RAM, with the memory cells arranged as a matrix of 64 columns × 64 rows. In the middle of the chip, between rows 31 and 32, is a row of refresh/sense amplifiers, each one connected to all the cells in its column via the sense/digit lines. To cut down on the number of wires, or pins, needed to access the memory's contents, addresses are coded as 6 bits ($2^6 = 64$), and applied to the chip via an address decoder and multiplexer. The 6 bit address specifying the required row is first applied, decoded and held in a buffer whilst the 6 bits specifying the column are applied and decoded. Once the whole address has been specified, the appropriate row and column lines are activated. On the row which is selected, the charges from the cell capacitors of each column are transferred on to the digit/sense line connecting the cells of that column to the respective sense/refresh amplifiers. Only on the selected column will that line be enabled, and thus for read access the charge from the selected memory cell will be amplified and output via the data out line. For writing, the input data is applied to the data in/out line, thus setting the sense/refresh amplifier to the required state and causing that state to be applied via the digit/refresh line to the required cell. The memory constantly cycles through a Read-Write-Modify cycle; reading and refreshing occur in the same action, that is, when a value is read, it is automatically written back to refresh the cell contents. To make a 4 KByte memory,

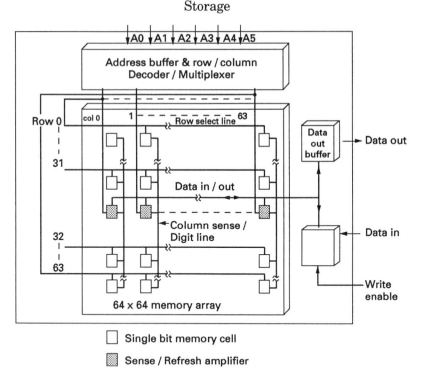

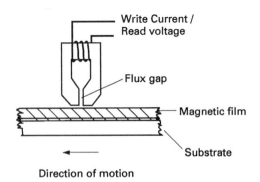

FIG. 4.6 Dynamic RAM Block Diagram

eight 4 KBit chips like the one in Fig 4.6 are wired in parallel and selected simultaneously.

Magnetic Surface Memory: Basic Principle

The basic principle of magnetic surface memories is the same as that used in audio tape recording. The recording medium has a strong base or substrate, which is coated with a thin film of magnetic metal oxide. A mechanical arrangement is required in order to bring the magnetic surface either into direct physical contact with or very close to a reading and writing head, as shown in Figure 4.7. The coils

FIG. 4.7 Magnetic Surface and Read/Write Head

in the head are energised by electrical currents generated by circuitry within the storage device, in response to the data presented to it. The currents produce magnetic fields, which magnetise the domains of the oxide surface. In this way, the data are 'written' to the magnetic surface. The reading action depends upon the induction of voltages in the head by the magnetic fields of the magnetised domains in the oxide surface, as they pass by the head. The voltages are amplified and interpreted by circuitry within the storage device.

Types of Magnetic Surface Device

The different varieties of magnetic surface recording devices are distinguished by the mechanical arrangements used to bring the surface and the heads into contact. Magnetic tape units are similar in principle to those devices used for the recording of analogue audio and video signals. In the disc unit the magnetic surface is deposited on to a flat disc, which is spun about an axis passing through its centre. Information is recorded in concentric tracks by a head which is arranged to move in and out at right angles to the direction of rotation of the disc, parallel to its surface. A magnetic surface recording device which is more or less obsolete now is the drum, in which the magnetic oxide layer is on the outside surface of a rotating drum. The information is recorded in tracks which go around the circumference of the drum. There is one head per track, arranged to lie close to the magnetic surface, parallel to the drum's axis of rotation. In the magnetic strip device, the recording medium is, in essence, a short length of magnetic tape attached to some stiff backing, which is read by sliding it through a slot in the reading device. The strips attached to some types of credit and identity card are examples of this technique. Of all these devices, the tape and disc are the most important from the computer system point of view, and they are described in more detail in the following paragraphs.

Magnetic Tape

Tape is essentially a serial storage medium. Recording starts at one end of the tape and goes on until the tape is full. To find a given piece of information on a tape, one must start at the beginning and read through the tape serially until the required information is found. Thus the time taken to access any given item of information on a tape depends entirely upon where on the tape the information is recorded. Tape is therefore not a random access storage medium. This important characteristic obviously governs the way tape storage is used, and its most common application is in archiving and off-line storage of large quantities of data. For archiving purposes, its serial characteristic is no drawback. Data will be dumped to the tape archive from mass store in one serial operation, and when it is required to use the data thus stored, they will be read back into mass store in a serial operation. When used as an on-line archive, as introduced earlier in this chapter, its serial operation is still appropriate. Changes to the data held on mass store are copied onto the tape, where they are stored sequentially in time order. If the tape has to be used following a failure to bring a database back up to date, the changes are simply read back from the tape in the order in which they were recorded.

Just as in the domestic audio market, there are various methods of packaging tape for use as a data storage medium. The earliest tape drives were reel-to-reel machines, using open-reel tape. Drives which are designed to enable the computer to search the tape for given items of data must have mechanisms for stopping the tape rapidly when the required place on the tape has been found, and for accelerating the tape quickly to resume searching for further data. Some quite complicated and therefore expensive servo-controlled mechanisms are needed to achieve this on the fast tape drives found in large data processing installations. Where the tape is only ever used as an archive medium such complication is unnecessary, and more simple tape streamer devices can be used. Various sizes of tape cartridge and cassette are used for data storage, bringing the advantages of ease of use and some protection of the tape against the effects of dirt and moisture.

A form of data recording on tape which was developed for the home computer industry relies on the conversion of data into audio frequency signals which can be recorded on domestic audio tape cassettes. This has the advantage of great cheapness, since the instrument required is an ordinary domestic cassette tape-recorder, which can be bought for a few tens of pounds. Its major disadvantage is speed, or rather lack of it, as anyone who has waited several minutes for a program to load from an audio cassette into a home computer will testify. For this reason alone, data recording on audio cassettes has no serious application in the CIS field. It is interesting to note, however, that the technique of converting the data into audio frequency signals for recording on the tape has much in common with one of the techniques used to transmit data over audio frequency communications channels, a point which is returned to in Chapter 6.

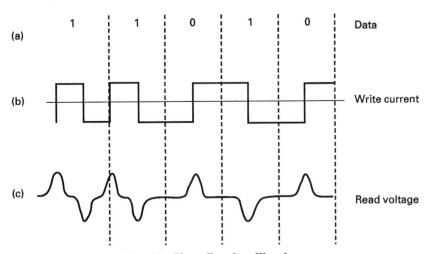

FIG. 4.8   Phase Encoding Waveforms

In digital data recording systems, data are recorded on tape in the form of parallel tracks using a pulse recording technique. The 'industry standard' is a nine track format, with a recording density of 1600 bits per inch. With nine parallel tracks, it is possible to record a byte at a time in parallel across the tape. One could calculate quite easily that with this standard, a 2400-foot reel of magnetic tape can hold well over 40 Mbytes of data. The recording mechanism specified by the standard is phase encoding. In this method the head current to write a '1' is a positive followed by a negative pulse, and that to write '0' is the other way round. Figure 4.8 shows the head current waveform to write the binary pattern '11010', and the voltage generated when reading this pattern off the tape. The benefit of this technique lies in the fact that signal timing can be derived directly from the recorded signal itself. As the read voltage waveform at Figure 4.8 (c) shows, there is a pulse (either positive or negative going) in the middle of every bit period.

Magnetic Disc Stores

The general arrangement of a disc storage device is shown in Figure 4.9. The disc is rotated about its axis, and the heads (normally one on either side of the

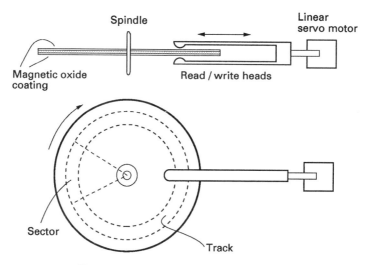

FIG. 4.9   Disc Drive: General Arrangement

disc, so that both sides may be in use at the same time) can move in and out over the recording surfaces at right angles to the direction of rotation. The disc store is a random access device. Data are stored on the disc in concentric tracks, which are further subdivided into sectors. The software used to access the disc by the processor (the disc handler; part of the operating system) addresses the disc by track and sector. Addresses are translated by hardware, i.e. circuitry in the disc drive unit, into commands to the head to place itself over the correct track, and start reading/writing when the correct sector is under the head. The time taken to access a given item of information on the disc is thus the sum of the time taken to get the head into the right place (the seek time) and the time for the right sector to come under the head. This latter time is referred to as the 'latency'. The average latency of a disc drive is equal to half a period of revolution.

Discs are used in a variety of different guises. Amongst the earliest types to be developed, and still in extensive use, is that which uses removable rigid discs.

These discs are often found in a multi-platter configuration with up to 12 discs on the one spindle, each one served by a pair of read/write heads.

FIG. 4.10   Disc and Head Assembly of Multi-Platter Winchester Disk Drive
(*Vermont Research Limited*)

The construction and operation of this type of disc unit demands mechanical precision of a very high order. The discs themselves must be made to close tolerances, as must the mechanism controlling the movement in and out of the read/write heads. The more precisely can the positioning of the heads be controlled, the closer together can the tracks be placed, and hence the greater the storage capacity of the unit. In this type of drive the heads actually 'fly' over the surface of the discs, planing on a viscous film of air thinner than the thickness of a human hair. The need to operate such devices in a dust-free atmosphere is one of the main environmental constraints on computer systems of this generation. A failure dreaded by data processing managers using this type of equipment is the 'head crash', where due to the ingress of some foreign matter—a few grains of dust would be enough—the head no longer planes but crashes into the surface of the disc, causing severe physical damage and loss of data.

The advent of the rigid disc in a sealed unit has greatly reduced the likelihood of this sort of problem. The 'Winchester' disc unit has a rigid disc and head unit inside a sealed package. There is some divergence of opinion over the origin of the name Winchester for this device. There seems little doubt that it originated within the IBM company, but the name appears to have no association with either Winchester, Hampshire, nor, except indirectly, with any of the seven towns named Winchester in the USA. The most plausible explanation is that the original IBM product number was 3030, and, as every Western fan knows, that is the calibre of the famous Winchester '73 repeating rifle . . .

Because the unit is sealed, the environmental problem which afflicted the type of unit described above no longer applies. Taking away the need for the disc platter to be removed and instead fixing it into the device makes it easier to achieve the close tolerances needed for high storage densities. Winchester units with discs only 3.5 inches in diameter are found in personal computer systems, offering storage capacities of up to 70 MBytes. Units with larger diameter discs, e.g. 5.25 or 8 inches, can hold several hundred megabytes. Multi-platter Winchester discs have now been introduced, pushing up the storage capacity further still. Should there be a need to remove the mass storage from the machine, removable Winchester disc drives are available, where the whole disc and head assembly may be taken out of the machine, just as easily as taking a cartridge out of a tape cartridge device. This is very useful for systems used for processing classified information; instead of having to keep the whole machine in a suitably protected environment, when it is not in use the Winchester drive may be removed and locked away securely. Figure 4.10 shows the disc and head assembly of an 8-inch multi-platter Winchester drive.

Floppy Discs

The development of the personal computer has been largely responsible for the establishment of the floppy disc as the most commonly used computer mass storage medium. The disc itself uses a non-rigid (i.e. floppy!) substrate such as Mylar coated on both sides with a film of magnetic oxide, and is enclosed within a cardboard or plastic sleeve. Once inserted into the drive, the disc is engaged and rotated within its sleeve. A slot in the sleeve allows the head to come into contact with the disc's surface. Early floppy discs were 8 inches in diameter, but the most common floppy disc size today, and a 'de facto' industry standard is 5¼ inches. The discs of this size used with the original IBM Personal Computer (PC), introduced in 1981, had a capacity of 360 KBytes. Nowadays such discs can be formatted to hold up to 1.2 MBytes. An even smaller floppy disc, of 3½-inch diameter, has come on to the market in recent years. Its future has been ensured through its adoption as the standard for IBM's new personal computer, the Personal System 2 (PS 2), but 5¼-inch devices are now so numerous that they will be in use for many years to come.

Floppy discs serve a number of roles. In small computer systems they are the mass storage medium. A typical small PC configuration would be a machine with 640 KBytes of main memory, and two 5¼-inch floppy disc drives.

Going up the scale in PCs, one finds that the built-in Winchester disc drive provides the main mass storage, with floppies relegated to an auxiliary role. They may be used for archiving and back-up (although it takes a lot of floppies to hold the full contents of some of the larger Winchester devices; for serious archiving, a tape streamer is a more practicable proposition). Probably the main use for the floppy in this context is as a data-transfer medium. Data and program files may be transferred between machines via floppy discs, which underlines the importance of common disc standards, so that discs written by one model of machine may be read by a different one.

(a)

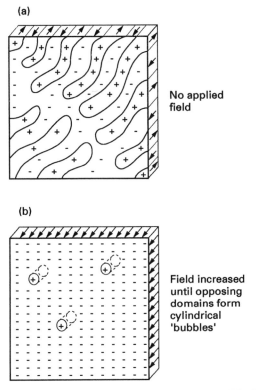

No applied field

(b)

Field increased until opposing domains form cylindrical 'bubbles'

FIG. 4.11   Bubble Formation in Thin Garnet Film

Bubble Memory

The magnetic tape and discs described earlier in this chapter were examples of the magnetic surface type of storage device. There is another class of storage device which makes use of the property of certain magnetic materials to organise themselves into small cylindrical domains, or bubbles, under the influence of a magnetic field. This is the magnetic bubble memory. The material which exhibits this property is synthetic garnet, arranged as a thin, single crystal film on a suitable substrate. When no magnetic field is applied to the film, the domains organise themselves into random patterns, but, when a magnetic field is applied at right angles to the film, the domains first of all shrink in size, and, as the strength of field increases, eventually become tight, cylindrical areas of magnetisation. It is these areas, or bubbles, which can be used to store information. The process of bubble formation is shown in Figure 4.11.

To be of any use as a memory, there must be some means of writing to and reading from the device. The technique adopted is to cause the contents of the memory to move, through the application of a rotating magnetic field. The bubble 'stream' thus moving through the garnet layer is arranged at one stage of its journey to pass a read/write 'head' which in writing mode can set or destroy bubbles, and in reading mode can sense the presence or otherwise of a bubble. The bubble memory can therefore be regarded as a serial store, organised as a continuous loop. In practice, in order to speed up the access time to its contents, the memory is organised as a number of loops, each one with its own read/write mechanism. For example, a typical 1 MBit bubble memory is organised as 512 loops, each with 2048 bit storage locations, i.e. 2048 areas which may or may not contain a bubble. To achieve the necessary organisation of the memory into such loops, a layer of magnetic material, usually Permalloy, is deposited on top of the garnet bubble layer via a spacing layer of silicon dioxide. This spacing layer also contains the conductors for the read and write 'heads'. The Permalloy layer contains a template for the pattern into which the bubbles are required to organise themselves.

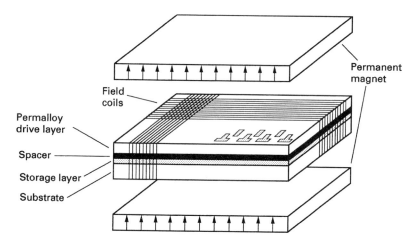

FIG. 4.12   Bubble Memory Construction

The whole structure of the bubble memory device is shown in Figure 4.12. The bubble layer, on its substrate, topped by the silicon dioxide spacing layer and the Permalloy pattern layer, is wrapped by orthogonal drive coils which produce the rotating field required to move the bubbles. Finally, the device is sandwiched between two slices of permanent magnet which produce the strong perpendicular field needed to create the bubbles in the first instance.

Bubble memory devices offer faster access than magnetic disc stores, but much slower than semiconductor memories. At 1 Mbit per bubble 'chip', they are approaching semiconductor memory in storage density. They have the advantage of being non-volatile; when the power is removed, the bubbles stop rotating but remain in existence because of the presence of the permanent magnets sandwiching the device. An obvious application for bubble memory is as mass storage, particularly when the mechanical fragility of conventional (i.e. rotating magnetic disc) mass memory could be a disadvantage. However, because the storage density of semiconductor memory continues to increase, because the volatility of such devices is easily overcome where needed through resort to battery back up, and because the mechanical reliability of rotating disc memories is increasing, the relative advantage of bubble memory is decreasing.

Optical Memory

Another example of the adaptation by the computer industry of techniques first developed by the electronic entertainments industry is the use of optical discs for data storage. These devices were first introduced for the storage of video signals in a lower cost, playback-only alternative to the now all-pervasive video cassette recorder (VCR). More recently the same technique has been applied to high fidelity musical recording in the form of the compact disc (CD). Both devices use essentially the same process. The disc, made of a rigid material, is coated with a highly reflective film, which contains the information to be stored in the form of microscopic 'pits' in the reflective surface, arranged in concentric tracks. Thus the presence or otherwise of a pit represents the two binary states. The pits are read by aiming a laser beam at the surface of the disc, which is arranged to rotate.

The reflected beam, now modulated by the pattern of pits, is received by a photodetector. Circuitry within the disc player converts the received signal, in the case of a device used for computer data storage, into a bit stream in a form which can be passed, via a suitable interface, to the processor. Video and audio disc players contain circuitry to convert the digital signal received by the photodetector into the analogue video and/or audio signals required by the rest of the playback system. Both the video optical disc, and the audio CD are now seen in data storage applications. The 12-inch diameter disc can hold up to 2000 MBytes per side, whilst the 12-cm CD has a potential capacity of 600 MBytes. This represents a very high storage density indeed, and the mass production for the electronic entertainments industry of the devices required to 'play' these discs has brought their price down. The medium itself is cheap to produce and very robust. Its main limitation as a data storage medium is its read-only characteristic, but there are many applications which call for the presence of large volumes of fixed data. The example of terrain data to support map display and related systems has already been mentioned as an application of this technology which is particularly relevant to CIS.

The technique has been extended to overcome the read-only constraint in a limited way through the introduction of the write-once-read-many (or WORM) memory. WORM memory devices contain a laser writing 'head' which can be used to create the necessary pits in the surface of the disc to record data. Unfortunately, the nature of the medium is such that the creation of these pits is an irreversible process. Once the data have been recorded on the disc's surface, they are there for ever. WORM memories are becoming a cost-effective alternative to magnetic tape for archiving purposes.

A new development is the application of the optical recording technique in a tape format. A flexible, polyester-based material is used for the optical tape. Information is recorded as pits, just as on the optical disc, arranged in parallel tracks. On a tape 880 metres long, 1 terabyte (a million megabytes) of information may be stored.

Some Typical Memory Configurations

Before we leave our examination of the physical aspects of computer data storage, it would be helpful to look at some typical computer systems and how their storage needs are satisfied.

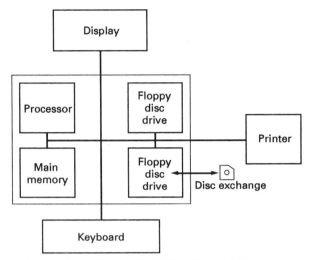

FIG. 4.13.   A Simple Single-User Personal Computer

Figure 4.13 shows a single-user, personal computer system of modest capability; a system of this type can be purchased, at the time of writing, for under £1000. Its main memory is a semiconductor dynamic RAM, of 640-KByte capacity assembled from an array of 256 Kbit chips. Most systems of this type offer the capability of increasing the size of main memory simply by plugging more circuit cards into vacant expansion slots inside the computer's casing. However, the significance in this case of the figure 640 KBytes is that this is the maximum amount of memory which can be used directly by applications running under the most common operating system for this class of machine—MSDOS, or Microsoft Disc Operating System. This point is returned to later in the chapter. Our simple PC uses 5¼-inch floppy discs as the 'mass' storage medium, and the machine is equipped with two such drives.

Organisation of storage

Figure 4.14 shows a small, multi-user system, consisting of a number of personal computers connected via a communications network to each other and to a central file server. The file server is a computer in its own right, but its main function is to provide the user's personal computers with access to the central store of data, held on a high capacity Winchester disc. The individual PCs are each fitted with semiconductor main memory and exchangeable floppy disc drives, in much the same way as the simple, stand-alone device described before. The file server will have a certain amount of main memory to serve its own processor, and the Winchester disc provides data storage for all the system users. To enable back-up copies to be taken of the contents of the Winchester, so that the system may be

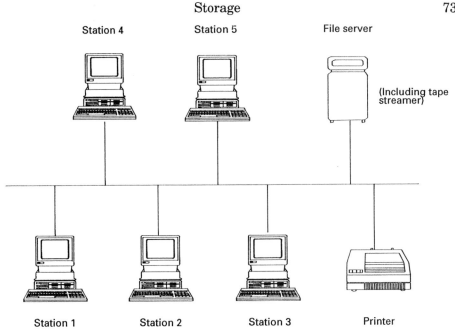

FIG. 4.14.   Multi-User System with File Server

protected from data loss in the event of failure, the file server is fitted with a tape streamer, capable of accepting the entire contents of the disc on one tape cartridge. The final example is shown in Figure 4.15. This is a rather specialised configuration, and is typical of what might be found in a processing installation within a battlefield information system.

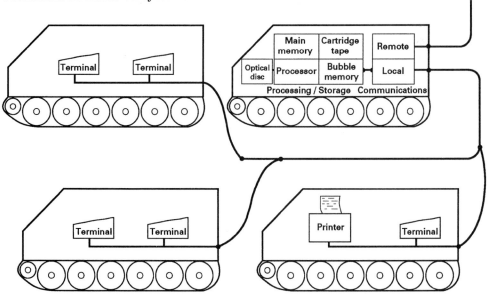

FIG. 4.15.   Battlefield CIS Processing Installation

The processor is supported by a semiconductor dynamic RAM as main memory, and the capacity of this memory is likely to be several megabytes. Bubble memory has been used instead of disc drives to provide mass storage, and the installation is fitted with 100 MBytes of this type of memory. A high capacity, tape cartridge unit is used for archiving and recovery purposes, and an optical disc unit is included to hold terrain data used as the basis of tactical map displays.

We have now laid the foundations: all the physical storage devices which are likely to be encountered in battlefield CIS have been described. The remainder of this chapter builds on this foundation and considers how one might organise the many millions of binary digits held by the various classes of storage device into an

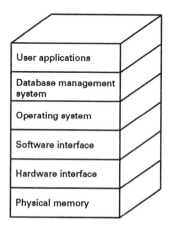

FIG. 4.16   Layered Approach to Information Storage

information store which could support the CIS processes. The diagram at Figure 4.16 shows that, just as in the case of processors and processing, a layered approach is taken.

Hardware and Software Interfaces

Whatever device is used to store data, it must have some interface through which to exchange data with the rest of the system. Main memory has a direct and tightly coupled interface, normally via the processor 'bus'. A bus is no more than an internal, high-speed communications channel, which is used by the processor to exchange data with its main memory and other peripheral devices. The software interface with the main memory is an integral part of the processor's hardware instruction set, that is, there are 'built-in' instructions (the 'memory reference' instructions) which deal with the exchange of data between the processor and main memory.

Mass storage devices will normally be connected via a hardware interface which allows the parallel transfer of whole bytes of data. This interface will be connected to the processor bus. The management of data exchange between the mass storage device(s) and the rest of the system (almost invariably via the main memory) is controlled by software modules within the operating system. A similar arrangement usually exists for backing storage devices, such as magnetic tape.

File Storage

The first stage of data organisation above the fundamental bits and bytes level is its organisation into files, a function normally provided by the operating system. A file is a collection of data treated as an entity by the operating system. At this level it is not necessary for the software responsible for organising the file storage to have any concept of the internal structure of the file—this comes later, in a higher level of software. The operating system will be concerned about such things as the maximum size of the file, and the size of the records into which it is subdivided. It may also be concerned with ownership of the file, and rights of access to it; that is, which users are entitled to read/write access, which are entitled to read-only access, and which users are not entitled to access the file at all. Files may therefore contain information in many different guises; it may be structured data, such as records in an information system, which are further broken down into fields, each one of which contains some discrete item of information. This form of organisation is covered later in the chapter. It may be formatted text, produced by word-processing software, or it may be unformatted strings of ASCII characters. It may be program code, either source code which will almost certainly be intended for interpretation as ASCII characters, or object code which has a lower level, binary interpretation. Files may be used to hold the symbols which represent digitised images, such as those produced by computer-based drawing programs, or by optical image scanners. They may even be used to hold digitised speech. The point is that the file holds some arbitrary assembly of bits, the meaning of which is generally the responsibility of some layer of software which resides above the operating system. The operating system does not have to understand what is in the files; its job is to organise their storage on whatever medium is appropriate, to make them available to applications programs and other higher level software (possibly subject to access controls, as discussed above), and to carry out other utility tasks on them, such as copying, and moving them from one medium to another.

Most operating systems have a method of organising files into groups, or directories, to ease the task of finding the right file. The principle followed springs directly from the organisation of paper files in an office; files may be kept in folders, which are kept in drawers of filing cabinets. To find a file in a well-organised office I might consult a directory which tells me in which folder of which drawer of which cabinet I will find the file. The distribution of files in this way will usually be carried out according to the types of file concerned and their subjects. Thus, for example, in an estate agent's office one might find a cabinet full of client files, with the drawers divided up according to the initial letter of the clients' surnames, e.g. clients A–G in the top drawer, and so on. A different cabinet, or cabinets, might hold details of properties for sale, including both written descriptions and photographs. This will probably be arranged by geographical area, perhaps by allocating a drawer to each district or street. Exactly the same sort of approach is taken to the organisation of filestore. Figure 4.17 illustrates a typical directory structure of a hard disc unit on a personal computer used for general office automation tasks. The operating system in this case is MSDOS (MicroSoft's Disc Operating System). The top level directory, indicated by the backslash symbol '\', is known

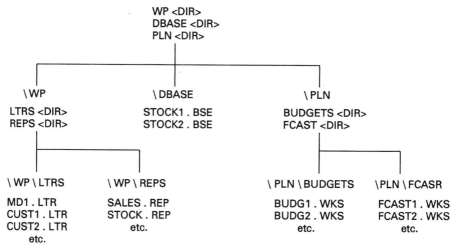

FIG. 4.17   Typical Directory Structure Using MSDOS

as the 'root' (in keeping with the 'tree structure' analogy). It contains three further directories, one for word-processing files, one for database files, and one for spreadsheet files.

At the next level down the database directory (\DBASE) contains two database files. The other two directories at the second level refer to a third level of directory. There are two word-processing directories, one for letters and one for reports. The spreadsheet directory is split into two, for 'budgets' and 'forecasts'. At the bottom level of these four directories are actual files containing letters, reports, budget spreadsheets and forecast spreadsheets. The full 'identity' (or 'pathname') of one of the letter files, assuming that the directory is on the disc drive designated as the 'A' drive by the operating system, would be 'A:\WP\LTRS\CUST1.LTR'.

File Organisation for Information Systems

It should be stressed at this stage that the structure imposed by the use of the operating-system file directory imposes its own discipline on the user. It is not, by itself, a mechanism for the creation of an automated information system, although it is an important foundation for such a system. We have stressed previously that the filestore is not concerned with the internal structure of the files for which it is responsible. To see how information systems organise their data, we must first go back to the time before the introduction of magnetic disc storage, when commercial data processing (DP) systems based on the use of magnetic tape were the order of the day. As we have already seen, tape is a serial storage medium; to find a particular item of information on a tape you must start reading at the beginning and carry on through the tape until you find it. This, of course, imposed a major constraint on the way in which information was organised and processed. Data files were designed to support specific applications; for example, one might have found in most commercial DP installations a payroll processing application, which would have been supported by a serial file on tape, containing details of employees, their rates of pay, hours worked, etc. The file would have been organised into records, each record holding information relating to an individual employee. Records would have been subdivided into fields, each field holding a single item of information about the employee to whom the record referred. The processing would have been carried out in batches, at regular intervals. Details of occurrences to employees, such as hours worked and time off due to sickness, or changes to rates of pay would have been entered from data entry forms completed by the appropriate department. Such details would have been written to a temporary transaction file, on tape. When all the transactions from a particular batch had been entered, the transaction file would have been sorted, to put the records into the same order as they appear on the master file, and then the information in the transaction file would have been merged with the master file, thus creating a new version of the master file which could then be used to support the processing of the actual payroll. If some other application were required, say to produce details of the manpower allocated to particular projects, a new set of programs and their supporting files would have had to be designed and created.

The advent of the magnetic disc store revolutionised the DP industry, because it provided a means of storing large amounts of information which could be accessed directly. This information could then be made accessible to remote users (i.e. be 'on-line'), which opened the way for the distribution of computing out of the strictly batch-processing environment in which it had been confined. At first applications and supporting files continued to be written in the same way as they had been for tape-based systems, but designers soon started to exploit the direct access capability of the disc, through such techniques as the indexed sequential access method (ISAM). Data were still held in sequential files consisting of individual records, but direct access to records was possible using one of a number of prede-fined key fields, stored in a separate index file containing the key field and the location on disc of the indexed record. Another technique is the direct access file, where the location of a record on the disc is established by performing some calcu-lation on the value of the data held in one of the fields of the record. Some form of randomisation algorithm is used to ensure an even distribution of records on the disc.

Whilst the techniques described in the last paragraph went some way towards exploiting the advantages of disc storage, they were still used mainly to create files to support individual applications. In the late 1960s and early 1970s there started to emerge a number of techniques for organising information in a way which was more general and largely independent of individual applications. The whole body of information which was required to support a wide range of appli-cations could be stored in a systematic way, in which each item of information, though it may be used in a number of applications, is stored only once. Such an organisation of data is known as a database, and the software used for its organisation and access is called a database management system (DBMS). DBMSs have made possible the transformation of 'data', very much the preserve of the DP department and used to support specific, routine tasks, into 'management information'. The bringing together of information into a database can enhance its total value; for example, by making possible the sort of *ad hoc* enquiry which would have been very time consuming and probably impracticable using separate files. Other major DBMS benefits are reduced data redundancy and concurrent access to the data by a number of users. The advantages must be paid for, of course. More effort is required at the design stage, to produce a database which can satisfy a large proportion of the organisation's needs, and be able to meet new and changing requirements. Databases need to be positively managed, information must be seen as a resource in its own right, which needs as much husbandry as any other of the organisation's resources.

The Hierarchical Model Database

Figure 4.18 shows a simple database used to hold information on employees and projects, organised according to the hierarchical model of database structure, the oldest of the data models. The information is organised as it would be in a paper file or card box.

The diagram shows that there are two possible ways to organise the data; in Figure 4.18 (a) there is a record for each employee, showing the projects he or she is working on. Figure 4.18 (b), on the other hand, organises the data differently,

(a) *Employees*

Emp_No	Name	Address	Proj_No	Title	Location	Assigned_Date
12	White	1 Black Road	13	Wizzbang	A Bldg	01/06/88
			24	Zap	A Bldg	12/09/88
14	Brown	3 Green Lane	21	Kerplunk	B Bldg	01/04/88
15	Green	17 Brown Street	21	Kerplunk	B Bldg	01/04/88
17	Black	22 Blue Drive	21	Kerplunk	B Bldg	01/04/88
			22	Wowee	C Bldg	30/06/88
18	Redd	2 Yellow River	24	Zap	A Bldg	01/11/87
19	Gray	37 Purple Patch	24	Zap	A Bldg	01/11/87
			25	Zonk	A Bldg	01/02/88

(b) *Projects*

Proj_No	Title	Location	Emp_No	Name	Address	Assigned_Date
13	Wizzbang	A Bldg	12	White	1 Black Road	01/06/88
21	Kerplunk	B Bldg	14	Brown	3 Green Lane	01/04/88
			15	Green	17 Brown Street	01/04/88
			17	Black	22 Blue Drive	01/04/88
22	Wowee	C Bldg	17	Black	22 Blue Drive	30/06/88
24	Zap	A Bldg	18	Redd	2 Yellow River	01/11/87
			19	Gray	37 Purple Patch	01/11/87
25	Zonk	A Bldg	19	Gray	37 Purple Patch	01/02/88

FIG. 4.18   Hierarchical Database Structures

by holding a record for each project, and showing the employees associated with it. Readers will be familiar with this approach from searches of library card-indexes, where subject and authors are usually separately indexed.

Searching hierarchical databases can only be done efficiently from top to bottom, e.g. to find which projects employee WHITE is working on, using the layout of Figure 4.18 (a) one must search through the employee names in order until WHITE is found. If there is a frequent need to search through projects to find which employees are working on them, a more efficient organisation of the database is that shown in Figure 4.18 (b). Searching a hierarchical database 'against the grain', for example, looking for the employees associated with a given project using the structure of Figure 4.18 (a), is a very inefficient process. There is a data redundancy penalty to be paid too. In the example, all the information for Project 21 is stored in BROWN's, BLACK's and GREEN's records. If we were to change any of the Project 21 data in GREEN's record, we would have to change them in BROWN's and BLACK's too, or else the database would become inconsistent. The problem arises from the inability of the hierarchical database to cope with many-to-many relationships. It can handle one-to-one relationships, e.g. one person linked to one address, and one-to-many, e.g. where one person is linked to a number of projects, and the converse of the letter, i.e. many-to-one. In our example the projects may be linked to more than one person, which turns the relationship into a many-to-many, which as we have seen is not very efficiently represented by the hierarchical database.

The Network Model Database

In the network model, each 'entity' type, i.e. Employee or Project, is stored in a separate file, which contains a record for each instance of that entity type. Thus in our employee/project example, we would have a file of employees and a file of projects. This is shown in the network diagram in Figure 4.19, which also shows the link between the two files, depicted as a many-to-many link. There is effectively a one-to-many link in either direction, i.e. an employee-project link and a project-employee link. The links are stored in the individual records of each file, as a pointer or some other means of indicating the physical location of the record at the other end of the link.

The advantage of the network model is that it can efficiently represent any relationship. Links can be created between any records in the database, in order to support specific applications. The major disadvantage is that database users must know the structure of the database and its linkages in order to use it efficiently. This makes the network model very efficient for supporting pre-

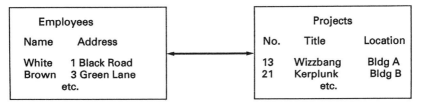

FIG. 4.19   Network Model Database

planned applications where the linkages have been tailor-made for the application, but much less efficient for answering *ad hoc* enquiries.

The Relational Database

Network model DBMSs are still in widespread use, but the majority of new database applications nowadays can be traced to a paper published in 1970 by E. F. Codd, of IBM, on the concept of what he termed the 'relational database'. Relational databases consist only of 'flat files', or tables, known as relations. Continuing our example from above, in a relational database we would have a table of employees, and a table of projects as shown in Figure 4.20 (*a*) and (*b*). So far, it

Employee (a)				Project (b)				Assignment (c)		
Emp_No	Name	Address		Proj_No	Title	Location		Emp_No	Proj_No	Date
12	White	1 Black Road		13	Wizzbang	A Bldg		12	24	12/09/88
14	Brown	3 Green Lane		21	Kerplunk	B Bldg		12	13	01/06/88
15	Green	17 Brown Street		22	Wowee	C Bldg		14	21	01/04/88
17	Black	22 Blue Drive		24	Zap	A Bldg		15	21	01/04/88
18	Redd	2 Yellow River		25	Zonk	A Bldg		17	21	01/04/88
19	Gray	37 Purple Patch						17	22	30/06/88
								18	24	01/11/87
								19	24	01/11/87
								19	25	01/02/88

FIG. 4.20   Relational Database

looks very similar to the two files of the network database; the employee table says nothing about projects and vice versa. The link between the two is not in the form of specific links or pointers, as in the network model, but in the form of a third table, or relation, which we shall call 'assignment', as shown in Fig 4.20 (*c*). Each record of the assignment table relates an employee to a project.

A simple query might be answered from one table only, for example, where does employee GREEN live?

SELECT ADDRESS FROM EMPLOYEE WHERE NAME = 'GREEN'

The question above is expressed in a form of structured query language (SQL), which is a feature of relational databases. SQL provides a way of composing queries of any complexity, which does not rely on a knowledge of the way in which the database is constructed. To take a more complex query: what are the names and addresses of all the employees working on Project 24?

SELECT NAME, ADDRESS FROM EMPLOYEE, ASSIGNMENT
WHERE PROJ_NO = 24 AND ASSIGNMENT.EMP_NO =
EMPLOYEE.EMP NO

This query is answered by performing an operation known as joining two relations (i.e. assignment and employee). Each row, or record, in the assignment table which contains Project 24 is matched with a record in the employee table which contains the same employee number. Finally, the employee's name and address are selected from the matched records in the employee table.

The answer to a query like the one above can be regarded as another relation, consisting of the records which matched the query criteria. Temporary relations, usually known as 'views', may be created, and treated as virtual relations. Although they have no physical existence, they may be used in queries in just the same way as the permanent relations of the database. For example, if we wanted to ask a lot of different questions about the employees working on Project 25, we could create a view which was effectively an extract from the employee table containing only the details of those employees working on Project 25. We could then refer to that view in our subsequent queries if it were a table in its own right.

The major advantage of the relational model is its flexibility. It is easy to create new relationships and to add to the database as requirements change. Also the programmer, or *ad hoc* enquirer using the database, does not have to specify the way in which to find the data, as he would in a network database.

Summary

This chapter has covered the whole spectrum of issues concerned with the storage of information, from the technologies of the devices used to store digital data to the operational considerations of database design and organisation. Later chapters, particularly Chapter 7, will deal with some of the practical difficulties of using some of the devices described here in the harsh physical environment of the land battlefield. We shall also be looking at the problems of software design encountered when one applies the techniques described to the organisation and distribution of information in real battlefield systems.

5.

Input and Output

Introduction

Almost without exception, the systems which are the subject of this book must at some stage interface with a human user—the 'man in the loop'. The design of this, the man machine—interface (MMI), will be crucial to the efficient working of the system. The MMI provides the user with a 'window' through which he may view the system and a set of controls to enable him to 'drive' it.

The approach taken in this chapter is the by-now familiar 'layered' approach. At the lowest level are the devices used to put information into computer systems and to get it out again. The higher layers consist of techniques developed to use the basic devices to establish a dialogue between the user and the machine, in a way which is optimised for the performance of the job in hand.

Fundamental Techniques

It is not surprising to find that the techniques for exchanging information between human beings and computers are based on the sensory capabilities of the human being. Sight and hearing are the main senses used by the human to detect output from the computer, whilst input mostly depends on the human's manipulative skills to operate such devices as the keyboard. The sense of smell is normally only called into play when something has gone badly wrong!

Input Devices

Although human beings convey surprisingly large amounts of information to each other through non-verbal means (so-called 'body language'), most overt, interpersonal communication is carried by the spoken word. It would seem to be very convenient therefore, if we could use the same means to communicate with machines. As we shall see later, computers which can recognise speech in a limited way are possible now, but the general recognition of human speech, particularly under difficult acoustic conditions, has yet to be achieved reliably. Thirty years ago, when the use of computers in commerce and industry was first becoming widespread, the idea of speaking to them directly was about as realistic as Buck Rogers's death ray. In any case, there was already a strong tradition of 'communicating' with machines through the pressing of buttons and twiddling of knobs, i.e. through manipulative means. To this day therefore, human input to the computer is mainly manipulative, and the most commonly used input device is the keyboard, which is, after all, no more than an organised collection of 'buttons'. In recent years input techniques based on the ability of the operator to point at some area of the computer's display have been developed and refined. Pointing methods include the mouse, the touch-sensitive screen, the light pen and the tracker ball, all of which are described later.

A number of specialised input devices have a role to play, including bar-code readers, magnetic-strip readers and optical-character readers. These are all examples of devices used to input pre-prepared data to the computer, and some of their everyday and commercial applications will be familiar to readers.

Keyboards

The keyboard is such a familiar item that it may seem hardly worth devoting any space to its description. Like most familiar objects, though, it tends to be taken for granted, and there are some aspects of keyboard design which are well worth considering. The reason for the keyboard's familiarity is, of course, its association with the typewriter, and the vast majority of computer keyboards use the typewriter's QWERTY key layout. The layout has been retained because of the specialised skills needed to learn to touch type, i.e. to use all the fingers of both hands on the keyboard. But are all CIS users necessarily touch typists? Recent experience in the USA has shown, not surprisingly, that for tasks involving much text input, touch typing skills are a considerable advantage. At the same time, it is instructive to watch someone who is a trained touch-typist using a keyboard in an interactive session with the computer in the sort of task where the input required involves only a few key depressions at a time. It is surprising how many seem to revert to the 'hunt and peck' mode of typing, although in doing so they are still relying on a conditioned familiarity with the keyboard layout. For an operator who has never been trained to type, and who has never used a QWERTY keyboard, a key layout which follows some other familiar pattern, such as one with the keys laid out in alphabetical order, would seem to offer some advantage. This principle has been embodied in a number of tactical data devices in recent years, and works perfectly well when used by the non-QWERTY indoctrinated personnel for whom it was designed. However, to give an ABCDE keyboard to a QWERTY person is to invite severe frustration. It seems likely that QWERTY is going to be with us for the foreseeable future.

There are a few other design aspects of the humble keyboard worth looking at before we move on to less familiar devices. For instance, the type of key is very important. The 'feel' of the key when it is depressed (so-called 'tactile feedback') and the effort required to operate the keys make a vital contribution to the ease of use of the keyboard. On most commercial keyboards designed for use in the normal office environment, the keys take the form of spring-loaded plungers, which have an appreciable 'travel' (2 to 3 mm) when operated, which contributes to the feel. This type of keyboard is not ideal for battlefield use; it is not particularly robust, and the gaps between and under the keys are refuges for nuclear or chemical contamination. For that reason, totally sealed keyboards operating on the principle of contact between two membranes when a key is pressed have been

FIG. 5.1   Membrane Keyboard (*Plessey Naval Systems Ltd*)

developed for use with field systems. Figure 5.1 shows a typical membrane keyboard. It suffers from the drawback of poor feel—it is hard to make it behave like a 'normal' keyboard. Because the keys have negligible travel, there is little tactile feedback to the operator to tell him that he has pressed a key successfully. To help to overcome this, many systems use an electronically generated audible click to indicate the depression of a key.

Pointing Devices

Every well brought-up child knows that it is 'rude to point', but, as the child knows, pointing is quite an effective means of communication. It is a well-known technique for making oneself understood when the normal medium of spoken language is not available, such as when shopping in a foreign market place, or when trying to get one's point across in a noisy environment. Various artefacts have been designed to allow people to communicate with computers by using this simple technique. The full exploitation of pointing as a means of computer input demands more than the gadget or other physical technique; it calls for a different approach to the design of the whole dialogue between person and computer. This wider aspect is covered later; for the present we shall just look at the different devices which make this type of MMI possible. They fall roughly into two classes:

the devices used to move some form of pointer symbol on the display to a desired position, and those which allow direct indication of the position required on the screen by pointing at the screen itself with a finger or with some instrument.

FIG. 5.2   Tracker Ball (*APRICOT Computers Ltd*)

The tracker ball (Figure 5.2) was one of the earliest forms of pointing device of the first type, and was first used in conjunction with radar displays. The ball itself is set either into the surface of the display console, or in a free-standing housing which may be positioned to suit the operator. Part of the ball, whose typical diameter is of the order of 30–40 mm, protrudes through the housing and may be rotated by the operator's finger tips in any direction. As the ball is rotated, a symbol on the screen known as a pointer, or cursor, moves in sympathy with the rotation. Most tracker-ball systems have one or more buttons built into the same housing as the ball, which are pressed, or 'clicked' by the operator to select some action once the ball has been used to position the pointer in the required place on the screen. The whole device is designed so that ball and buttons fall conveniently to the operator's hand. The mouse is a very similar device to the tracker ball, but instead of using one's fingers to rotate the ball in a fixed housing, the whole device is moved around on a convenient flat surface near to the display. Many types of mouse actually work on exactly the same principle as the tracker ball. They are rather like an upside down tracker ball housing, where the ball is rotated by moving the housing in contact with the working surface. More recent 'mice' work on an optical principle. The mouse is moved on a small, flat 'mouse pad' which has a light-reflecting surface on which a fine grid of non-reflecting lines is marked. Light from a light-emitting diode (LED) in the under surface of the mouse is reflected back into a photodetector to detect movement over the grid. Just like the tracker ball, the mouse is fitted with a number of buttons for the selection of choices. It should also be mentioned here that the keyboard can be used in conjunction with the pointing technique, by using specially designated keys to move the cursor left/right and up/down.

In the direct-pointing technique, pointing and selection are carried out in one movement. In one variety of touch screen (see Figure 5.3) piezo-electric devices are used to generate and detect a pattern of acoustic waves on the surface of the screen. The action of touching the screen disturbs the wave pattern, and the detectors are able to locate the point of disturbance.

A light pen is used to achieve much the same effect. The pen, which contains a sensitive light detector in its tip, is connected to the computer via a cable and interface. When the device is pointed at the desired place on the screen, by pressing a button on the pen itself, or by pressing a special function key, the computer is

FIG. 5.3   Touch Screen (*Hewlett Packard*)

instructed to calculate the position of the pen. This it does by noting the time that the area of screen immediately under the pen's light detector receives the display 'refresh' pulse, relative to the refresh cycle time for the whole display. The refresh pulse, which should normally be undetectable by the human eye, is detected by the light pen as a momentary increase in brightness of the phosphor immediately under the pen's tip. By knowing the time it takes the display to 'paint' a whole screen, the scan pattern used, and the time at which the indicated spot was painted, working out its position on the screen is straightforward. If the pen is then left in contact with the screen and 'dragged' to a new position, the computer can track its movement. In this way the light pen may be used to 'draw' on the screen.

Voice Input

As introduced earlier, the most direct means of input from a human being to a computer is the way in which he or she communicates with other human beings, namely by speech. Direct speech input is now feasible, but vocabularies are limited, as is the ability to interpret 'joined-up speech', or whole sentences. The performance of current systems in a noisy environment is somewhat unreliable, and any marked change in the characteristics of the speaker's voice, perhaps as a result of stress, further decrease the reliability with which current systems can recognise speech input. Taken together, these limitations do not bode well for the use of direct speech input where it would be most valuable, that is, for use by troops engaged in fighting the contact battle, where their hands and eyes are likely to be occupied with tasks of a higher priority than the operating of a computer keyboard.

Output Devices

Like input devices, output devices may be classed according to the human sense upon which they rely, and by far the largest class of device is that which uses the sense of sight. A classification of visual output devices is shown in Figure 5.4.

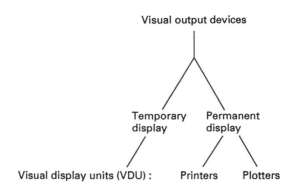

FIG. 5.4   Visual Output Device Classification

Temporary Displays

Used in conjunction with a keyboard, and possibly with one of the pointing techniques outlined earlier, the visual display unit (VDU) is the basis of the MMI in the majority of computer systems. The term 'temporary' is used to indicate that the display is transient; it is visible only when the machine is switched on and in use, and is an integral part of the device. If a permanent visual record of the information displayed is needed, then one of the permanent displays, or to use the jargon, 'hard copy' devices must be used. Temporary displays are therefore an essential element of the dialogue between user and computer.

Display Characteristics

The choice of a temporary display will be governed mainly by the nature of the tasks to be performed. For example, applications whose display requirements are confined to straightforward text will demand a different, more simple type of display from those where there is a need to show detailed representations of three-dimensional objects in colour. To compare displays, we must identify the individual characteristics which define their capabilities.

RESOLUTION

It is resolution which determines the detail with which images can be displayed. There are several different techniques used by displays to 'paint' the image, but the standard means of measuring resolution is to regard the image as being composed of a number of picture elements, or pixels. A pixel is the smallest element of the image, and thus its size determines the degree of detail the display is capable of showing. Individual pixels may or not be addressable directly by the programmer using the screen, to set them 'on' or 'off', or to cause them to be displayed in a number of colours. It is usual to describe the resolution of a screen in terms of the number of pixels displayed in the x and y axes of the display. As a guide, a screen which displays less than 600×200 pixels would be termed low resolution, between this and 600×350 pixels medium resolution, and above that high resolution. Very high resolution screens display more than 1000×1000 pixels. In the case of displays which are used only to display text, it is generally more meaningful to describe their resolution in terms of the number of lines of characters displayed, the number of characters per line, and the way in which the characters are generated. A typical standard for text displays is 24 lines of 80 characters each, with the characters represented by a 7×9 dot matrix.

CONTRAST

Taken together with resolution, the contrast of the display, or the brightness of the displayed information relative to the background, determines the overall clarity of the display, and therefore the ease with which the information may be read by the user. Contrast is also concerned with the performance of the display under a variety of ambient lighting conditions, and it is normal to find some means of adjusting the display to cope with changing conditions.

COLOUR

Displays may either be monochrome (in which case the choice of the single colour and the number of different density levels is important) or they may display more than one colour at a time. The number of colours which may be active on the screen at any one time is a function of the computer system rather than of the screen itself. Normally the screen is capable of responding to whatever combination of colour signals (based on the primary colours of red, green and blue) is sent to it. The actual combinations are generated by the hardware and the software of the computer, and limitations in memory size or a need to reduce complexity, and hence cost, may cause the designer to limit the extent of the colour palette which is available.

SCREEN SIZE

The majority of display screens use a horizontal format, in an approximate 4:3 aspect ratio. The quoted size of a screen is normally the length of the diagonal, expressed in inches. Screens of between 12 and 15 inches diagonal measure are common for general purpose use. For specialised applications, particularly those involving very high resolution graphics, 19-inch screens are becoming popular. Where larger displays are needed, for example, when the display must be seen by a number of persons at the same time, projection techniques developed in the television industry provide an effective solution, but they are not generally suitable for use in the harsh environmental conditions encountered in tactical systems. The difficulties of designing a large screen display for use in the field are returned to in a later chapter.

POWER CONSUMPTION

For systems which are only ever used indoors, with a reliable mains electricity supply readily available, the amount of power consumed by a particular display design has not been critical for the choice of display. For military tactical systems, which must either operate from self-contained power supplies or be supplied by field generators of limited capacity, power consumption becomes an important factor. In the commercial world, the growth in popularity of portable, so-called 'lap top' computers capable of running from an internal power supply has increased the relative importance of low power consumption in the choice of display technique.

Display Technologies

Table 5.1 lists the most commonly encountered display technologies and their characteristics.

By far the most common display technology is the cathode ray tube (CRT), which had its origins in the design of radar displays and television receivers. The images are formed on the inside surface of a glass screen, through the impact of a beam of electrons on a coating of a phosphorescent material. The means of steering the electron beam to form the characters varies between displays. Many, but by no means all, use a scanning technique which is exactly the same as that used in television receivers. Monochrome displays use a single phosphor coating, which may glow white, green, orange or some other colour under the influence of the electron beam. Full colour displays must use phosphors corresponding to the three primary colours, grouped on the screen to suit the scanning technique employed. Most colour displays use the 'shadow mask' technique developed for TV receivers, in which a mask behind the phosphor layer is aligned in such a way that the areas of phosphor of a particular colour can only be illuminated by the electron 'gun' dedicated to that colour.

CRT displays are now highly developed, and when combined with the necessary electronic control circuitry, can provide an enormous range of capabilities from the simple, text-only display to large screen, full colour, very high resolution graphic displays. The limitations of the CRT display are, chiefly, its relative size, particularly its depth, fragility and power consumption, but for a wide range of applications these limitations are not significant. The depth problem arises from the geometry of the electron beam arrangement inside the tube. This is illustrated in

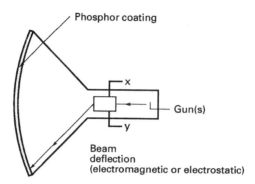

FIG. 5.5　Cathode Ray Tube

Figure 5.5. There is a limit on the angle through which the beam can be turned by the control circuitry. Hence for a given screen size there must be a minimum distance between the electron gun and the screen, which in turn determines the depth of the display housing. The power supply problem mainly arises from the requirement to generate a very high voltage—so-called extra high tension (EHT) to attract electrons from the gun(s) with sufficient force to make the phosphor glow at the required level. Another drawback of the presence of high voltages in the CRT display is that they tend to cause the device to radiate electromagnetic signals which can be received over a surprisingly long distance. As the information being displayed can be recovered from these signals, it is important in systems processing sensitive or classified information to take steps to reduce the radiation.

The development of most of the other display technologies has been in response to a need to overcome the drawbacks of CRT displays mentioned above in order to meet some particular requirement. One avenue of development has been the search for a large, flat screen display as a space-saving substitute for the projected display. The other main direction has been to find small, flat screens of low power consumption for use in portable equipment. Both of these lines of development are relevant for military CIS.

A display technology which may have the potential to serve both requirements is the gas-plasma panel, such as that shown in Figure 5.6. The space between two layers of insulating material is filled with a suitable gas, such as neon. The sandwiching layers each contain a mesh of conducting wires, arranged so that a voltage can be applied between points on the top and the bottom layer, causing the small volume of gas between them to glow. This individual glowing area of gas represents one pixel on a plasma screen. Resolutions of 24 pixels per centimetre are possible with modern plasma panels, which may be up to 1 metre × 1 metre in size. The larger panels need to have inert spacers between the two layers to

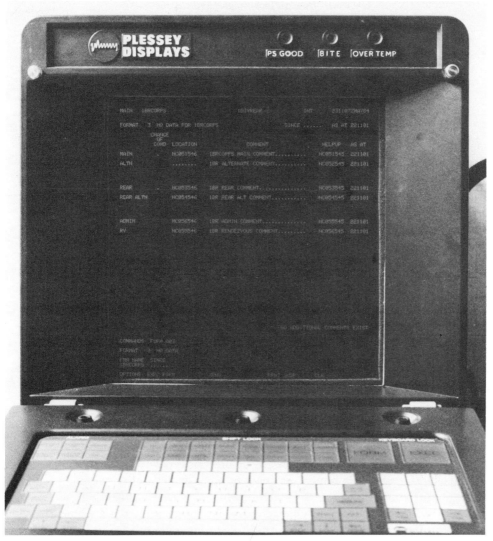

FIG. 5.6   Plasma Panel (*Plessey Naval Systems Ltd*)

maintain their separation, and these tend to intrude into the available image area.

The liquid crystal display (LCD) relies on the properties of certain crystalline materials to align themselves in a particular way when a voltage is applied. The LCD is probably the most widespread, single variety of digital display, as it used in most digital wrist watches. There can be few readers who are not familiar with the appearance of an LCD display, and all will be aware that it is a passive form of display, that is, it needs an external light source to make it visible. LCD displays are now commonly found in portable computers. Improvements which have been made in recent display devices are the availability of colours other than the ubiquitous grey, and better low temperature performance.

TABLE 5.1   *Display Technologies and Characteristics*

Display Type	Resolution	Colour	Screen Size	Power Cons	Remarks
Cathode ray tube	Low Medium High Very high	Mono or full colour	up to 30-in diagonal	High	Depth of housing may be a limitation
Plasma panel	Low/medium	Mono only	up to 1 m^2	Medium	Flat screen
Liquid crystal	Low	Mono or colour	up to 12-in diagonal	Low	Poor at low temperature passive
Light emitting diode	Low/medium	Mono or colour	Very large (several m^2) possible	Medium	Colour matching may be difficult

Permanent Displays: Hard Copy Devices

The choice among hard copy devices—printers and plotters—available today is truly enormous, and reflects the wide variety of different uses to which these devices can be put. The selection of a device for a particular role will be governed by the requirements of its task, and of course the available budget.

Printers

Some of the key technical parameters which distinguish between the various types of printer are discussed below.

PRINT QUALITY

The range of quality available varies from the highest quality—so-called 'letter quality', equivalent to that produced by an electric typewriter, through near letter quality (NLQ), which is almost as good, to mere draft quality, which is readable but not particularly elegant. The factors which determine the quality of print are the clarity of the individual characters and the accuracy with which they are placed on the paper. A true letter-quality printer will produce crisp, hard-edged characters of dense and even tone, lined up precisely on the paper. In a draft quality machine, the individual dot structure of the characters will probably be visible, which means that their appearance will be neither crisp nor dense and even in tone. Their alignment may appear to be somewhat ragged.

PRINT SPEED

How fast can the printer do its work? This factor is expressed variously in characters per second, lines per minute, or pages per minute, according to the type of printer. In most machines, especially those based on an electromechanical principle, there is an inverse relationship between speed and quality of print. This is clearly shown in some multi-mode machines, which offer a choice of print qualities, the penalty being that the higher quality print takes longer to produce.

Range of Characters

In printer's terminology, this characteristic is concerned with the number of founts, or character styles available. Simple printers are limited to one style of character, with a standard set of alphanumeric characters and symbols, such as punctuation marks, available. At the other extreme, some printers operate at a level below the character, that is, they can be used to print any pattern of the basic dots which are used to make up characters. Thus they may be used to print any pattern which the driving computer is capable of generating, which includes any size and style of printed character, as well as graphical images.

Robustness and Reliability

As a general principle, the smaller the number of moving parts, the more robust the machine. The reliability aspect depends upon the environment in which the machine is used. Thus a very fast line printer of high mechanical complexity may not be at all robust in a general sense, but when permanently installed in a computer room may be extremely reliable. The same machine is not likely to perform satisfactorily if put in the back of an armoured vehicle and taken on a bumpy cross-country ride.

Type of Paper

Some printers depend on the use of thermally sensitised paper, or paper with unusual absorbency. The need for a special type of paper can be a disadvantage, not least because such paper is probably more expensive than normal paper types. In a military system, the need to stock special types of paper is an additional logistic burden. Figure 5.7 is a 'family tree' of printer types.

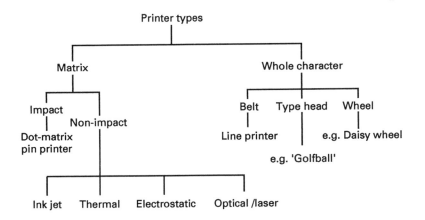

FIG. 5.7   Printer 'Family Tree'

Plotters

The term 'plotter' is normally used to describe a device which draws an image in much the same way as a person would, using a pen or similar instrument. The movement of the pen is controlled in two orthogonal directions—the x and y axis, giving it the capability to draw any two dimensional image. In some plotters, the same effect is achieved by allowing the pen to move in the x direction, and moving the paper or other drawing medium in the y direction. The resolution of the plot is determined by the smallest distance, or step, through which it is possible to move the pen. A good test of a plotter is to have it draw a circle: the better the plotter, the smoother will be the line tracing the circle. In a low-resolution plotter, the individual steps will be clearly visible. Plotters may draw in several colours, through the use of different pens.

The laser printer is a recent development which combines many of the qualities of both printer and plotter. Although shown in the Figure 5.7 as a 'matrix' printer, it is a device which is 'dot addressable', that is, the image it produces can be controlled through the switching on or off under software control of the individual dots of which the image is composed. The image to be printed is 'painted' as an electrostatic charge on to a rotating drum by the action of a laser which is modulated by the data signal from the computer. The charged areas of the drum then attract toner (i.e. ink) which is transferred to the paper to produce an image of very high quality. The electrostatic drum and printing mechanism are the same as those used in a photocopier; one often reads in the literature of laser printers being based upon some manufacturer's copier 'engine'. Current laser printers are capable of resolutions around 300 dots per inch, which produces a quality of print approaching that of electronic typesetting machines. It is a far higher resolution than any display screen can match; 300 dots per inch equates to a resolution of better than 3000×2500 pixels on a 12-inch diagonal screen! The laser printer is bringing about a revolution in the printing and publishing industry, through the development of desk-top publishing systems based on personal computers, with software for the organisation of both text and visual images into pages for printing by the laser printer. It has yet to make an impact in the CIS field, where quality of output is not as important as, say, mechanical robustness.

The LCD shutter printer is a combination of an LCD screen display and a photocopier. The LCD screen is in the image plane of the copier, and the image is formed on it by the computer in the normal way. Light is passed through the LCD screen on to a photosensitive film, which is then used to transfer an ink (or 'toner') image to paper via an adapted photocopier mechanism, as described above for the laser printer.

Speech Output

We have already touched on the difficulties of designing computers which can recognise spoken input with a useful degree of reliability under a wide range of operating conditions. It is much easier, however, to design computers which can produce speech output. Speech synthesisers are now highly developed and are seen in a wide range of applications, from educational toys to help children with

FIG. 5.8   Desk-top Plotter (*Hewlett Packard*)

their spelling and arithmetic, to talking instruments in motor cars and aircraft. Synthesisers can be used incorporated in general purpose computer systems, and used by the programmer to produce output in spoken form just as easily as he can direct it to the screen or to a printer. The most likely application of synthesised speech to military CIS is probably at the combat level, where one could envisage synthesised spoken messages from the information system being relayed to, say, a tank commander through the same headset as he uses for the tank's voice radio and crew intercom system.

Design of the Man–Machine Interface (MMI)

Once again we have taken in this chapter the approach of describing the fundamental 'nuts and bolts', to lay the foundation for an examination of how they can be applied to real tasks in military CIS. The design of an effective and efficient interface between man and machine demands more than just the input and output devices we have been looking at so far. Using the devices as building blocks, the MMI designer's task is to provide the means for the users to interact with the system, in a way which is intended to help them to carry out their functions as efficiently as possible. The physical interface between the operator and the system may well be a keyboard and one of the display devices described earlier in this chapter; the definition of the MMI includes both these devices and the techniques—implemented by software—to allow the user to find his way around a complex system.

It might help us to get a clearer view of exactly what the MMI is if we attempt to set out three 'golden rules' for its design, and illustrate those rules with some examples.

MMI Rule 1: The MMI Must Be Easy to Use

Taken literally and absolutely, the application of this rule could lead to almost certain failure. There is a degree of subtlety at work; perhaps the rule should be amplified to say that the MMI should be easily used by those for whom the system was designed. A 'simple' MMI, which takes an accustomed user by the hand and leads him in a deliberate way through the various options offered by the system would become tedious and frustrating the moment the user starts to become familiar with it and know his own way around. It is rather like finding one's way around a new town or district. At first it is helpful to be shown round by a guide with good local knowledge; after a while though, the guide can be dispensed with and all one needs is a good map to which one can refer in moments of uncertainty. Eventually even the map can be put aside, as navigation around the district becomes second nature. There are some systems in which it is possible to identify a narrow range of user 'types', and design the system to suit their experience. An example at the 'easy' end of the spectrum might be an information-retrieval system designed for occasional use, say in a library. It may be assumed that the majority of users will be relatively unfamiliar with the system, and hence a very explicit MMI design would be appropriate. At the other extreme, in a system which is used continually in direct support of the user's main task, such as an airline booking-system, one would expect to find a very abbreviated MMI which would seem distinctly 'unfriendly' to a newcomer and to call for a degree of training in order to use it efficiently. A military CIS may have to encompass both extremes. The system may well be used by persons with differing amounts of experience, and hence the MMI must be flexible enough to provide a degree of 'hand holding' and guidance for the newcomer, whilst at the same time allowing the 'expert' to navigate directly around the system's features. One way of catering for the needs of users of mixed experience is to provide a number of different levels of system help. For the beginner, the most detailed help level will give an unsolicited explanation of all the system's features as they are encountered. At the other extreme, help is given only when requested. For example, if an unfamiliar option is presented, the user should be able to press a 'help' key and be given a few lines of guidance on what the option is and how to use it. Help should be offered in context, that is, the response to pressing the 'help' key should be information relevant to the task the user is trying to perform, and not simply a screenful of general information, or even a help menu.

MMI Rule 2: The MMI Must Be Consistent

There can be few features of a badly designed MMI which are more likely to cause extreme user frustration than inconsistency in the way the MMI calls for things to be done. Probably the simplest example is that of a program which invites single-character responses to select options from a list on the screen. On some screens, the single character has to be followed by a depression of the 'Return' or 'Enter' key, whilst on others the desired action happens as soon as the selected character key is pressed. Frequently one is asked to enter 'Y' for 'yes' or 'N' for 'no' to select or reject some option. It is highly irritating to find that at some points in the program the single letter 'Y' or 'N' will suffice, whilst in others the computer will reject anything but the fully spelled-out 'YES' or 'NO'. These are trivial examples, which should never be found in professionally developed CIS programs, but they serve to illustrate the point. There are less obvious, more subtle forms of inconsistency which are harder to detect at the design stage, but which can cause equal misery for the user if they are present in the deployed system.

The main application of this rule concerns the self-consistency of a given program or system. An extension which would take us more into the field of standardisation would be to say that it is highly desirable that the MMIs of different systems should be consistent with each other. For example: a highly interactive, graphics-based program with a menu-and-pointer style of MMI using a mouse, always uses the left-hand one of two mouse buttons to make a selection from a menu list. Another, very similar program designed by the same organisation and using exactly the same hardware and style of MMI, demands that the right-hand mouse button be used for menu selection. In this case the left-hand button is used to exit from the program. Just imagine what happens when someone accustomed to using the first program starts to use the second one. . . (this is a true story!). In the CIS case we shall be arguing in a later chapter that the same system should be used both in the field and back in the barrack, office environment, so that users may become thoroughly familiar with its operation. If this desirable state cannot be attained, for whatever reason, and separate systems have to be used, there should at the very least be a common MMI between the systems.

MMI Rule 3: The MMI Must Be Optimised for the Task Being Performed

A staff officer in a headquarters preparing a report, an operation order, or other routine task should be able to access the information needed to assist him in that task as directly as possible. If he needs a certain number of different items of information, it is desirable that they be presented to him either all on one display, or on a number of displays which have been designed and organised with that specific task in mind. He should not have to access a large number of general purpose displays to pull together the required information. Obviously, the wider the range of tasks which the system can perform or support, the more difficult it is to obey this rule, although, as we shall see below, it is quite possible and frequently desirable to have a number of different MMI 'styles' in the same system. (Provided of course they are implemented with due regard to Rule 2.)

Examples of MMI

Three styles of MMI are presented below. They are all representative of the MMI styles available on today's systems, and all are capable of being designed to conform with our rules above, to a greater or lesser extent. Although one style of MMI may lend itself to the design of a simple-to-use system more than the others, it is the actual design which counts in the end. A poorly designed MMI using all the modern gadgets and sophisticated techniques can be much harder to use than a well designed MMI using just a keyboard and screen.

KEYBOARD-BASED MMI

It is impossible to generalise about a particular style of MMI under this simple heading. The actual style (obeying Rule 3) will be determined by the task to be performed. We can, though, identify a few of the basic techniques used to build MMIs based on the keyboard and simple display.

Menu selection is a favourite way of indicating a range of choices to the user. The choices or options are listed on the screen, normally accompanied by an identifying number or letter, and the user is invited to enter the number or letter of the selected option. Figure 5.9 shows a typical menu screen. The response to the selection of a particular option may be another menu, and this situation could be repeated at a number of different levels until the desired action has been accomplished. The layout of a menu-driven system may be described as a tree structure, with the main menu at the top and subsidiary menus branching out of it at a number of different levels. It may be useful to give the user a copy of this structure as a diagram, to help him to find his way around it. Having due regard to our ease-of-use rule introduced above, a menu-driven system with a number of layers should normally allow the experienced user to jump between layers. At the very least, he should be able to jump directly back to the top menu from any depth within the structure, rather than have to return through the intermediate menus.

Form filling is a technique used in many systems to ease the task of entering information. As the name implies, its basis is the display on the screen of a struc-

```
┌─────────────────────────────────────────┐
│  ╔═══════════════════════════════════╗  │
│  ║   Battalion office automation system  ║  │
│  ╠═══════════════════════════════════╣  │
│  ║              Main menu              ║  │
│  ║                                     ║  │
│  ║        1. Personnel records         ║  │
│  ║        2. Stores accounting         ║  │
│  ║        3. Transport management      ║  │
│  ║        4. Word processing           ║  │
│  ║        5. Quit                       ║  │
│  ║                  Enter choice 1-5   ║  │
│  ╚═══════════════════════════════════╝  │
└─────────────────────────────────────────┘
```

Fig. 5.9   Menu Screen

ture or format, with blank spaces into which information is to be entered. The layout of the form, and the words used on it can all assist the user to enter information correctly. For example, a difference in brightness level, or inverse video (i.e. dark characters on a bright background as opposed to vice versa) can be used to distinguish between the fixed words on the form and the information entered. It is normal to use the 'TAB' (tabulate) key to move the cursor from one entry field to the next. The size of the space allowed in each field will normally reflect the maximum size of entry allowed. Other validation may also take place at this stage; for example, if the entry is meant to represent a date, a simple check can be carried out to see if the data entered represent a valid date. For repetitive data-entry tasks, form filling is a useful technique.

Command languages are potentially the basis of a very flexible MMI. All the options for action available to the system user may be indicated by commands, which may be accompanied by one or more parameters, which specify the way in which the command is to be used. Some systems allow commands to be abbreviated and also strung together in combinations. From an ease-of-use viewpoint, command language-based systems tend to lie at the expert, trained user end of the spectrum, although, through the availability of carefully designed 'help' information in the right places, inexperienced users can be guided.

One should not get the impression that the three techniques outlined above are mutually exclusive MMI styles. Some systems use all three; a typical combination might be a basic menu structure to guide one through the facilities offered by the system, with form filling used to implement certain of the functions, particularly data entry. A command language could be used for other functions, and possibly as an alternative to the menu structure for the more experienced user.

A Touch Screen Based MMI

Touch screens lend themselves to a menu-selection approach, using graphical or diagrammatic menus. A box diagram of the system's functions may be presented, and the user is invited to touch the box on the screen which describes the desired function. Just as in the text menu, there could be several layers of graphical menu. The technique can also be used in conjunction with either form filling, command language, or both.

The Windows, Icons, Menus and Pointer (WIMP) Approach to MMI

Menus and pointers have already been described in this chapter, so to complete the scene setting for a description of the WIMP environment we need to say a few words about 'windows' and 'icons'. A 'window' is an area of screen which is dedicated to a particular task. It may be of any size, up to and including the whole screen. If the information to be displayed in a particular window is too much to be seen all at once, it may be scrolled (SCreen ROLL) within the window, in the same way as one scrolls information on a whole screen display. A number of windows may be 'open', or active at any one time, the actual number being determined by the operating system concerned. Open windows may be displayed on the screen simultaneously; their size relative to each other is controlled by the user, as is the way they are juxtaposed on the screen. In some systems, windows are 'tiled' together, that is, their edges adjoin and they do not overlap. In other systems—propably the majority nowadays—windows can overlap each other, and if required, totally eclipse each other. Just as in the management of sheets of paper on a desk, a given window may be 'brought to the top of the pile', so that it overlaps or eclipses all other open windows and is not itself overlapped by any other window. This likening of the technique to moving papers on a desk is significant, as will become clearer shortly.

An 'icon' is a symbol representing some resource available to the system, or some action to be performed. A selection of typical icons is shown in Figure 5.10, which is the opening window of a typical WIMP-based office automation system. It shows that there are a number of tools available, such as a calculator, a word processor, and a spreadsheet program. Information is stored in drawers and files, which are indicated in a graphical, or 'iconic' representation of the file directory seen in Chapter 4. The window is organised to represent the user's desk top and other features of his physical office environment, such as the filing cabinets and even the waste paper basket (normally called the trash can, in American developed systems. As a trivial example of the use of the WIMP environment compared with a 'conventional' MMI, consider the operation of deleting a file, called JOHN. LTR. In the conventional system, say one based on MSDOS, one would type the command 'DELETE JOHN. LTR'. In the WIMP environment, the mouse is used to point at the icon representing the file JOHN. LTR, which is then 'dragged' to the waste paper basket icon. A button on the mouse is clicked to indicate that the 'Trash' option is to be exercised with respect to the file JOHN. LTR, that is, the indicated file is to be 'thrown' into the 'bin'.

It can be argued that the power of the WIMP technique lies not so much in providing a better way to do any specific task, but in integrating together a number of different tasks in a way which approximates to that in which a human operator organises his work. The real power of the technique is realised only when it is used with an operating system which can manage multi-tasking, that is, it allows more than one task to be active at any given time, sharing the resources of the system. Take another example from the world of office automation, a salesman using a personal computer to compile a sales report. The tool, used for the actual writing of the report will be a word-processing package. He may have some of the information needed for the paper held in a database on the PC. He may also need to include certain information which is held in databases in other locations, such as on the corporate mainframe computer. It is very likely that he will have compiled a table of sales figures using a spreadsheet, into which he can enter the required figures and have all the necessary totals, averages and other calculations performed automatically. He may need to display some of his figures graphically, for instance, as bar charts, pie charts or even exploded three-dimensional pie charts, if that is what he feels will present the figures in the most advantageous way. To do this he will use a business graphics package. On a 'conventional', single-tasking PC, to accomplish the above in a reasonable time demands a high degree of familiarity with the operating system and quite a lot of patience, because each program or package must be run separately. The common bond between the different applications is at the file level. Each program will produce its results and write them into a file, which can then be used by the other programs. The spreadsheet can be used to generate a file including the desired figures, which can then be read into the word-processing file. A similar train of transactions applies to the extracting of information from the database for incorporation into the document.

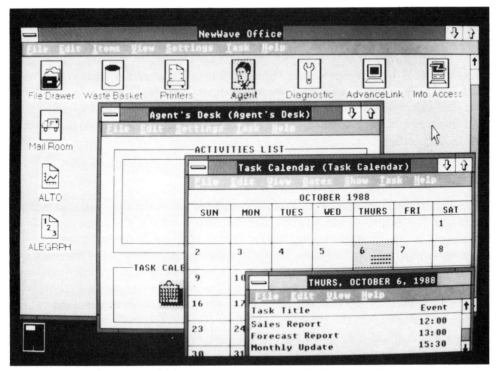

FIG. 5.10 A WIMP Desk-Top Screen (*Hewlett Packard*)

Enter the multi-tasking, WIMP-equipped business executive, with the same job to do. He can first of all open a window in which to run his word-processing tool to write the framework of the report. In practice he will probably use an existing report as a model, so he finds the file containing the existing report in his 'filing cabinet', and places a copy of it into the current word-processing window to be edited. To get the information from the local database is simple. He opens another window, this time for the database program, and finds the required information. Using his 'cut and paste' tools, he extracts the required information from the database window and puts it into the word-processor window in the right place in his document. Extracting information from the spreadsheet is done in a similar way. The information from the corporate database is slightly more difficult to obtain. He must first open a communications window, through which he 'logs on' to the mainframe computer, runs the database program, and finds the required information. This can then be 'cut and pasted' as before. Once he has a version of the complete report assembled in his word-processing window, he may choose to print it, by directing it either to a local printer, or to a different printer located somewhere else within the organisation. Alternatively, he may use the electronic mail option of his office automation system to send the whole document with a suitable covering memo in electronic form, directly to his sales director. Whilst he has been engaged in this task, his electronic mail facility could have been active in the background, and have received a number of incoming messages for him.

The sort of power described above has a price, of course, mostly in terms of processor speed and memory capacity, but also because of the requirement for high-resolution graphics. The system has a large processing overhead to manage the multi-tasking and the very flexible transfer of information between tasks. This style of computing is only available on machines based on the most up-to-date, high-speed, 32-bit microprocessor chips, supported by several megabytes of main memory, and a commensurate amount of mass storage. It has yet to make an impact on tactical CIS but will undoubtedly do so, particularly as more and more CIS users become accustomed to the power and flexibility of this style of system use in their offices.

Sensor Input and Output

So far in this chapter we have concentrated on human input and output. Although the details of the sensors themselves are outside the scope of the book, we cannot leave the subject of input and output without considering the interface to sensors and other 'automata'. This will most frequently take the form of input to the information system, although there will also be a need with some varieties of device to send controlling instructions from the information system to the device. Hence we must consider in many cases a two-way interface. In terms of the volume of data passing across the interface, the flow of information from the sensor into the system is invariably more significant than the movement of telemetry commands in the other direction.

Even though sensors have been declared to be outside of our scope, we should at least be aware of the various types which may be encountered, and of the characteristics which could have a bearing on their interface with the information system. All sensors have a common, general aim of gathering information on the enemy which cannot be obtained by direct human observation. The information can take a variety of forms, according to the technique employed by the sensor:

▶ *Area sensors* normally produce an image, usually in two dimensions, of their area of surveillance. They may do so by optical means, using either visible light or infra-red, or by one or more of a wide range of radar-imaging techniques. Imaging sensors are the most prolific generators of information; for example, using conventional television techniques, a monochrome TV signal requires a channel with a bandwidth of several megahertz (MHz) to transmit it. As we shall see in later chapters, this sort of high capacity channel is unlikely to be available on the battlefield.

▶ *Point sensors* are employed to detect the presence or level of certain phenomena in their immediate area. An example is the seismic disturbance sensor, which can detect the vibrations in the ground caused by passing vehicles or personnel. The most sophisticated devices of this variety now use a high degree of signal processing and pattern recognition techniques to distinguish between different stimuli. They can, for example, differentiate between human and animal footfalls, and recognise different types of armoured and wheeled vehicle. Acoustic sensors have been used to good effect in artillery sound-ranging systems since the First World War. An array of microphones is used to pick up the sound of gunfire from an enemy battery, and the location of the guns may be calculated knowing the locations of the microphones and the time of arrival of the sound of the gunfire at each microphone. Probably the most bizarre sensor in this category is the one used by the American forces in Vietnam as a detector of human beings, typically Viet Cong personnel moving along supply trails in the jungle. The sensor relied on the behaviour of a certain species of beetle, which became excited in the presence of human body odours. Its excitement was manifested as a pattern of movement of the creatures' legs, which was detected by a sensitive microphone built into the capsule containing the beetles. The sounds were relayed back to a central point for analysis.

It is also of some interest to us to know where the sensors are. Many forms of sensor will by definition be remote from our own forces. Some will be deployed in airborne platforms, such as manned helicopters, fixed wing aircraft or remotely piloted vehicles (RPVs). Others will be placed behind enemy lines, either through being left behind and overrun as the enemy advances, or possibly delivered by artillery or aircraft. Communications with remote sensors will always present difficulties, which in turn will impose constraints on the information flow across the interface with the system.

All the sensors, even the 'sniffer bug', produce their output in the form of electrical signals. Those signals will almost invariably be of a form which cannot be passed directly into the information system. At the very least, some conversion is required to turn the signals generated by the sensors into information in a form which can be understood by the CIS. In most cases it will be necessary to carry out a great deal of processing and interpretation to convert the raw sensor data into useful information for the command and control system. Where that processing is carried out is of vital importance to the communications system. To cut down the amount of data which must be transmitted, the processing should be carried out as near to its source as possible. Tactical communications systems, as shall be explained later, simply do not have the capacity to carry the masses of raw data which can be generated by sensors.

Summary

If the user of a computer system is to be able to interact efficiently with the system and to make the best use of it to support his work, there must be a well designed man-machine interface. The MMI will depend both on the characteristics of the devices used to get data in and out of the machine, and on the design and 'style' of the dialogue. In tactical CIS constraints may be placed on both of these aspects. The devices must be appropriate to their use in the physical environment, which may be extremely harsh, and the design of the dialogue must be appropriate to the user's circumstances. Both of these points are returned to in Chapter 7, when we look at the battlefield environment and the demands placed on the design of equipment and systems which must work there.

6.

Communications

Introduction

The command and control system model introduced in Chapter 1 illustrates the importance of communications; remove the communications links, and one is left with a collection of unconnected and therefore relatively useless items of equipment. Of course, in system terms, such a view is unfair since, to operate as a system, all the components are needed. However, it is worth reflecting on the historical perspective that today's CIS and those planned for the immediate future represent a convergence between battlefield communications systems and computer-based information systems. Before the coming of computers to the battlefield, the command and control process was supported by a combination of manual command and staff procedures and communications systems designed for voice and written messages. The legacy of voice-oriented communications systems will be with us for a considerable time to come, in the shape of adaptations of voice systems for data transmission. Only in recent years have the growing demands of computer-based information systems led to the development and deployment of systems specifically designed for data transmission.

An obvious starting point for our examination of communications is the nature of the signal. We have already seen in Chapter 2 how information may be represented in a binary, digital form. In Chapter 4 we saw how the digital representation of information may be stored, using a variety of electronic, electromagnetic and optical techniques. To communicate data electronically from one place to another we need to convert these static representations of information into dynamic pulses of electricity which can travel along conducting wires and other transmission media. When we need to transfer information between elements of a computer system inside the same box, e.g. from processor to main memory, the capacity of the interconnecting communication links is seldom a limitation. Internal data transfer rates of many tens of megabits per second are common place. What then is so different about sending such information beyond the confines of the box? As we shall see, there are major advantages in retaining the digital nature of the signal during its transmission through the communication system, but there is a vast difference between the movement of data inside the machine and in the world outside. Inside the machine transmission is invariably in parallel form, that is, whole bytes or even greater numbers of bits (e.g. 32-bit words in certain machines) are transferred simultaneously over relatively short, multi-wire connections or highways. When we go beyond the confines of the box, we find that transmission is serial, that is, one bit at a time, at relatively low speeds, and subject to many constraints. This chapter is mainly devoted to an examination of these constraints, and the techniques used to overcome them in military communications systems.

We shall take the same layered approach to the examination of communications as was earlier taken to the other components. Of advantage to us here is the fact that this layered approach has been described formally in recent years by the International Standardisation Organisation (ISO), in its model for 'open systems interconnection'. This is a topic covered in detail in Chapter 9 under the heading

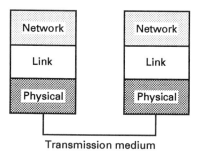

Transmission medium

FIG. 6.1   The Communications Model

of Interoperability. Figure 6.1 shows the first three layers of the ISO OSI model, interconnected by the transmission medium, or bearer. In this chapter, the description of data communications techniques is loosely based on the components in this diagram, namely the transmission medium and the first three layers of the model.

The transmission medium, or bearer, may be anything from a short length of copper wire to a radio link established via a geostationary communications satellite. The physical layer is concerned with the representation of individual bits by suitable symbols, or electrical conditions, and their presentation to the transmission medium. The link layer describes the techniques for the transmission of data over a link between two points, in a way that enables the receiver to recognise the organisation of the received data into words or other meaningful groupings. The network layer recognises that most communication systems are more complicated than simple one-to-one links, and makes provision for the connection of more than one such link into a network. It must therefore cover such aspects of switching and addressing.

Before we start on this journey up the layers of the model, it would be useful to consider first of all the demands which will be placed on the communications system by the information system which requires its services.

Communications requirements

The role of the communications component of CIS may be stated simply as 'the timely, accurate and secure distribution of information between dispersed elements of the information system'. To get an insight into the nature of the communications system, we must look more closely at the requirements placed on it and the ways in which they are met.

Capacity

The communications system must meet the demands for data transmission capacity placed on it by subscriber information systems, but assessing and specifying those demands is seldom a straightforward task. It would be an unusual information system which had a steady communications requirement of so many kilobits per second (kbit/s) over a long period of time. The demand for communication is normally anything but steady; although there will always be a certain amount of routine traffic, such as standard reports and returns which are predictable in both quantity and time of generation, the major peaks of traffic will occur as a result of events, such as the first contact with a major enemy thrust. It is almost axiomatic that the time when it will be most vital for a message to be delivered very quickly will be when all other users are generating high levels of traffic. This is why most information systems are more concerned with the response time available from the communications system than with the average capacity. From the common user's viewpoint, however, the overall capacity of the communications system is important, since the fast response times demanded by some systems must be provided against the background load of all the other traffic. Overall required capacity is a critical factor in the sizing of the communications network.

Response Time

Response time is a measure of how long it takes the communications system to deliver information from one user to another. Precise definitions of response time are obviously concerned with what is being delivered, i.e. how much data, and the exact points between which it is to be conveyed. As introduced above, for many users of the communications system, especially those with time-critical applications, such as the control of weapon systems, the response time is far more important than the overall throughput.

Connection and Addressing

The communications system must provide connection between the required users and a means of identifying the intended recipient of a particular transmission, i.e. of addressing. In all but the simplest communications system this requirement involves some form of switching and a mechanism for routing traffic between subscribers. Some of the different approaches to switching and network interconnection are outlined later.

Integrity

A general rule is that the communications system must preserve the integrity of the information it handles. Just as one expects the postman to deliver letters which are still in one piece and in a readable state, so a data communications system must not corrupt the data which it carries. 'Must not corrupt' needs to be precisely specified; a typical requirement might be that the probability of a bit being received in error should be less than one in a million. This is described as a bit error rate (BER) of one in 10^6, which can be quite a tall order when the raw BER of a noisy VHF radio channel may be one in 10^2, or worse. Measures are therefore needed to combat the effect of noise in the channel. Many schemes have been devised for error detection and error detection and correction (EDC), but they all have in common the need to add redundant information to the transmitted data. Some of the techniques used are described later.

Control

The human user of a communications channel controls his use of the channel by following a set of predefined procedures, e.g. voice procedure, containing such basic rules as 'listen before sending', to ensure that no other station is transmitting. For automated communications between the distributed elements of computer-based information systems, similar rules must be applied to control the use of the channel and the communication between the two parties. Such rules are generally termed 'protocols'.

Security

The communications system must preserve the security of the information handled by taking steps to ensure that it is only seen by those who have a right and the need to do so. Once launched into a radio system, information is in 'free space' and thus open for interception by the enemy. Some form of encryption is called for, to render the information unreadable to those not in possession of the appropriate encryption 'key'. Schemes involving end-to-end or user encryption are possible, but are complicated by the fact that the routing of information must be left accessible and readable by intermediate switching points or nodes in the communications network. The most common technique is link-by-link encryption, where the information is encrypted only when it is passed over a transmission link. The basic technique used to encrypt digital signals is covered further on under the description of the link layer and the whole topic of security is examined in Chapter 10.

The Transmission Medium

The transmission medium used to establish a link from one point to another is known as a communications bearer. Bearers may be radio links, which can be further subdivided into single- or multi-channel, by frequency band (e.g. HF or VHF), or by method of propagation (e.g. line of sight, ionospheric reflection, tropospheric scatter or satellite relay. Cable bearers include both wire conductors and optical fibres.

Radio Systems

In a radio system, a signal at radio frequency (RF) is used to 'carry' the signal representing the information that is to be transmitted through a process known as modulation. The RF signal is known as the carrier, and its frequency is chosen as a compromise between the propagation characteristics available at a particular frequency (which govern the physical range of the link, i.e. the distance over which it can be established), and the information carrying capacity or bandwidth available. Whilst the latter is directly proportional to the radio frequency, i.e. the higher the frequency, the greater the information carrying bandwidth, the former varies according to the dominant mode of propagation at the frequency concerned. Table 6.1 identifies the various frequency bands and their characteristics.

TABLE 6.1   *Frequency Bands for Communications*

Band designation	Frequency Range	Propagation Mode	Main Application
Extra low frequency (ELF)	below 3 kHz	Surface wave	Communication to submarines
Very low frequency (VLF)	3–30 kHz	Surface wave	Radio navigation
Low frequency (LF)	30–300 kHz	Surface wave	Broadcasting
Medium frequency (MF)	300 kHz–3 MHz	Surface wave	Broadcasting
High frequency (HF)	3–30 MHz	Surface wave Sky wave via Ionosphere	Broadcasting, Long-range Communications
Very high frequency (VHF)	30–300 MHz	Space wave	Short-range communications Broadcasting
Ultra high frequency (UHF)	300–3000 MHz	Space wave	Communications, TV broadcasting
Super high frequency (SHF)	3–30 GHz	Space wave	Communications, Radar
Extra high frequency (EHF)	30–300 GHz	Space wave	Communications, Radar

The use of the frequency spectrum is governed by international treaty, which divides up the available frequencies into bands, which in turn are designated for specific purposes. Military tactical communications systems are found in the following bands:

SINGLE-CHANNEL RADIO

Frequencies in the range from 1.5 to 30 MHz are used for long-range communications using skywave propagation, and sometimes over shorter ranges, using surface-wave propagation, as an alternative or back-up to VHF radio. Most VHF combat radio is found in the 30–88 MHz band. The low UHF part of the spectrum is used for short-range communications, typically in urban areas, and for air-ground-air links.

MULTI-CHANNEL TERRESTRIAL RADIO RELAY

This form of point-to-point communication is found mainly in the UHF and low SHF regions of the spectrum. The higher the frequency, the more closely must the path between transmitter and receiver approach true line-of-sight. Whilst the higher frequencies are suitable for civil, or static military applications, in tactical systems where the links must be established rapidly in temporary locations, use of the lower frequencies makes siting less critical. Where connection is required beyond the range of a single link, relay stations may be inserted to join links together in a chain. A form of terrestrial radio relay which is not limited in its range by the line-of-sight propagation mode is tropospheric scatter, which makes use of the phenomenon of scattering of frequencies in the VHF and the UHF bands by discontinuities in the troposphere to achieve communication beyond the horizon, typically up to ranges of 120 km. This propagation method is very inefficient; large amounts of power must be transmitted to produce an acceptable signal at the receiving end. It is most useful for establishing links in terrain where the positioning of relay stations is either undesirable or impossible, such as links across water.

SATELLITE COMMUNICATIONS

A satellite communications link is essentially a radio-relay link, with the relay in space, normally in a geostationary orbit, some 36,000 km away from the Earth. Frequencies in the UHF and the SHF are used for satellite communications. Satellite communications terminals capable of being carried by one man are now in military service.

Modulation

The most elementary way to impress information on to the RF carrier is to switch the carrier on and off in a way which conveys information to a receiver of the interrupted RF signal. This is exactly how the characters of the Morse code are transmitted; the action of the operator in keying the dots and dashes of the code simply switches the carrier on and off, which is why this form of communication is called carrier wave (CW) mode. Morse is not a binary, but a three-state code, the states being short pulses (dots), long pulses (dashes) and the space in between pulses. For the transmission of signals more complex than the simple on/off signalling of the Morse code, a form of modulation which varies one of the parameters of the carrier in sympathy with the applied signal is used. Hence we have amplitude modulation (AM), in which the amplitude of the carrier is varied, frequency modulation (FM) in which the frequency of the carrier varies in proportion to the amplitude of the applied signal, and phase modulation (PhM) in which the carrier phase is varied. These forms of modulation are illustrated in Figure 6.2.

Non-Radio Bearers

In static communication systems, a significant proportion of the long-distance, as well as local traffic is carried by cables, which may either be buried in the ground or carried on overhead routes suspended from poles or pylons. In military, tactical systems, the use of cables is generally confined to local interconnection, such as that between the vehicles of a formation headquarters. Cable takes time and effort to lay and recover, and is vulnerable to damage both from one's own

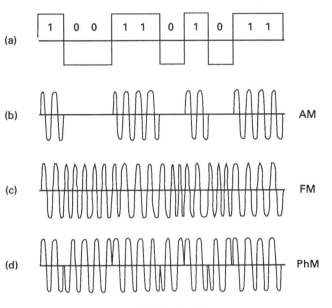

FIG. 6.2   Modulation Types

troops and by enemy action. Such is the expected pace of battle that the laying of field cable over distances more than one or two kilometres is not contemplated by most armies.

Copper Cables

Within a headquarters complex, it is common to find multi-pair cables used for interconnection, with each pair carrying one speech channel or its equivalent. Other types of cable include the single twisted-pair field cable used to connect single field-telephone extensions, and the high frequency cables used to carry multiplexed groups of speech channels. The introduction of local area networks (LANs) to headquarters could involve the use of coaxial cables, which are similar in design and construction to the cables used to carry RF signals between radio equipments and antennas.

Optical Fibres

Optical-fibre cables contain one or more fine strands of optical glass, encased in a suitable cladding to make the cable robust enough for use in the field. The electrical signal to be transmitted down the cable must first of all be converted into a light signal through the use of a transducer, based on a photo-emitting device. It is detected at the receiving end by a transducer based on a photodetecting device. The principle of fibre-optic transmission is shown in Figure 6.3. The main advantages of optical fibres over copper cables are the very high relative bandwidth of the optical fibre and the facts that there is no electromagnetic radiation from the fibre, nor is it susceptible to external electromagnetic fields. These factors

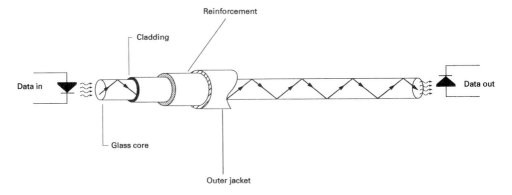

FIG. 6.3   Fibre Optic Transmission

make it particularly suitable for use in military vehicle installations and for applications involving classified information.

The Physical Layer

The problem addressed by the physical layer of the communications model is essentially that of transferring data stored in electronic form on to a transmission medium and vice versa. The data in the store are held, as we saw in Chapter 4, in the form of electrical charges. The simplest way to transfer those data on to a transmission medium, such as a pair of wires joining two parts of a computer system, would be to transfer the contents of each store location to the wire in turn, where the '1's would be represented by a pulse of electricity, and the '0's by no pulse. The speed of transmission across this simplest of links has little to do with how fast a pulse can get from point A to point B, because it travels at something approaching the speed of light. This is analogous to a machine gun; the number of bullets which can be fired at the target in a given time is a function of the gun's rate of fire and has little or nothing to do with how long it takes a single bullet to reach the target. The rate at which the contents of store A can be transferred across the link to store B depends upon how quickly the digits can be transferred out of the store and on to the link. Hence we express transmission rates in terms of bits per second (bit/s), and use the normal prefixes to indicate faster transmission rates, e.g. kilobit/s (KB/s: one thousand bit/s) and megabit/s (MB/s: one million bit/s).

Transmission Rate and Bandwidth

The faster the transmission rate, the shorter the duration of the individual pulses, and the higher the frequency content of the signal which represents the bit stream. It is common to see bit streams represented in diagrams as a series of rectangular pulses, but in practice they are not perfectly rectangular. If they were, they would contain infinitely high frequencies, since the vertical elements of the pulses would represent changes of voltage or current in zero time. In practice, pulses are smoothed out to produce more gradual rise and decay slopes. Taken to an extreme, this introduces a problem known as 'intersymbol interference'. The process of smoothing out the near-rectangular, high-speed pulses also causes them to 'spread' and merge into one another. This is shown in Figure 6.4.

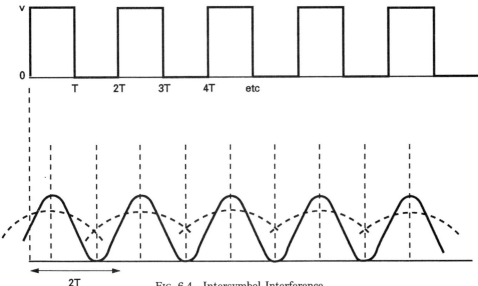

FIG. 6.4   Intersymbol Interference

This effect occurs when signals are sent down channels with inadequate bandwidth. The attenuation of a channel (i.e. the amount by which the strength of a signal is reduced) increases with the frequency, so that when a signal with components at different frequencies is passed down the channel, the higher frequencies are attenuated more than the lower frequencies. This causes the sort of distortion of the pulse shape described above, and leads to intersymbol interference. There comes a point at which the individual symbols are indistinguishable and hence the signal is unreadable. The solid line waveform in the lower part of Figure 6.4 is the result of passing the series of on/off pulses over a channel with a maximum frequency response of 1/2T Hz, where T sec is the duration of a single pulse. Another way of expressing this set of facts is to say that the maximum digital signalling rate possible without intersymbol interference over a channel with a cut-off frequency of B Hz is 2B bit/s. This is known as the Nyquist rate. The dotted waveform in the lower part of Figure 6.4 is the result of passing the pulse stream down a channel with a cut-off frequency below 1/2T Hz; the spreading of the pulses into the adjacent pulse 'slots' can be clearly seen. Another channel characteristic which can cause pulse distortion is group delay, that is, the difference in propagation speed through the channel of signals at different frequencies. The actual amount of attenuation and group delay depends, in the case of a wire or cable connection, on the length of the cable. For very short connections, such as those inside the computer assembly, attenuation is not a great problem and signals of very high bit rate, and therefore high frequency, can be exchanged. For digital transmission over cables beyond the immediate boundary of the computer the distance achievable for a given cable type is inversely proportional to the bit rate. The choice of cable type is significant; for example, coaxial cables generally have a better high frequency performance than twisted-pair cables.

Serial versus Parallel Communication

Within the confines of the computer and between the computer and some periph-erals, such as external disc drives and certain types of printer, it is normal to use parallel transmission, that is, the simultaneous transmission of several bits down parallel communications paths—normally a multi-wire cable. This obviously increases the transfer rate, but is not a practicable technique for communications beyond the immediate surroundings of the computer installation, because of the need for parallel channels. In serial transmission, the data are sent to the channel

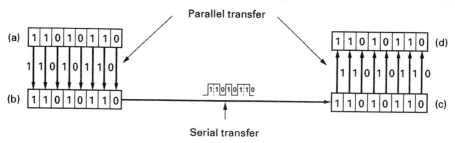

FIG. 6.5   Serial and Parallel Transmission

one bit at a time. Figure 6.5 illustrates the difference between serial and parallel transmission.

Digital versus Analogue Communication

So far we have considered the presentation to the transmission medium of data in digital form, that is, as on/off pulses of electricity. Many of the older, voice-based communications systems cannot cope with the data in this form, because they were designed to handle information in an analogue form, that is, as continu-ously variable signals. For example, a single voice channel in an analogue system will carry signals which are electrical representations of the variations, in both frequency and amplitude, of the speech which was input by the user through a microphone. In telecommunications systems these analogue speech signals are normally confined to a 3.1 kHz bandwidth, from 0.3 to 3.4 kHz. A channel with these characteristics is totally unsuitable for the transmission of data in a raw, digital form of on/off electrical impulses. Faced with an analogue channel, the data system must convert its digital signals into an acceptable form for the chan-nel, that is, into signals in the 0.3 to 3.4 kHz audio bandwidth. The device used to perform this transformation, and to reverse it at the receiving end is known as a modem. (MODulator-DEModulator). Figure 6.6 shows a link between a computer terminal and a host computer using a 'dialled-up' connection through the public switched telephone network, using modems. In its simplest form, the connection is first established by the human operator at the terminal end. Instead of a voice at the other end of the line, an audio tone from the modem will be heard, at which point the terminal-end modem is connected to the line and data transmission can

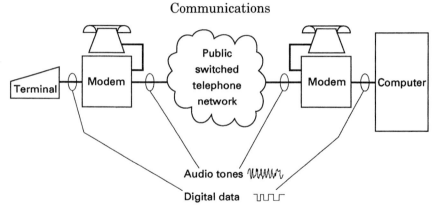

FIG. 6.6.   Communications Link with Modems

begin. The simplest form of digital-to-analogue (D to A) conversion used by modems is frequency shift keying (FSK). A signal in the audio range, known as the carrier, is shifted up in frequency by a set amount to represent a binary '1' and down by the same amount for a '0'.

There are other aspects of voice-oriented communications which must be addressed by the designer of data communications systems, which we shall come to later. At this stage it would be useful to highlight the main advantage for voice and data users alike of using communications systems which handle signals in a digital form throughout. This is the performance of digital signals in the presence of noise.

Digital systems have an inherent degree of immunity to the effects of noise in the channel. In an analogue system, the receiver must follow the continuous variations in amplitude to produce a faithful representation of the transmitted signal. Any noise in the channel will be added to the wanted signal, and will reduce its 'readability' by the receiver. The digital receiver simply has to distinguish between two states of the received signal, that is, the state which represents the digit '1' and that which represents '0'. It does so by sampling the received signal, say at the midpoint of each bit period, to see if the signal is above or below a given threshold value. The receiver has a simple binary decision to make, i.e. the received signal may either be a '1' or a '0'. Once correctly received, the signals may be reconstituted perfectly, thus removing the noise completely. Of course, should the noise exceed the threshold level, it may cause the digit to be interpreted incorrectly, that is, it causes an error in the received bit pattern. This process is illustrated in Figure 6.7. As we shall see, there are techniques available to detect and correct errors in received signals.

The Link Layer

This section deals with the functions which must be provided in order to allow the transmission of meaningful groups of bits across a communications link.

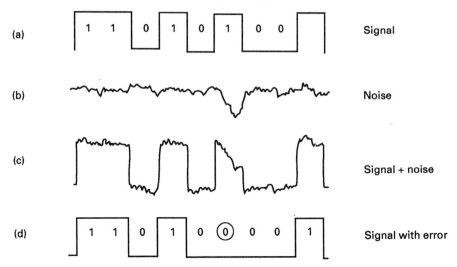

FIG. 6.7   Digital Signal in Presence of Noise

Synchronisation

A mechanism must exist which enables the receiving end of the link to recognise the individual bits as part of some organised grouping of data. For example, if the data are structured into bytes, each one representing an ASCII symbol, the receiving end must know when looking at the incoming stream of pulses where one byte starts and another one finishes. There are two basic approaches to this problem.

In asynchronous transmission, each byte, or other grouping of bits, is sent as an entity bounded by pulses known as stop and start bits. This form of transmission is useful for character-oriented tasks, such as computer terminals and printers. In the case of a computer terminal, each character typed by the operator is sent to the computer individually, as a character in the ASCII or other code, enclosed by the start and stop bits.

Synchronous transmission relies on timing signals, normally derived from the data-pulse stream itself, to determine the boundaries between symbols. The data are sent in blocks, the boundaries of which are marked by special control characters. Figure 6.8 shows a typical synchronous data block.

S Y N	S Y N	S O H	Other header and control characters	S T X	Message text	E T X	B C C	P A D

FIG. 6.8   Synchronous Data Block

Error Detection/Correction

Noise on the transmission link, whether emanating from natural sources or man-made, can cause errors in the detection of symbols. Techniques are available to combat these effects. The simplest error detection scheme, capable of detecting single bit errors, is the parity check, which is commonly used in conjunction with the asynchronous, one character-at-a-time mode of operation described above. To each group of bits representing a character, a further bit is added to make the total number of '1' bits an even number. The character is checked on receipt, and if it is found to have an odd number of '1' bits it is rejected as containing an error. Take as an example the transmission of the character 'A', represented in ASCII as the bit pattern 01000001. This has an even number of '1's, and so the parity check mechanism at the sending end will add as the ninth digit a '0'. Thus the pattern 010000010 will be transmitted. If this pattern should be corrupted and received as 011000001, the receiver will immediately detect that it has an odd number of '1's , reject it and request a retransmission. What has been described is an 'even parity' system. The opposite is also possible, that is, one in which an odd number of '1's is expected.

Parity checking is a simple technique to detect single bit errors, and the 'overhead' imposed, i.e. the extra redundant information added to the transmitted data, is just one bit per block. There are much more complex and powerful techniques, capable of detecting and correcting multiple errors, and imposing a correspondingly higher overhead. In the synchronous transmission method already described, the control character 'BCC' is a block check character which is used to perform an error check on the whole block of data. If the block check fails at the receiving end, the whole block is rejected and a retransmission is requested. In a system designed for transmission over VHF radio channels, the EDC overhead may typically reduce the information carrying capacity of the channel by a half. Thus a channel with a data rate of 16 Kb/s might have an information rate of only 8 Kb/s. Systems designed to survive both heavy congestion and deliberate interference (jamming) may have variable, dynamic EDC schemes in which the worst case performance may be only a few hundred bits per second.

Encryption

As we saw above, one of the requirements placed on the communications system is that of preserving the security of the information entrusted to it, even though that information may be transmitted through free space and therefore be open to interception by the enemy. This requirement is met by encryption, and another advantage of digital transmission is the ease with which signals may be encrypted. The process is shown in Figure 6.9. A key, which is known only to the sender and the authorised recipients of the message, is added to the transmitted bitstream using modulo-2 addition, as shown. At the receiving end exactly the same process is performed to recover the original signal.

Control

There is a need to control the flow of data over the link, normally accomplished within the link through the use of special control blocks or frames, as they are known in the terminology of one of the more commonly used data-link protocols. This is the high level, data-link control (HDLC) protocol. The term 'handshaking' is used to describe the process used by the two ends of the link to establish each

Plain text: 1 1 0 1 1 0 0 1 1 0 1 1

Encryption key: 1 0 1 0 1 1 0 0 1 0 1 1

Cypher text: 0 1 1 1 0 1 0 1 0 0 0 0

Encryption key: 1 0 1 0 1 1 0 0 1 0 1 1

Plain text: 1 1 0 1 1 0 0 1 1 0 1 1

'Truth table' for the modulo-2 addition used in the above process

$$1 + 1 = 0$$
$$1 + 0 = 1$$
$$0 + 1 = 1$$
$$0 + 0 = 0$$

This is also known as the 'Exclusive-OR' function

FIG. 6.9   Digital Encryption Technique

other's presence and readiness to accept data. HDLC also provides a frame-numbering scheme which can be used, amongst other things, to detect out-of-sequence frames, or detect the fact that a frame has not been received.

The Network Layer

Once the communications system becomes more complicated than a simple, one-to-one link, some consideration must be given to the way in which subscribing stations are to be connected together. A broad division between network types is the distinction between switched and non-switched networks. A familiar non-switched network 'topology' or layout, for voice communications is the 'all-informed' radio net in which all stations share access to a common transmission medium (in this case, a radio frequency). Stations are identified by call signs, and calls may be made to one or more stations at once, including all-stations calls. Stations listen before sending, in order to prevent their transmissions clashing with others. The all-informed characteristics of the radio net can also be achieved in networks where the stations are interconnected by some form of cable. This type of connection is encountered in the computer local area network (LAN), described in more detail below.

Switched Networks

Probably the most commonly encountered switched network is the public telephone system, in which calls are routed from one subscriber to another via one or more exchanges or switches. The switches perform their routing operation in response to instructions from the calling subscriber. In an automatic telephone system those instructions consist of a telephone number—the called subscriber's 'address' on the network—which is entered by the calling subscriber via the telephone dial or key pad. In both civil and military systems, computer-controlled (so-called stored program controlled, SPC) switches are replacing electromechanical automatic exchanges which may have many moving parts and are far from ideal for use on the battlefield. In the typical tactical SPC system, such as the UK's Ptarmigan, the user is relieved of the problem of knowing exactly where on the network his called subscriber is connected. All he has to do is enter a fixed number to identify the subscriber from a 'deducible' directory, that is, the digits of the telephone number indicate the level of command, formation/unit and the appointment of the subscriber. The system locates the subscriber using a technique known as 'flood searching', whereby a request to locate the called subscriber is propagated through the network from node to node. When the reply is returned, the calling node will select the shortest route to the called subscriber. The routes used to contact frequently called subscribers are stored in the switches' memory, to avoid wasting time on unnecessary flood searches.

For data communications, the broad principles are the same, but the differences between data and voice traffic call for a different approach to switching.

Circuit Switching

Just as in the case of the voice telephone circuit, where a connection between two human users is established through exchanges or switches by the action of the user who initiates the call, it is possible to establish a connection between two equipments for the transfer of data. The connection is maintained throughout the transfer of data and is broken once transfer is complete, at the request of one of the participants. In some cases, the connection may be established by human operators, in exactly the same way as they would dial a voice connection, in which the case the data equipments are only connected once the circuit has been established. It is more usual today for the data equipments to establish their own connection (sometimes referred to as 'auto-dialling'). This type of connection is common where systems which were originally designed for voice traffic are adapted for data transmission, and it has the advantage that exactly the same switching mechanism as was used for voice may be used for data transfer. The disadvantage lies in the difference between voice and data traffic. Whereas the typical voice call, even on a military, tactical telephone system may last several minutes, the typical duration of a data transmission is of the order of a few seconds. For the voice call, the fact that it takes a few seconds to establish the call is not usually significant, because it is a short time in relation to the length of the call. In the case of the data 'call', the time taken to establish the call may be longer than the call itself, and so the connection time 'overhead' is very significant. Thus for a data system in which most of the transmissions are very short, circuit switching is an inefficient method of connection. For the occasional transfer of relatively large amounts of data (i.e. where the transmission time is significantly longer than the connection time), circuit switching is an acceptable technique.

Message Switching

Message switching systems were developed for handling written messages, where the user writes his message, normally on a pre-formatted pad and hands it into a message centre for transmission. The message, together with the necessary addressing and other control information, is typed on a teleprinter and transmitted into the system in digital form. In an automatic message switching system these digital messages are routed by computer-based message switches, which act on the routing information contained in the message. Messages may be held within the computer store of a switch until it is possible to deliver them to their final destinations, which gives rise to the term 'store-and-forward' often applied to such systems. It is possible to use store-and-forward systems to carry traffic between data equipments, treating the whole of a data transmission as a message. In most battlefield information systems the average length of a transmission between elements of the system is very much shorter than the average length of a written signal message, so message switching is an inefficient means of connection.

Packet Switching

The first two switching systems were both developed to cope with forms of human transmission, and their adaptation to carry data traffic between elements of computer-based information systems involves a degree of compromise. The technique of packet switching, however, is one which has been developed specifically for data transfer. Data to be transferred are assembled into packets, the size of which is optimised for the switching system concerned, after taking into account such factors as the capacity or transmission rate on the interconnecting circuits, the amount of store available at the switches, and the likely transmission delay time. In a typical system, the packet length is 128 bytes. The switching principle is illustrated in Figure 6.10.

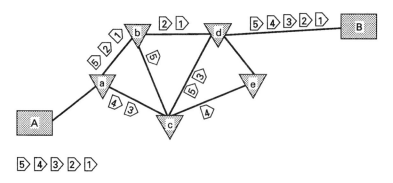

FIG. 6.10   Packet Switching Technique

The data to be transmitted between points A and B in the network have been split into five packets. Each packet is routed through the network independently, with the result that they may be received at the distant switching 'node' in the network in a different order to that in which they were sent. If the system is one which guarantees 'ordered delivery' to the user, the packets will be re-ordered before they are sent on to their final destination. The major advantage of packet switching is that it makes for efficient use of the communications channels available. Because the packets are so short and may be independently routed, the system can keep the traffic flowing by sending packets which are part of different transmissions consecutively down a given circuit, instead of having to keep the circuit open until a whole transmission is complete, thereby holding up other transmissions.

Two basic types of packet switching service may be offered. The first of these is the 'datagram' service, where the network undertakes to accept and deliver one packet of data at a time from the user. These packets, the 'datagrams', are routed independently through the network and may be delivered out of order at the receiving end; it is the receiver's responsibility to re-order them. In the virtual circuit service, the user has the impression that a physical circuit exists between sender and destination. Packets are received in the order in which they were sent; even though they are not necessarily all routed in the same way through the network, the action of the software at the sending and the receiving end switch makes it appear to the user that they are.

Non-Switched Networks: Local Area Networks (LANs)

The 'local area' is normally taken to mean a single site or building. In the case of a tactical system, the group of vehicles comprising a formation or unit headquarters would count as a local area. The stations in an information system LAN could be individual users' terminals or work-stations, or shared resources such as mass storage, printers and plotters. In some office systems the same LAN is used to carry all forms of information, i.e. voice, images and data.

Configurations

The LAN, as already introduced, is a form of non-switched network. The basic configurations which may be used to connect stations are shown in Figure 6.11.

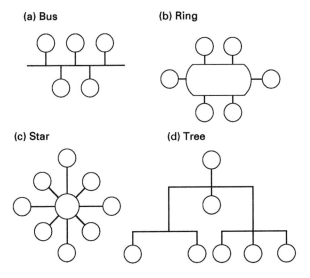

FIG. 6.11   LAN Configurations

Baseband vs Broadband

In a baseband LAN signals are sent over the network at the frequencies in which they are produced by their sources. In a broadband LAN signals are transformed in frequency through the modulation of a carrier signal. By using a number of different carrier frequencies, several signals may be sent simultaneously in a

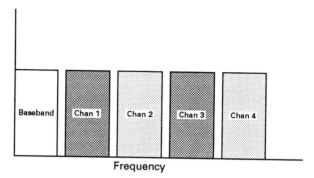

FIG. 6.12   Frequency Division Multiplex on Broadband LAN

process known as frequency division multiplex, illustrated in Figure 6.12. Thus a broadband LAN has a greater capacity than a baseband LAN, at the cost of the complexity of equipment needed for multiplexing and de-multiplexing.

Transmission Media

The simplest LANs use twisted-pair cable, but this is limited in its frequency response and hence data-carrying capacity. Coaxial cable, that is, cable with a central conductor surrounded by an insulating layer and an outer conducting layer, can provide higher capacities, and is commonly used in broadband LANs. Optical fibres offer a number of advantages for use as a LAN transmission medium; they do not radiate electromagnetically, an important feature where security of information is a consideration, and they are not vulnerable to interference from electromagnetic radiation. Optical fibres have a much higher information carrying capacity than metal conductors.

Control

As introduced above, there is much in common between the LAN and the all-informed radio net. All the stations are connected to a common medium, and when one transmits it is 'heard' by all the other stations. On a voice radio net it is up to the human operator to listen out for his station's call sign, indicating that a transmission is intended for his station, and, when he wants to send a message, to listen to the net to ensure that no other station is sending. In a LAN, where the stations are computers and other data processing devices, these features must be automated. Station selection is very much a computer version of the human process described above. Transmissions contain an address field; all stations on the network monitor all transmissions, but they respond only to those transmissions which contain their own address. The process of controlling access to a LAN is often referred to as 'arbitration'.

There are several ways of controlling transmissions on a LAN, but most are variations of two basic techniques: carrier sense multi-access (CSMA) and token passing. CSMA is basically an automated listen-before-sending process. The sending station monitors the network (i.e. it 'senses the carrier') for a given time, and, if no transmission is detected, it assumes the network to be free and sends its transmission. A refinement of this simple technique involves collision detection. A collision occurs when two or more stations transmit at the same time. Having detected that this has occurred, the stations involved 'back off' and try again. The 'back off' is arranged to be different for each station. It can either be a random time period (within a set limit), which over a period of time will not favour any one station over the others, or it can be governed by precedence, that is, the more important a station, the shorter its 'back off' time.

In 'token passing' systems, a special control packet known as the 'token' is continually passed from station to station, or passed to stations in turn from a central control unit. A station may only transmit when it has the token. The main advantage of this technique is that stations are guaranteed a share of access to the network, even when traffic is heavy; a CSMA system may 'lock up' under heavy traffic. However, when traffic is light stations may waste time waiting for the token, even though the net is quiet. Clearly the expected traffic loading on a LAN must influence the choice of control technique. The 'intelligence' needed to implement the control measures may either reside in the subscriber device itself or in a LAN interface unit. There are several variations on the token passing theme, mainly depending upon the physical configuration used. In the token bus, stations are all connected to the same physical medium in the manner shown in Figure 6.11 (a). The token is passed from station to station in a manner which may be varied according to the priority of stations. In the token ring system all stations are connected to a ring cable, as shown in Figure 6.11 (b), and the order of token passing is determined strictly by the physical order of stations on the ring. A further scheme, which is related to the token ring but does not use tokens, is the 'slotted ring'. The physical configuration is that of a ring, but arbitration is by a form of time division multiplex or time slotting.

Standards

As with many developments in the information-technology field, standards for LANs were devised independently by equipment manufacturers. This has led to the existence of a large number of different, incompatible LAN standards. The difficulty caused by this situation is that it creates 'islands' of communication which must either remain isolated from each other, or communicate, probably with some constraints, via 'gateways'. Standard interfaces to LANs make it easier (and cheaper) for manufacterers to incorporate the necessary measures in their equipment, often as standard hardware. The situation has improved in recent years, with the emergence of the IEEE 802 series of standards for LANs. Standards and interoperability are dealt with in more detail in Chapter 9.

Summary

In this chapter, we have looked in a general way at the important principles of data communications. It is difficult to divorce the underlying concepts from their practical application, which is strongly influenced by the environment in which the communications must operate. Of all the 'enabling technologies' covered in the last few chapters, communications is the one which is most affected by the operating environment. This is hardly surprising since communications must, by definition, provide the links through the outside world between the distributed elements of the information system. However, we have tried to confine this chapter to the general issues which would apply to any communications system, whether civil or military. We have left for Chapter 7 the description of communications systems designed to cope with the battlefield environment.

7.

Design for the Battlefield Environment

Introduction

Anyone who has read the opening chapters of this book has now been introduced to the 'enabling technologies' of battlefield CIS. Indeed, Chapters 2 to 6 could stand alone as an introduction to the general field of information technology used to support a wide range of administrative and business applications. These chapters describe the enormous advances which have been made in the capabilities of computer hardware in recent years. The advent of microminiaturisation has in itself brought about a considerable increase in the reliability and robustness of equipment: compare the room full of thermionic valves of the 1950s, or even the box full of printed circuit cards of the 1960s with the single silicon chip of the 1980s. In the very early days, the sheer size of computer hardware made its use on the battlefield an impracticable proposition. We have overcome the size problem, and commonly put processors of a power hitherto unavailable outside of an air-conditioned computer room into hand-held devices which can be used anywhere. But how do even these seemingly robust commercial devices stand up to the expected environment of the battlefield? This chapter will examine the features of the battlefield environment, and the ways in which the designers of CIS must respond to them.

The Physical Environment

Probably the most obvious features are physical; most battlefield CIS equipments have to operate outside the protective shelter of buildings, and some without any shelter at all. Even those installed in vehicles are in a far more testing environment than is found in the office setting. Equipments are shoehorned into the seemingly impossibly small space available in the vehicle. In the worse case they may be subjected to the extremes of temperature, humidity, dust, smoke, shock and vibration which would very soon render unprotected equipment useless.

The Electromagnetic Environment

An equally important but less obvious set of constraints operates in the electromagnetic environment (EME). All CIS equipments radiate electromagnetic energy to some degree, and are themselves susceptible to radiation. An extreme form of electromagnetic interference with the correct working of equipment is the electromagnetic pulse (EMP) emitted as a side effect of a nuclear explosion. An extemely intense EM field of very short duration is created, which can induce destructively large pulses of current in conductors, causing severe damage to unprotected equipments. Less physically destructive, but potentially just as disruptive, are the electronic counter measures (ECM) which may be taken by an enemy, such as jamming or deception. Even without such deliberate interference, the EM environment is crowded. Radio equipments of allies and enemy alike share the same frequencies, and may cause interference well beyond the ranges at which they are designed to communicate.

If all the above were not bad enough, the designer must also ensure that equipments are electromagnetically compatible with each other, so they can coexist in close proximity. An obvious example of EM compatibility is that between two radio equipments. They may be operating on different radio frequencies, but because of the intermediate frequencies used inside the equipment and the relatively higher power of the nearby transmitter, signals may break through and cause interference. Less obvious is the interference which can be caused by radiation from digital processing equipments. Very fast pulses in such equipment can cause radio frequency radiation, and careful design at the component, circuit, equipment and installation level is needed to reduce the radiations to an acceptable level. Thorough testing of equipments and installations is necessary to ensure EM compatibility.

Human Factors

We have already looked in some detail at the design of the man-machine-interface (MMI). This is one of the range of what are termed human factors, which deal with the way in which systems are used by their human operators. Ergonomic design, covering such aspects as the positioning of controls and the layout of installations, is an important aspect. An added dimension in battlefield systems is that the operator must be able to use the system effectively under a wide range of prevailing conditions, and whilst wearing all or any of a range of protective clothing, including gloves to protect against nuclear, biological or chemical (NBC) contamination and an anti-gas respirator.

So far we have taken a 'bottom up' approach to the subject, dealing with the nuts and bolts first and building up to descriptions of whole systems. This is as appropriate here as it was earlier, and we shall start by looking at the environment in some detail, and how the designer must respond to the various effects and phenomena to be encountered there. Having established these equipment-level design constraints, we can go on to look at the wider, system-level implications of the environment.

The Physical Environment

The physical environment in which military CIS equipments have to operate can pose an impressive variety of threats against which the equipment must be protected. Even in the so-called temperate zones, such as north-west Europe, the range of climatic extremes is fairly dramatic. It can be as hot as the tropics or as cold as the Arctic, and although the conditions may not persist for long periods at a time, the fact that they can exist at all is reason enough to take account of them in the design of equipment. Not all tactical CIS equipment has to be able to work when completely exposed to the rigours of the weather. It is normal to group equipments into environmental categories, the most extreme of which is the totally unprotected category, which obviously includes man-portable equipment, such as radio sets and data entry devices used by the foot soldier away from the protection of vehicles. Equipment mounted in cross-country vehicles is afforded some protection from the elements, but is subject to the full range of shock and vibration effects. The class of equipment requiring the least in-built protection is that installed in vehicle containers which themselves offer a high degree of environmental shelter. In the paragraphs which follow each of the main environmental phenomena is considered in turn, with attention being paid to the nature of the phenomenon and its likely intensity, its effect on electronic equipments and systems, and the protective measures available.

Temperature

There are two aspects to the effects of temperature on equipment: the static effect of operating at a given temperature, and the dynamic effect of changes in temperature. Large changes of temperature over very short periods of time constitute thermal shock which may be damaging to certain materials. Less rapid cycling between extremes of temperature, such as the normal diurnal cycle, can also cause deterioration.

HIGH TEMPERATURE EFFECTS

The basic measure of temperature is the meteorological or ambient air temperature, measured out of the direct rays of the sun and sheltered from the wind. The actual operating temperature of equipment may be quite different; for example, the temperature inside equipment exposed to direct sunlight may be far higher than the ambient temperature. Even in temperate areas, where ambient temperatures of 30°C are relatively uncommon, the interior temperature of equipment exposed to the sun can rise to around three times that figure. This is well above the upper limit at which a person can work, particularly if the humidity is also high. Given that the equipment inside the enclosure or container is also generating waste heat, reaching this sort of temperature, i.e. 80–100°C, is not difficult. Individual, simple electronic components may be able to work at temperatures of this order, but in complex components, such as silicon integrated circuits, the effects are multiplied, and the devices are likely to operate outside their specified parameters, causing incorrect operation of the equipment. At temperatures above

100°C, the choice of insulating material, e.g. for cable sleeving becomes critical; polyvinyl chloride (PVC), a widely-used sleeving material, starts to deteriorate at temperatures above 85°C, and a dangerous by-product of this deterioration is the emission of a poisonous gas. The measures available to maintain the temperature of equipment at a safe working level rely on the mechanisms of heat transfer, namely convection, conduction and, to a lesser extent, radiation. Convection cooling relies on a flow of air over the surface of the components, which can either be naturally induced, i.e. by ventilation of the case, or be generated by fans. The air flow in the case must be carefully designed to provide the right amount of cooling in the right places—some components get much hotter than others. The effects of convective cooling can be increased by attaching metal heat-sinks, often multi-finned, to hot components to increase their surface areas. Conductive cooling is used in confined, sealed equipments where there is not enough air flow to achieve cooling by convection. In this case, the critical components are bonded to the internal structure of the equipment by heat-conducting materials so that the whole enclosure acts as a heat sink. Heat dissipation is achieved from the outer surface of the enclosure by a combination of convection and radiation.

LOW TEMPERATURE EFFECTS

   Ambient temperatures below –15°C are not uncommon in a north-west European winter. The effect of wind (the wind chill factor) is significant. In still air a temperature of –15°C is quite tolerable. The increased rate of heat loss caused by even a moderate wind can be equivalent to a much lower still air temperature. For example, with a still air temperature of –15°C and a wind of 5 m/s (about Beaufort scale force 3—a 'gentle breeze'), the cooling effect is about the same as that for a temperature of –50°C in still air. With a still air temperature of –15°C and a gale force wind (Beaufort scale force 8; 45 knots or 20 m/s), the effective temperature is low enough to freeze exposed flesh in a matter of seconds. Thus the extremes of low temperature possible in a temperate region should on no account be underestimated. Although individual electronic components may continue to operate down to as low as –55°C, the correct functioning of complex circuits cannot be guaranteed much below 0°C. Liquid crystal displays are generally unusable below that temperature. Even CRT devices are not immune to cold weather effects; one of the authors has experienced conditions where, in a visual display unit with an external, protective glass screen in front of the actual CRT, moisture trapped between this glass and the front of the screen had frozen and rendered the screen display unreadable. This was at a temperature of about –5°C, inside a vehicle office container when the outside temperature was around –10°C. Other major casualties of cold weather are chemical batteries, whose performance falls off markedly as the temperature drops. One good point is that the waste heat which may be the problem for high temperature operation can help to keep up the internal temperature of the equipment under cold conditions. Some equipments are fitted with internal heaters, but these consume power which is at a premium in portable equipments.
   If the designer were simply designing equipment for either hot or cold conditions the task would be relatively straightforward. To design equipment which must

operate over a wide temperature range involves the resolution of many conflicting design factors.

Humidity

Atmospheric humidity can vary between the absolute extremes of 0%, i.e. totally dry air, and approaching 100%, or air totally saturated with water vapour. 'Microclimates' may be created inside equipment enclosures if the internal temperature and pressure differ from those outside. The problem of high humidity is that it leads to condensation, that is, water in its liquid state inside the equipment. This may lead to corrosion of metal components and short-circuiting on printed circuit boards. Two basic approaches are available to the designer to combat humidity. Equipment may be sealed, to prevent the ingress of humid air from the atmosphere outside, but this measure can be in conflict with the need to keep the equipment cool. The other approach is to apply moisture-resistant, so-called 'conformal' coatings to components and sub-assemblies. This has the penalty of making equipment repair at the component level more difficult.

Sand and Dust

Should sand, dust or other foreign matter enter equipment, the consequences will be most serious for those components with moving parts. Thus electromechanical devices, such as disc or tape drives and printers, are especially susceptible. All connectors, be they 'edge' connectors on printed circuit boards or external, plug-and-socket connectors, are vulnerable. One way to reduce the chances of dirt ingress is to maintain a higher than ambient pressure inside the equipment housing, i.e. an overpressure. However, to achieve that requires a source of forced air, e.g. fans, which must be fed with air from the outside. This air intake must therefore be filtered. Particularly vulnerable are apertures in the equipment housing for the insertion and removal of storage media, such as floppy discs or tape cartridges. The use of overpressure, and a suitable cover over the aperture when access is not required, are the primary counters to this problem.

Air Pressure

Static air pressure by itself is seldom a problem; it is the combination of pressure, temperature and humidity which can lead to trouble, normally in the form of internal condensation of water vapour, as described above. One area where static air pressure is of concern is in the design and use of Winchester discs. As introduced in Chapter 4, the reading and writing heads of these discs actually 'fly' over the surface of the disc at a very low 'altitude' indeed (a few microns). One of the factors which determines the magnitude of the force which supports the heads above the disc surfaces is the static air pressure. If the air pressure is too low, the heads fly too low and crash into the surface of the disc, with disastrous consequences. This is not likely to be a problem at ground level. Discs capable of operating at pressures down to 730 millibars are available; under conditions of standard pressure at mean sea level, this equates to an altitude of about 3,000 metres.

Whilst it is unlikely that equipment will be deployed on the ground at these altitudes, there is a serious problem for equipment mounted in aircraft. However, most aircraft environments are artificially pressurised to a safe working level. Equipments installed in aircraft are commonly fitted with pressure sensors which cause the equipment to shut down without catastrophic consequences should the pressure fall below the safe level, such as in the event of an accidental decompression.

Shock and Vibration

The shock loads imposed on equipment mounted in cross-country vehicles can be extremely severe. Accelerations of 20–30 g, sustained for several milliseconds are commonly encountered whilst travelling over rough terrain. When the gun of an armoured fighting vehicle is fired, shock waves are propagated throught the vehicle. The most significant vibration is that generated by the vehicle's propulsion system, and this can be particularly severe in tracked vehicles. Regular loads of up to 2 g at frequencies up to 2,000 Hz are probable. The effects of shock and vibration depend upon the physical characteristics of the equipment, that is the size and the mass of its components. Large components with inadequate support will tend to flex or bend under load, leading to mechanical failure, and probable electrical failure through the breaking of connections. The greater the mass of a component, the greater the kinetic energy that is generated through the application of the shock or vibrational acceleration, and hence the greater the potential for damage. In this respect the trend to microminiaturisation increases the ruggedness of equipment. Electromechanical equipments which rely on moving parts and connectors are much more vulnerable to shock and vibration effects than electronic assemblies. There are two levels of protection available to the designer. First, the design at the component level should ensure that individual components are securely assembled in a way which causes the least physical stress. For example, components on a printed circuit board will be mounted as close to the board as possible, using a high quality soldering technique. Secondly, at the equipment level the designer will build in resistance to shock through the use of shock-damping materials, such as elastomers, in the mounting of the internal sub-assemblies, and the fixing of equipments in vehicle installations using shock-isolating mountings.

It is normal to distinguish between the shock and vibration loads which must be sustainable by equipment whilst it is operating and those which must be sustained when equipment is being moved from one place to another. In the interests of retaining an ability to move at short notice, extensive preparation of equipment such as packing it into transit cases will not usually be acceptable, but some degree of preparation will undoubtedly increase the tolerance of the equipment to the shocks of movement. As usual, it is the electromechanical devices which are the most vulnerable. For example, if Winchester disc drives have their heads safely 'parked' before being transported, they can withstand much greater shocks. As a rule of thumb, the sustainable shock level during transportation will be around double that which can be sustained by the equipment when operational.

The Electromagnetic Environment

Electromagnetic Pulse (EMP)

EMP is one of the side effects of a nuclear explosion. As well as blast, heat and nuclear radiation, the explosion causes large electric fields to be generated in very short times, typically up to a peak of several tens of kilovolts per metre in a few nanoseconds. This EMP field can cause very short pulses of extremely high current to be induced in conductors within the field. Without protective measures, such currents can cause severe damage to electronic equipment. The location of the explosion has a significant effect on the characteristics of the EMP. A high-altitude, exo-atmospheric explosion can produce fields which cover an area of the Earth's surface many thousands of miles in diameter. A ground-burst nuclear explosion produces strong fields over a much smaller area, whilst air bursts (endo-atmospheric explosions) have the least significant EMP effect.

The main effect of EMP on unprotected equipments is to cause component failure, particularly of semiconductor devices. These may fail through a breakdown of the junctions between negative and positive regions of semiconductor, on whose existence the devices rely for their operation, or through straightforward burn-out of metal connections inside the device through current overload.

As with many of the phenomena studied here, there are two approaches to EMP protection. The first is the containment, or isolation approach, which relies on the presence of electrical screening around the equipment. This is also demanded for the reduction of other phenomena discussed later, that is, radio frequency interference (RFI)/electromagnetic compatibility (EMC) and TEMPEST. Also, for equipments housed within metal-skinned vehicles, the outside of the vehicle provides a significant degree of screening against EMP. However, to be of any use in a system, CIS equipments and installations must have connections to the outside world. Such connections for both communications and power represent possible points of penetration of the EMP screening, and therefore the second approach to protection, at the component level, is required. Clamping devices to keep voltages and currents below pre-set safe minima, and filters to smooth out the extreme sharpness of the EMP may be used on the conductors which penetrate the screen. Also, since some types of semiconductor devices are notably 'harder', i.e. less susceptible to the effects of EMP than others, the choice of component is important.

Ionising Radiation

Another side effect of a nuclear explosion, better known for its physiological effects on human beings, is the emission of radiation and charged particles, such as gamma rays, alpha particles and neutrons. These can disrupt the operation of microelectronic devices. The effects tend to be temporary, although the speed with which devices recover once the radiation has diminished varies widely according to the semiconductor fabrication technique used. Also, some fabrication techniques produce chips with are intrinsically 'harder' from a radiation point of view than others. Bipolar devices tend to be harder than MOS, but their relatively high power consumption is a drawback. Specially hardened MOS devices, such as

CMOS (complementary metal oxide semiconductor) built on to a substrate of silicon on sapphire, can be made but are not widely available and are relatively expensive.

Electromagnetic Compatibility (EMC) and Radio Frequency Interference (RFI)

All electronic devices are potential radiators of electromagnetic energy, and all are potentially susceptible to interference from unwanted radiations. EMC/RFI problems occur when an equipment which is susceptible to radiation is installed in proximity to another equipment which radiates electromagnetic energy within the frequency band to which the former is susceptible. Examples of this abound, such as radar transmitters interfering with radio receivers, radio transmitters interfering with radio remote-control devices, and so on. The problem is by no means exclusively a military one. The term 'electronic smog' was coined recently in the British press to describe the electromagnetic pollution caused by the high concentration of electrical and electronic devices in some urban areas. In the military field the problem is often made worse by the need to install a number of different equipments in the very restricted space of, say, an armoured fighting vehicle.

The electrical screening of equipment can both reduce its susceptibility to RFI and help to contain any spurious radiations which it may generate. The same applies to the use of filters on conductors which penetrate the screening. At a lower level, the prevention of unwanted radiation is largely a matter of good circuit design, although compromises are necessary. One of the most common causes of spurious radiation is the generation of pulses with very fast rise times. As we saw in Chapter 6, fast rise times mean high frequencies. Hence to avoid unwanted radio frequency (RF) radiation, filters are employed to smooth off the sharp edges. However, from the point of view of circuit operation and timing, clean, sharp pulses are all to the good, so there is a limit to the smoothing which can be applied.

Radiation Security (TEMPEST)

TEMPEST is essentially a 'special case' of EMC. The concern here is not that unwanted radiations are generated which can interfere with other equipment, but that radiations are generated which can convey information to an unauthorised recipient. If the sharp-edged pulse stream which is generating spurious RF radiation is an information-bearing pulse stream, then the likelihood is that the information will be extractable from the spurious radiation. This radiation may be carried some way from its source, either by direct RF propagation, or by conduction along signal cables or power lines. The measures used to suppress this type of radiation are similar to those used for EMC/RFI purposes. What is normally applied is a combination of prevention through good circuit design and layout, and containment through screening and filtering.

The Design Process

The designers of computer hardware for use on the battlefield are faced with a series of difficult compromises. For example, from an electromagnetic shielding point of view, it would be a good thing to enclose equipment in a totally sealed, metal casing, whilst the need to keep the equipment down to a safe working temperature calls for ventilation. To protect equipment against the effects of shock and vibration, it would be sensible to avoid mechanical connections as far as possible, and encapsulate as many components as possible. Taken to an extreme, this approach would make the repair and maintenance of equipment very difficult. Computer-aided design (CAD) techniques are used to optimise component layout, and to solve some of the problems of compromise faced by the designer. Such techniques may help to reduce, but not remove entirely, the need to build a number of stages of pre-production models of equipment. The earliest of these will be laboratory 'breadboard' models, used to define the electronic functionality of the equipment. Later models will concentrate on the actual component layout and fabrication techniques to be used in the production models, in order to meet the environmental criteria.

Testing

Any equipment or installation which has been designed to meet a particular set of environmental criteria must be tested to give a measure of assurance that the design has been successful. It is normal to carry out the full range of tests on first-of-type equipments only, and to carry out a more limited set on a sample of production equipments as they are manufactured. Testing is an extremely time consuming and painstaking process. The EMC/TEMPEST testing of data processing equipment is especially complicated because of the extreme complexity of the equipments and of the signals generated inside them. Nowadays it is common to find automated test rigs used for this type of testing. The test rigs themselves are computer-controlled, and can, for example, run a series of tests over a pre-set range of radio frequencies without the need for operator intervention. The results can also be recorded and analysed by computer techniques, which greatly reduces the time required. In spite of these advances, testing remains a costly business which contributes to the extra cost of equipment designed for the battlefield environment.

The Selection of Hardware

It can be seen from the foregoing that the design, construction and testing from 'the ground up' of special purpose military hardware is an extended and expensive process. Nowadays however, the designer may be able to exercise an option which does not involve the design of 'bespoke' hardware. In order of 'ruggedness' (although the final two are equivalent), the range of choices of hardware types is as follows:

▶ Standard, commercial hardware

▶ 'Ruggedised' commercial hardware
▶ Standard, military specification (MILSPEC) hardware
▶ 'Bespoke' MILSPEC hardware

Standard Commercial Hardware

Some of the better quality commercial hardware, especially portable equipment, is surprisingly rugged, but it has to be remembered that such equipment is designed for the relatively benign environment of the office, and is designed to a price. If the right equipment is selected and it is not used in the worst extremes of the military environment, commercial equipment can provide a useful service. However, its use will normally be confined to trials of prototype systems, where, for example, it is desired to evaluate the software-implemented functions of a system before the development of more appropriate hardware. There is always a risk that equipment introduced on that pretext comes to be accepted as an operational system, especially when there are financial pressures. Such a situation should not be accepted without acknowledging the risk that the hardware might not survive in a realistic battlefield environment.

Ruggedised Commercial Hardware

The principle behind 'ruggedised' hardware is that it is based on sub-assemblies such as printed circuit boards (PCBs), disc drives and other peripherals which are identical to those found in commercial equipments. It is their assembly and packaging which is changed to meet the demands of the environment. Hence ruggedisation is essentially a containment approach. The photograph at Figure 7.1b shows a typical, ruggedised, commercial computer unit. The PCBs have been mounted in a specially designed backplane, using connectors of greater mechanical reliability than the original commercial components. The Winchester and the floppy disc drives are mounted in their own isolating containers within the main container. All the sub-assemblies are held together by a rigid metal frame, which is mounted inside an external casing using shock-damping mountings. The commercial power supply unit has been replaced by one which has a much better tolerance of the fluctuations in input power which are inevitable in field power supplies. Finally, the whole unit is sealed, with electric fans providing a source of cooling air which also maintains an overpressure in the box to keep out dust and dirt. The sealing is also designed to be an EMC/RFI/TEMPEST containment measure. All external connections are of a proven rugged design, with a mechanism for positively locking together the two halves of the connector.

With the increasing density and reduced cost/bit of semiconductor memory devices, there is a trend to replace electromechanical memories, such as Winchester disc drives, in ruggedised systems with solid-state mass memories which can be plugged directly into the disc interface and be treated by the processor in exactly the same way as disc memory.

FIG. 7.1(a)   Commercial Computer Unit (*Photograph Digital Equipment Corporation*)

Standard MILSPEC Hardware

The production of 'standard' MILSPEC hardware involves the re-creation of the architecture of some widely-used commercial equipment, designing it *ab initio* to meet the environmental specification. The process starts at the component level, and only components which have passed the rigid selection criteria can be used. The PCBs themselves will probably bear no resemblance to their commercial counterparts; their size, layout and construction may be quite different. Typical equipments which have been subjected to this redesign (by a number of different firms) are the Digital Equipment Company's VAX and Data General's Eclipse ranges of 32-bit computer.

Bespoke MILSPEC Hardware

The most 'tailor-made' approach of all is to design specific items of military hardware from scratch. Even this type of equipment is likely to be based on commercial microprocessor chips (using MILSPEC versions, of course), but may con-

FIG. 7(b)   Ruggedised Commercial Computer Unit
(*DICOLL Electronics Ltd*)

tain quite a large amount of 'custom made', very large scale integration (VLSI) circuits.

Comparison of the Approaches

Table 7.1 below summarises the approximate cost and development times of the different approaches. The baseline used is the commercial hardware.

TABLE 7.1   *Comparison of Hardware Types*

Hardware Type	Relative Cost	Development Time
Commercial	1	'Off the shelf'
Rugged Commercial	2	<1 year from availability of commercial hardware
'Standard' MILSPEC	5	3–5 years from availability of commercial hardware
Bespoke MILSPEC	5+	3–5 years

The balance of advantage would seem to favour the ruggedised commercial approach, and this is certainly true for general purpose items, such as computers

FIG. 7.1(c)   MILSPEC Computer Unit (*Marconi Command and Control Systems Ltd*)

and their associated storage devices. The use of ruggedised commercial equipment, and to some extent of the standard MILSPEC units, has the great advantage that elements of standard software, such as operating systems, may be used, thus reducing costs and development times. Software can be developed on the normal, commercial, equivalent hardware on the development site, and then loaded into the rugged units for use in the field. The drawback of the MILSPEC units is their cost, and the fact that they are already several years behind the 'state-of-the-art' by the time they are introduced into service. It has to be recognised, of course, that there are devices required on the battlefield which have no direct commercial equivalent. Devices which must interface directly with sensors, or with weapon systems will almost certainly have to be built using the bespoke MILSPEC approach.

Environmental Consequences: Communications

Before going on to look at the system-wide, as opposed to the effects of the battlefield environment on individual equipments we must have another look at communications. Of course, the communications equipment itself will be subject to all the design constraints covered so far in this chapter. There is another, more important dimension: the consequences of the environmental constraints on the performance of the communications system. The fact that the communications system will be unable to produce a constant level of performance, and will on occasions be severely limited is a significant factor in the design of the overall information system. It is probably the single most important difference between civil and military systems. In the next few paragraphs we shall look again at some of the communications techniques introduced in Chapter 6 and see how they are applied to battlefield systems.

In the military system, the final limit is often imposed by the laws of physics. Where reliance must be placed on radio communications, as in the forward area of the battlefield, the available performance is limited by the nature of the terrain, and especially by the occupancy of the all too finite electromagnetic spectrum.

Classification of Communications Systems

The scene has now been set for an examination of the different communications systems available for use on the battlefield. The general characteristics of each communication type will be described, followed by an assessment of its data-transmission capabilities.

Multi-Channel, Switched Trunk Systems

Multi-channel, switched trunk systems are based on a network of switching centres or nodes, interconnected by multi-channel bearers which are most frequently implemented using UHF or SHF point-to-point radio relay, although cables, both copper and optical fibre, are found in some more static systems. Headquarters and other communities of users are served by access centres providing local switching, and connection into the trunk network via the same type of multi-channel bearer as is used to interconnect the trunk switches. An important feature of the modern battlefield trunk system from a tactical viewpoint lies in its description as an area system. The switching nodes are located to provide communications cover to a geographical area, and they are sited independently of the headquarters and other users they serve. The area to be served will, of course, be dictated by tactics; it would be unusual to find a situation in which the trunk network was deployed to give even area coverage without any concern for the likely progress of the battle. Examples of trunk systems in use today include Ptarmigan (UK), RITA (France), Autoko (Germany) and Zodiac (The Netherlands). A generic tactical trunk system is shown in Figure 7.2.

The needs of data subscribers may be met by one or more of the switching techniques described in Chapter 6, that is, circuit, message, or packet switching. The British Ptarmigan system provides both packet and circuit switching. The packet-switched network (PSN) is superimposed on the circuit-switched network. Primary packet switches (PPS) at switching nodes are interconnected by digital channels within the multi-channel bearer which would otherwise be used by the circuit switched network. Subscribers are connected to the network via secondary packet switches (SPS) located at access nodes.

The circuit switched option is available for use where it is more appropriate than packet switching, such as bulk data transfers between elements of an information

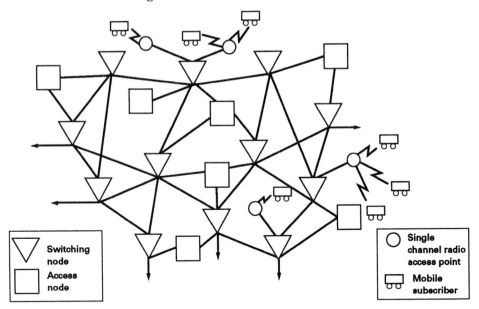

FIG. 7.2   Generic Trunk System

system. A typical use for this sort of transfer would be the restoration of a database which had become out of date during a period of disconnection from the network.

Single Channel Mobile Extension of Trunk System

Many trunk systems, Ptarmigan and RITA among them, feature a single channel radio access (SCRA) sub-system for mobile subscribers. These are based on VHF or low UHF omnidirectional radio, with sophisticated switching mechanisms to 'hand-off' subscribers from one central, or SCRA access point to another, as they move through the area of coverage. This is akin to the technique used in civil cellular radio systems.

Once a connection has been established, the services provided for the SCRA user are the same as those available via normal, static access to the network, including data transmission, although this latter may be restricted in performance. Because the connections are made via VHF or UHF mobile radio, which is subject to interference and propagation difficulties, and because there will always be more subscribers than there are channels available, it is by no means certain that an 'instant' connection can be made, and, even when a connection has been made, interruptions are possible. The delays involved should not normally be significant for the voice user, and the time taken to effect a 'hand-off' between base stations or centrals is too short to be noticed by a human operator. However, these delays and interruptions to service pose more severe problems for the data user, and may limit the performance available from a SCRA connection.

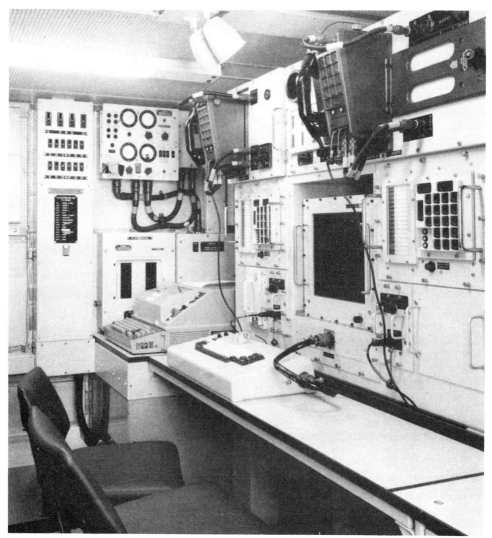

FIG. 7.3(a)   Ptarmigan Installation (*Plessey Defence Systems*)

Single Channel Combat Radio

Single channel combat radio, operating in the VHF or the HF frequency band has for many years been the mainstay of battlefield communications below the brigade level of command. Above this level it is still to be found, but often as a back-up to the trunk system or for specialist users. The term combat net radio (CNR) is often used to describe this type of radio system, because the traditional method of operation is for a community of stations, or net, to interoperate using the same radio frequency. In recent years the word 'net' has tended to disappear from the title, implying that other, non-netted architectures are being developed to suit the changing user need, especially in the data communications area.

FIG. 7.3(b)   Ptarmigan SHF Radio Relay (© *M. Rice*)

FIG. 7.4   Ptarmigan SCRA Control (© *M. Rice*)

FIG. 7.5   Combat Radio (*Plessey Military Communications Ltd*)

Vulnerability

A particular feature of combat radio is its vulnerability to electronic counter measures, such as jamming, and to interception. It is, by definition, an all-informed medium which implies omnidirectional transmission. It is therefore relatively easy to intercept, although a wide range of both technical and procedural measures have been developed to reduce the vulnerability.

Technical ECCMs

FREQUENCY HOPPING

Conventional radio systems operate on a single pre-selected frequency per net. Once an enemy has detected signals on that frequency, he can either exploit them for intelligence purposes or apply ECM, e.g. jamming. In a frequency-hopping system, a transmitter spends only a short time on any given frequency (the dwell time, typically a few milliseconds) as it 'hops' over a band of frequencies in a predetermined sequence. A net is defined as the group of users who share the same group of frequencies in the same hop order (or hopset). For maximum security the sequence will be pseudo-random, i.e. a complicated and apparently random order of frequency selection which makes an interceptor's job very difficult. Of course, a penalty of the system is that the sequence must be known to friendly receivers, which must stay in synchronism with the transmissions.

FREE CHANNEL SEARCH (FCS)

FCS, also known as automatic channel selection is another multi-frequency technique. Instead of allocating a single, fixed frequency to a radio net, a group of frequencies is allocated. When a station has a message to transmit, it selects a free channel and uses it for the transmission. Receivers must continually scan the group of allotted frequencies, and will only lock on to a particular frequency when a transmission addressed to that station has been detected. Thus, unlike frequency hopping, for a given transmission only one frequency out of the group is used.

STEERABLE NULL ANTENNAS

The antenna of a combat radio station is normally designed to be omni-directional, that is, it radiates power equally in all directions in the horizontal plane, and is equally sensitive to signals received from any direction. In a steerable null system signal processing techniques are used to reduce the sensitivity of the antenna in the direction of an unwanted signal, such as that from a jammer.

Data Transmission

MODULATION

Most combat radio data transmission systems in use today are adaptations of voice combat-radio for data. Some form of modulation is used to convert the digital signals into an acceptable form for transmission over a channel designed primarily for voice, and to reconvert the signals back into their digital form at the receiving end. A widely used form of modulation is frequency shift keying (FSK), in which a signal in the audio frequency range is shifted up in frequency by a set amount to represent the digital '1' condition, and down by the same amount to represent a '0'. In digital radio equipments, the digital signals modulate the carrier directly without the need for any prior conversion into an audio frequency signal.

Fig. 7.6   Data entry device (DED) (*Marconi Command and Control Systems*)

ERROR DETECTION AND CORRECTION (EDC)

Comprehensive EDC schemes are needed to achieve data transmission with an acceptable error rate over what can be a very noisy channel. The performance of the EDC is designed to match the expected characteristics of the channel, and it is not unusual to find a combination of measures used to provide the performance required. The price of an effective EDC scheme is the reduction in the information carrying capacity of the channel, which is brought about by the need to add redundant bits. Half-rate schemes, in which, for example, the information rate of a 16 Kbit/s channel would be reduced to 8 Kbit/s, are common, but much lower efficiencies than this must be tolerated if an acceptable performance is to be achieved under the severe conditions which may be expected in the VHF combat radio-spectrum in wartime. It is most important that the system deteriorates 'gracefully' in the face of increasing interference, rather than fails catastrophically once a certain threshold has been reached. This calls for dynamic EDC schemes, where the power of the technique is increased (and hence the information throughput is decreased) as the raw error rate worsens. 'Last ditch' systems may have link capacities as low as a few hundred bit/s.

CONTROL

The techniques used to control data transmission on combat radio are very similar to those used on LANs, as described in Chapter 6. Some applications use a form of CSMA, where stations monitor the net and only transmit when they detect that it is free. Just as on the LAN, 'back off' techniques are used to resolve contention between stations whose transmissions clash. Token passing, as used on LANs, is not a suitable technique for combat radio, since the regular transmissions required to pass the token would greatly increase the intercept vulnerability of the net. A technique akin to token passing which is used on combat radio is time division multiple access (TDMA). In a TDMA system, each station is allotted a specific time 'slot' in a regular cycle during which it is permitted to transmit. Thus the first requirement of this technique is that stations remain in synchronism with the control cycle. The performance of TDMA relative to CSMA is similar to that of token passing relative to CSMA on a LAN. Access to the net is guaranteed during busy periods, but stations must wait for their turn to come round before they can transmit, even when the net is quiet. Some hybrid, slotted CSMA techniques exist which attempt to combine the advantages of the two basic methods.

OTHER NETWORK TOPOLOGIES

What we have considered so far is the adaptation of the conventional, all-informed, voice combat-radio net to data use. For data transmission within a relatively small and geographically concentrated group of users, such an adaptation may produce acceptable results, and has the great advantage that it can be achieved with existing radio equipments, with a fairly simple interface unit. Where wider distribution of data is needed, the voice net adaptation is not completely satisfactory. Relay between nets must be considered, and, given the normally hierarchical organisation of combat radio nets, routing can be inordinately tortuous. An alternative network topology which can provide much more direct routing and hence faster distribution is packet radio (Figure 7.7).

In this scheme, each radio station in a given area acts not only as a terminal for its user, but also as a switching node within the network, relaying transmissions to other stations. The theoretical performance of such a system has been demonstrated, but a problem to which a practical solution has yet to be found is system management. In the conventional net, management of the system is the responsibility of the organisation which 'owns' the net, that is, the formation, unit or sub-unit served by the net. The intention in packet radio is that the communities of users which represent the packet network will include units at different levels of command, and operating in different functional areas, such as artillery units or combat service support units. The basic management problem is how to organise

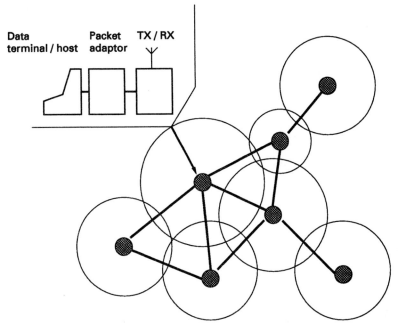

FIG. 7.7   Packet Radio System

such a potentially disparate group of users into a communications community, when they have different needs, different priorities and respond to a different chain of command. For example, given that stations are deployed for reasons associated with their own primary functions rather than to serve the needs of the packet radio community to which they belong, how is the network management authority to ensure that enough stations are in the right places to provide the required network connectivity?

Intra-Headquarters Communication

The analysis of networks so far has looked on unit and formation headquarters as indivisible sources and sinks of information. In fact, headquarters are made up of numbers of different users, who require interconnection both with the world beyond the headquarters and with each other. Thus the headquarters may be looked on as a network in its own right. A formation tactical headquarters normally consists of a group of vehicles, deployed in a location whose selection is a compromise between the requirements of concealment, defence against local attack, and the need to communicate both up and down the chain of command, but principally with the formations or units under command. Another critical compromise in the siting of the headquarters is that between the need for good internal communications and the dispersal of vehicles to aid concealment and to reduce the vulnerability to attack, especially from the air. The internal communications needs of a typical formation headquarters are listed below.

▶ Telephone and/or voice intercom between vehicles.

▶ Access to communications with the outside world, e.g. via the trunk system or via combat radio. In larger headquarters the radio equipments are often sited several kilometres away from the headquarters, and accessed remotely over cables.

▶ Connections between information system terminal equipments and other elements of the system, e.g. processors, shared storage devices, printers, plotters, and access to elements of the system outside the headquarters.

Currently it is common to find these needs satisfied by inter-vehicle cabling, normally using multicore cables. The most frequently used 'topology' is the star, connecting users separately to central resources, such as the local telephone exchange. The trend for the future is towards the use of LAN techniques in headquarters. All communication needs can be met by the LAN, which can provide a flexible and resilient means of connecting the components of the headquarters. For reasons of capacity and security, optical fibre cables appear to be the most promising transmission medium, although for maximum dispersion of the headquarters, millimetric wave radio, with a range of a few hundred metres, could provide a flexible alternative. Some of these concepts are illustrated in Figure 7.8.

Specialist Tactical Data Communication Systems

The adaptation of voice-oriented combat radio for data transmission in the forward areas of the battlefield is not fully satisfactory for all applications, particularly those where rapid and wide distribution of information is a requirement, as typified by command and control systems for air defence. A number of techniques have been developed, such as the American enhanced position locating and reporting system (EPLRS), which are designed specifically for battlefield data distribution, and are not constrained by any need to carry voice communications. EPLRS operates in the UHF region of the RF spectrum, and is based on a 'nodeless' connection architecture in which each station acts both as a user terminal and a relay station, in much the same way as the packet radio system described earlier. The transmission control mechanism is a form of TDMA, in which the time slots are allocated to the stations by a net control unit (NCU), according to their declared needs for throughput and response time. It is an expensive system compared to CNR. First of all there is the cost of developing and deploying a dedicated data-transmission system; the voice-adapted systems have the great merit that they make use of a large investment in voice radios and other existing equipment. Secondly, being UHF, a combination of high transmitter power and a greater density of stations on the battlefield is needed in order to produce the required range performance. The high transmitter power increases the cost and complexity of the individual equipments, and the increase in overall numbers obviously raises the total cost of deploying the system, and increases the problems of system management which were touched on briefly during the discussion of packet radio.

Use of Civil Telecommunications

The area over which the NATO armies would fight any future war is served by some of the most comprehensive civil telecommunications facilities available

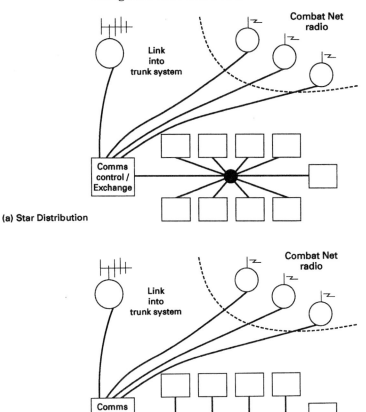

(a) Star Distribution

(b) Local area network (bus)

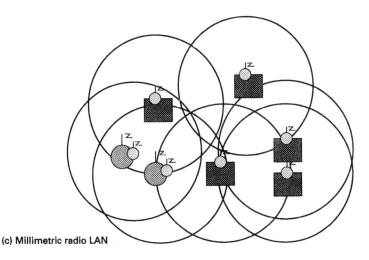

(c) Millimetric radio LAN

FIG. 7.8   Headquarters Layouts

anywhere in the world. These include the vast cable and microwave networks providing telephone and data services, and cellular radio systems providing services via portable or mobile equipments. Whilst it may be argued that the survivability of these services is questionable, particularly during all-out war, there is no doubt that the civil network offers many advantages for military use during the early stages of conflict. Amongst these is the ability to communicate between a force which is deployed, or partly deployed, and its static base areas, and to link the tactical area with the rear areas. In order to exploit these advantages military information systems must be able to operate to the appropriate civil communications standards.

Conclusions

The level of service which can be provided by battlefield communications systems will inevitably be variable, according to the prevailing conditions, and it is especially vulnerable to deliberate countermeasures. Even at its best and under the most benign conditions, battlefield systems cannot offer the same information-carrying capacity as their civil counterparts. There is a wide range of measures which can be applied to ensure that some degree of service remains, whatever the threat, and some of these have been described. An important principle to be observed, which has stood commanders in good stead over the years, is the provision of as many alternative means of communications as are available or can be afforded. Thus we are likely to see headquarters served by a combination of multi-channel trunk, combat radio (VHF and HF) and by connection into the civil telephone network. When all else fails, the use of the well-known 'FDMC' system ('floppy disc on a motor cycle') should not be discounted. (A motor cycle can carry several hundred megabytes' worth of magnetic media. If the average journey time between headquarters is, say, 20 minutes, this represents a channel of several Kbit/s capacity!)

Information System Design Consequences

The design of the overall information system has to take into account the need to use components which have been designed to meet the environmental specifications, and interconnect them in a way which minimises the effects of the communications limitations and maximises the survivability of the system. This latter aspect can be viewed from two angles; first, the function of the system must be preserved. This implies that its interconnection must survive, and that it can continue to carry out the processes necessary for the performance of its designed task. Secondly, both the integrity and the very existence of the information held by the system must be preserved. How well these requirements are met depends upon the way in which the system's elements are distributed.

Processing

Given the nature of modern processors, it is reasonable to apply the rule that processing power can be located where it is needed. This applies at all levels, down to and including hand-held devices used in the forward areas. Processing can therefore be regarded as fully distributed, and there should seldom be a reason to design a CIS which relies to any extent on centralised processing, accessed from remote terminals. The exception to this might be in a headquarters, where 'central' processing resources could be made available to user cells via a LAN. Remote processing over the tactical wide area network (WAN), i.e. between headquarters, should not be necessary.

Information Storage

The argument above cannot be applied to information storage. Information in the system is distributed by definition; it is a primary function of the system to move information from one place to another. What we are concerned with here is how to ensure that the information, once captured, is not lost or corrupted. The determination of where in the system information should be stored is not a trivial matter. To put the topic into context, we shall look first at two extremes, and then identify some options between the two which seem to offer realistic and practicable solutions to the problem.

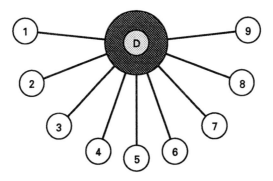

FIG. 7.9   Centralised System

Centralisation

The first extreme is the fully centralised case, shown in Figure 7.9. All the information held by the system is held in a database in one central location, to which all elements of the system are connected.

As information is captured by the several outposts of the monitoring sub-system, it is sent to the central database for storage. Whenever information is required to support the activities of any of the system elements, it must be demanded from the central database. The most obvious drawback of this arrangement, especially for a military system, is the vulnerability of the central database. Deny access to the central database to any user and you deny him the use of the system; destroy the central database, or cause the machine on which it is held to fail, and the system no longer exists. Even when the central database is intact and running, all users are wholly dependent on communications to gain access to any information. In a static, non-tactical environment where reliable, high-capacity communications can be taken for granted, and where a highly reliable machine can be used to hold the database, centralised systems are feasible, and have indeed been the norm in many commercial organisations for a long time. For the military, tactical application the vulnerability of a fully centralised system makes it an unacceptable solution.

Fully Distributed System

In the configuration shown in Figure 7.10, no information is distributed beyond its point of capture, except when needed to satisfy requests for information. Each

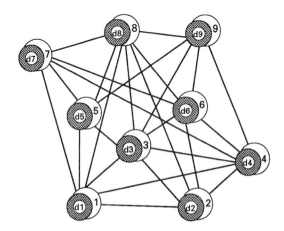

FIG. 7.10   Distributed System

element of the system holds a database which represents a picture of that portion of the 'real' world which it can 'see' directly. Looking at the total system from the outside, the whole body of information held by the system is the same as that held in the monolithic database of the previous solution, i.e. $d1 + d2 + \ldots + d9 = D$, i.e. the sum of all the distributed databases is equal to the whole database of the centralised, monolithic case.

The database in this case is relatively invulnerable to the destruction of any of the elements; only a small part of it would be lost through the destruction of any one element.

Its weakness is that it relies totally on communications to bring the distributed elements together into an apparent whole. Every time information is required which is not held by the cell which needs it, it must be requested from whichever cell does hold it. Both the request and the reply represent a load on the communications system. In an ideal environment, with perfect communications channels, this approach starts to be feasible and to offer some advantages. In a military tactical system, with unreliable, low-capacity communications it is scarcely feasible.

Replicated Global Databases

The main drawback of the centralised solution was that it put all the information eggs into one vulnerable basket. Its advantage is that the task of managing the information is made easier by having it all in one place, under the control of one

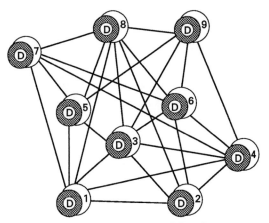

FIG. 7.11   Replicated Global Database

manager. The scheme depicted in Figure 7.11 is an attempt to make the most of the advantage of the centralised system and to minimise its disadvantages.

The essence of the idea is that every cell in the system which has a requirement to hold and process information holds a complete copy of the entire global database. In this configuration there are two types of communication associated with the creation and the maintenance of the database. First, there is the communication between the capturer of data, and its functional destination(s). An example of this type of communication would be typified by reports to the battlegroup level (assuming this to be the lowest level in the system at which information is held and processed) from its subordinates. The second form of communication is that between databases to ensure that they all hold the same information. For example, when a battlegroup database has been updated by the reports from its sub-ordinates, it must pass that information on to all other databases in the system. In practice, this scheme must make provision for the restoration of a database which has been out of contact with the rest of the system for a significant length of time. This may be achieved by bulk transfer over the communications system of data from an up-to-date database, or by physical transfer of storage media such as magnetic tape or disc. This approach to database distribution obviously scores heavily on resilience. Should access to the database at any location be denied, for whatever reason, provision can be made for users at that location to gain access to a database at another location. The price to be paid for this resilience is in three forms. First, there is the processing overhead involved in keeping the databases up to date. The processors must recognise when they have information to distribute to other database holders and take the necessary steps to send it. Secondly, the distribution of updates to other databases imposes a burden on the communi-cations system. The final snag is that in a system with imperfect communications there will always be a degree of uncertainty as to whether the several copies of the database are 'in step' with each other. There is a danger in this that staff at different headquarters may be acting on different versions of what purports to be the same information.

Limited Distribution and Replication

Another practical approach to the problem of database distribution is that shown in Figure 7.12. In this configuration elements of the system store locally

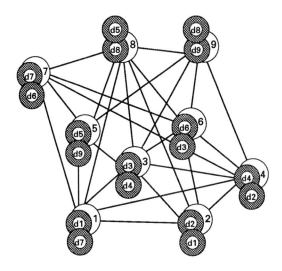

FIG. 7.12   System with Limited Distribution and Replication

those items of information which are needed for local processing, and send to other elements those items of information which those other elements need for their processing. The two classes of information just described are not, of course, mutually exclusive. The definition of the information exchange requirements (IERs) between the elements can either be fixed, that is, set into the system at some stage before deployment, or they can be dynamic and capable of being changed to suit changing tactical circumstances. Database resilience is achieved by replicating the database for each cell where information is held at one or more alternative cells. In this way the overhead imposed by the global replicated database approach is reduced, although so too is the degree of resilience.

Choice of Configuration in a Practical System

It is unlikely that either of the two extremes, of total centralisation or total distribution, could ever be implemented reliably in a military tactical CIS. Practical systems are likely to use something much more like one of the compromise configurations, and which one will depend very much on the nature and the requirements of the individual system. The choice of approach will have a significant influence on the processing power required by the system's elements and on the service required from the communications system. Looking at the problem the other way round, the availability of the necessary communications services may well prove to be a limitation on the choice of database distribution approach.

Summary

The stringent demands of the battlefield environment will call for a response in the design of equipments. For general purpose equipments, such as computers, there seems to be a balance of advantage in favour of using ruggedised commercial equipments. The environment also has a profound effect on the architecture of the whole system, primarily through its constraining influence on the communications links which interconnect the elements of the system. The limitations on communications comprise some of the main reasons why one cannot simply transplant whole systems designed for the civil world and convert them into battlefield CIS; the techniques used to 'militarise' civilian equipments simply cannot be translated up to the system level.

It may be that, apart from the communications constraints, we have given the impression in this chapter that all one needs to develop CIS is a selection of suitably hardened equipment, some standard system software, and a few 'applications programs'. Nothing could be further from the truth. Hardware is the easy bit; the development of software for CIS is a far from trivial matter, and we devote the whole of the next chapter to explaining why this should be so and what can be done about it.

8.

The Software Crisis

Introduction

In the previous chapters we have considered the fundamental concepts of information processing and of military command and control systems. We have examined the various components of such systems and we have looked at the special characteristics that are needed to make them work in the battlefield environment. The success of all of this, however, is dependent on our ability to write and implement the rules by which such systems must operate; that is, to develop the software that lies at their heart.

Real-Time Systems

This is not a trivial process. That major problems invariably beset the development of software for large, complex, military, real-time systems, is becoming an established fact. The outward manifestations of such problems are excessive budget over-runs, unacceptably long delays in delivery into service, and failure to meet user requirements; in some cases to such an extent that an entire project has to be abandoned. In recent months in the United Kingdom, airborne early-warning and fighter-attack radar systems have been especially prominent in this respect, with civil air-traffic control systems a current, major focus for concern.

As such systems typify vital aspects of the command and control process, it is important to understand why these problems occur in the development of software and what measures might be taken to limit their more damaging effects. It is these issues that we consider in this chapter.

Before doing so, however, we need to have a clearer view of the nature of software in order to see how and why the problems arise. We need also to recognise the differences between applications programs and systems programs, since it is these differences that give insight into the conflicting perceptions held by the agencies involved about the so-called software crisis and the measures needed to combat it. To do this, we must go back to the description of the simple processor and its operating system introduced in earlier chapters and look at it from a slightly different angle.

The Black Box Model

We start our discussion by referring back to a figure first introduced in Chapter 2: that of a simple 'black box' model of an information-processing system. To that original picture we have now added some indication of the response times for the various components of the system: the human operator carries out a few operations per second; the keyboard can be used at some tens of operations per second; the display can be driven at some hundreds of operations per second; the backing store some thousands of operations per second; whilst the processor and memory

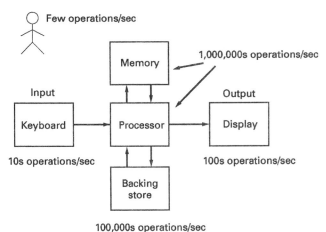

FIG. 8.1   Processing System Black Box Model

operate at some millions of operations per second (Figure 8.1). We shall be examining the relevance of these very different performance figures when we look at some of the issues surrounding operating systems software.

Initial Program Loading

At switch-on, the processor immediately starts to execute the rules that are contained in a pre-programmed ROM; this is the bootstrap, which was introduced in Chapter 3. As an example, a typical personal computer might exhibit the following messages on its visual display screen immediately after switch-on:

> Please wait . . .
> Insert a SYSTEM disk into drive A
> Then press any key

The rules in the pre-programmed bootstrap ROM have caused the processor, first to carry out a series of checks on the hardware of the system: 'Please wait . . .', and then instructed the system to read into its main memory patterns from a floppy disk loaded in its primary disk drive. In the example given, the wrong kind of disk has been found in the primary drive and the bootstrap program prompts for a system disk. This is a disk that has a set of patterns recorded at a particular place on the disk (the bootstrap or system tracks) that represent a comprehensive set of rules for managing the entire processing system. This set of rules is known as the operating system. The bootstrap program is designed to load automatically the operating system patterns from a system disk into the main memory and then cause the processor to start obeying the rules of the operating system. The pre-programmed rules of the bootstrap are rarely extensive enough to do little more than carry out this simple process.

The Operating System

Before the operating system has been loaded by the bootstrap program the computer system is simply an unco-ordinated collection of electronic black boxes. It is only through the execution by the processor of the rules of the operating system that the hardware becomes controlled and orchestrated into a cohesive and complete working system that can communicate effectively with its user and carry out tasks on demand. The electronic hardware of a computer system is of little value except when under the control of a full and comprehensive suite of operating system software.

Consider now that a well-known operating system for a popular personal computer has been loaded by the bootstrap loader into our model computer system (Figure 8.1). After a short period of time, during which the relevant operating system rules will have been executed by the processor to carry out a series of hardware assessment checks, a prompt similar to the following might appear on the visual display screen:

A>

This signifies that the primary disk drive is the A drive and provides an invitation to the user of the system to type in a command sequence. No other obvious activity will now take place until a command is typed in at the keyboard. The system is 'waiting' for its user. It is instructive to consider just what it is that the processor is doing at this stage.

Referring back to an earlier paragraph, we know that the processor is not halted; it is continuing to execute rules, for that is all that it can do whilst the computer is switched on. It must therefore be executing rules which themselves cause an effective 'wait', rules that are perhaps of the form:

Rule 1: Is there any keyboard input from the user?
Rule 2: If 'no' continue to next rule; if 'yes' process input from user
Rule 3: Go back to rule 1

The effect of this is a 'dynamic wait' during which the processor is constantly looping round a small sequence of rules until a keyboard entry is made by the user.

It is now that the relative timings shown in Figure 8.1 become interesting. The human user is operating at a few operations per second whilst the processor is running at some millions of operations per second, a timing mis-match between the processor and the user of the order of a million to one. Whilst the user, over the period of perhaps a second, has laboriously typed out the command 'DIR' in order to examine his disk directory, the processor has executed some million or so time-wasting instructions, In effect, the processor may spend much of its working life 'waiting', through the execution of such time-wasting instructions, for its user to type in the next command.

For a personal computer system that costs a few hundred pounds such gross inefficiency is no cause for concern. For a large mainframe computer system that costs several hundred thousand pounds however, such inefficiency is unacceptable and means have to be devised whereby the processing facilities can be used much more economically.

Time Sharing

The most usual way of utilising the processing resources more efficiently is by the application of some form of time sharing. If we refer back to Figure 8.1 we can conceive of not just one user with his keyboard input device and display output device being connected to the processor but many, say 50 or 100 or 150, or even more.

The set of 'wait' rules referred to earlier now has to become a little more complicated:

Rule 1: Is there any keyboard input from user 1?
Rule 2: If 'no' continue to next rule; if 'yes' process input from user 1
Rule 3: Is there any keyboard input from user 2?
Rule 4: If 'no' continue to next rule; if 'yes' process input from user 2

$$\begin{matrix} \vdots & & \vdots \\ \vdots & & \vdots \end{matrix}$$

Rule p: Is there any keyboard input from user n?
Rule q: If 'no' continue to next rule; if 'yes' process input from user n
Rule r: Go back to rule 1

Rather than 'waiting' for a single user to provide keyboard input, the new rules cause the system to sample each keyboard in turn, sharing the time of the processor between all the input lines. Because the processor is operating at millions of operations per second, the rate at which the sampling takes place is so fast compared with the human reaction time that no individual user should notice any degradation in service at his terminal; each appears to have a dedicated facility. Of course, the system management process is not as simple as this. It is not sufficient just to separate out the processing of the input from the different keyboards; associated output must also be sent to the appropriate displays. More important than this, however, is the fact that each user will require the system to be carrying out some process on his behalf that is typically unrelated to what any other user is doing. One may be involved in word processing, another using a spreadsheet, a third compiling a Pascal program, and so forth. The system management rules must be so designed as to keep all these, perhaps personal and unrelated activities entirely separate.

If each separate user activity is considered to be a task, then the system must consistently maintain as many tasks as there are active users, each task being implemented within the system by a separate[1] set of rules or program.

The operating-system rules must be so designed that they allocate some of the processor time to each task in turn, according to some predefined set of priorities. This should be done in such a way that all tasks appear to all users to be running simultaneously.

One approach often used is called 'time-slicing' where a few thousandths of a second of processor time (a time-slice) are allocated to execute a portion of each task in turn. If the switching process from one task to another is fast enough, all users appear to be being serviced simultaneously. That part of the operating-system rules responsible for this activity is often called the 'scheduler'.

Of course, for any set of rules to be executed by the processor, that set must be resident at the time in the main memory. One might consider that, even with the large memories available today, there is unlikely to be sufficient room in the main memory for the complete sets of rules for some one hundred or so tasks. This problem is normally overcome by holding in main memory only that portion of the set of rules relating to each task that is required for execution in the next few time-slices; the complete sets of rules for each task are held on the disk backing store. Another part of the operating system is responsible for ensuring that the relevant portion of each set of rules is, if necessary, recovered from disk and placed in main memory prior to the allocation to that task of the next time-slice. The reader will recall from Chapter 4 that the term 'virtual memory' is used to describe this method of operation.

A further problem that the operating-system rules must cope with is that of critical response times. Many devices that are connected to the computer require to be serviced within a critical time 'window' if they are not to corrupt or lose data. As an example, consider the simple case of a keyboard. When a user types in the letter 'D', say, then a serial pattern of pulses representing this letter will commence transmission down the line from the keyboard to the computer. If the user now follows this with another keystroke, 'I', a second set of pulses will be initiated. The operating system rules now have a critical time-window within which they must arrange to collect the pattern representing the letter 'D' and store it safely away in main memory before the next set of pulses representing the letter 'I' arrives and corrupts it.

This problem is typical of input devices, and whilst it is not particularly difficult to resolve for a slow device such as a keyboard, it can be much more serious for faster input devices such as disk drives. Although the problem may be reduced by using buffering and autonomous transfer techniques, the operating system rules must at some stage arrange for the buffers to be emptied and processed. The elements of the operating system that deal with all the vagaries of the various input and output peripherals that are connected to the system are called the device 'drivers' or 'handlers', and these are designed so as to ensure that the often unpredictable demands of the users and of the hardware devices are invariably handled correctly.

---

[1] In practice, the sets of rules need not be separate since it is possible to share the same program among a number of separate tasks by using common re-entrant code and separate data areas.

Operating Systems and Applications Software

A Benevolent Environment

Fundamentally, a multi-user operating system, when being executed, is providing all the housekeeping functions necessary for a number of tasks to be processed on behalf of a number of users apparently simultaneously, for all the hardware to be managed in a consistent and coherent way, and for the time-critical nature of the peripheral devices and their complexities to be hidden from all the users. It is also providing the means of communication between the system and its users. Without it, the hardware of the system is virtually unusable, other than by those with specialist training.

From a user viewpoint, such an operating system may be looked upon as providing a much more useful and benevolent environment within which to work than the hardware alone is capable of giving. It provides a number of high-level abstractions, such as file and database managers, command interpreters, and programming language environments. It is, in effect, converting the system hardware into some higher-level abstract machine: a virtual machine. Sets of rules, or programs, written for and used within this environment are known as application programs. Word processors, spreadsheets, compiling systems and so forth, as well as most programs written by the user, all come into this category.

Application Programs

Such application programs do not within themselves normally contain the detailed rules for managing the specific physical devices of the system, nor for resolving the complex timing constraints that are likely to arise. Such matters are invariably left to the operating system software, which provides a series of commands that an application program may call upon in order to have some difficult and complex process executed. For example, in order to output text to a printer, say, an application program would call upon a specific operating system function provided for that purpose, including with the call a reference to the place

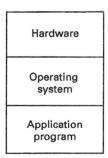

FIG. 8.2   System Hardware, Software and Applications Relationship

in memory where the application program had stored the relevant text characters. The operating system would then cause to be executed the relevant rules within its own body of code for the detailed and complex control of the line printer, issuing to it the text provided by the application program.

The relationships between the system hardware, the operating system and an application program are shown diagrammatically in Figure 8.2. The application program is designed to operate in the benevolent environment that has been provided by the operating system, itself designed for the specific machine hardware. The consequences of adopting this approach are important to recognise.

Consequences of This Approach

First, both the operating system object code and the application program object code work only within the particular hardware architecture and processor environment for which they were designed. This is because the patterns of the object code are specific to a particular processor system. There is no standardisation of processor order codes between manufacturers so a pattern that may represent a rule to 'add' in one processor type may represent 'multiply' in another, and may have no valid representation in a third. Object code programs are thus 'hardware' specific. Secondly, the application program object code generally works only within the particular operating system environment for which it was designed, since it must call on operating system functions to obtain access to required system facilities. Again, there is no standardisation of operating system interfaces between manufacturers, and so an application program is usually operating system specific. Most application programs are thus dependent upon and specific to both the particular operating system and the particular hardware architecture for which they were designed; that is, they are invariably specific to a particular manufacturer's product range of system hardware and system software.

This situation is often referred to as 'hardware lock'. An applications user can become locked into the product range of a particular manufacturer if he makes any significant investment in bespoke applications software. Say, for example, that a military pay and records applications system has been developed by in-house programming teams at a cost of some £100,000 in personnel and facility resource expenditure. Like most applications, it will have been programmed to operate on a specific manufacturer's hardware using the environment provided by a specific operating system supported by that manufacturer. When it becomes necessary, at some future date, to replace the computer system because the hardware can no longer economically be maintained, the applications user has little option but to upgrade the system to the latest offering from the same manufacturer. Any other course of action would mean that his existing system-specific applications code must be discarded, and he must either re-invest in new applications software or attempt to modify his existing software, both of which tend to be expensive options.

That is not to say that many applications users are not entirely satisfied with this arrangement. Most large system manufacturers provide economical and sensible upgrade paths for their user communities to replace their ageing systems and often thriving user groups exist which are able to bring pressure to bear whenever necessary on their manufacturer. For many applications users there is no software crisis; the manufacturer provides the operating system software that carries out all the difficult system tasks and market forces dictate that he looks after his user community reasonably well.

The Economics of Developing Operating Systems

Whilst it has not been the intention in this chapter to stray into a detailed discussion of the design of operating systems, it was felt that sufficient explanation needed to be given such that a sensible judgement could be formed about the degree of complexity, and thus the likely cost, involved in their development.

Another way of looking at the role of the operating system is to see it as mapping parallel, time-critical, real-world activities, whose behaviour cannot be predicted ahead of the events' occurring, on to a simple, sequential Von Neumann machine. The degree of intellectual ability and understanding needed to think through such processes in order that an unambiguous and correctly acting set of rules may be written down is high, and successful practitioners of this art are in short supply. Consequently the development of operating systems, a high-calibre manpower intensive activity, is a particularly expensive process.

Typical Costs

Typically, one major manufacturer has quoted his mainframe operating-system development costs as being in the bracket of £10 million to £100 million for a single system. How can such development be made cost-effective? Recognising that the hardware of a system is of little value to a user without an operating system being available, a manufacturer, on selling a system, provides both the hardware and the necessary operating-system software together as a bundled package. In practice, the total purchase price for a typical time-sharing system may be £500,000, of which only £50,000 is for the hardware; this latter, over the last decade, having consistently fallen. The remaining £450,000 is to offset the development costs of the operating system and to provide the supplier with a reasonable profit margin.

There is clearly a major advantage in a manufacturer retaining as large a user community as possible, since this will permit him to amortise his operating-system development costs across a greater number of systems. The larger the community, the greater the potential benefit to all, since there are no real 'production' costs with software. Copies of operating system software can be made for a few pounds; this is little more than the media costs of the disks on which they are distributed.

Sensible Strategy

This advantage suggests a strategy of not standardising on hardware architectures nor operating-system interfaces. To remove the hardware lock and to provide mechanisms whereby existing applications code could be run on other manufacturers' systems would permit users to migrate from their current manufacturer when they had to replace their ageing equipment. Proposals for such standards tend therefore not to be well supported nor well received.

The Military Operational Need

So far this discussion has concentrated on the commercial market. Many user communities are broadly content with the services that they receive from systems manufacturers, and there is little commercial pressure for standards that will permit portability of software between different systems. This same view tends to pervade the community of non-operational military users. Large, administrative, static, logistic systems invariably use commercially available hardware and system software and the reactions of their users tend to be similar to those of their civilian counterparts.

The picture is very different, however, for the military, real-time, operational community. Given the selection of some battleworthy, hardened, mobile, computer hardware for use in a command and control or weapon-control system, the first software issue that arises is the provision of a suitable operating system.[1]

As we have already seen, this is intimately concerned, amongst other things, with the detailed control of all the peripheral devices that may be connected to the processor. In the commercial field, such devices are likely to be standard disk drives, printers, visual display units, and so forth. In the operational military field they may include, for example, special non-standard display devices, such as those for radar pictures and map displays, weapon system controllers, and sensor input devices. The probability of a suitable operating system being commercially available to manage these kinds of devices is small.

In addition, the scheduling algorithms designed for a commercial peacetime system are unlikely to reflect the priorities required in a battlefield command and control system. Security too becomes a major concern and levels of assurance are required of the operating system that are unlikely to exist in a commercial product. In short, there is rarely going to be available much[2] operating system software that can be used directly to support the new command and control system.

One of the first software tasks that will invariably have to be undertaken, therefore, is the development of a full operating system for the specific hardware configuration.

The development costs for an operating system are, as we have already seen, of the order of £10 million to £100 million and, in this case, there is only one customer, Defence, which must shoulder the entire bill. On top of this comes the costs of writing the actual applications software; a somewhat easier and inherently less expensive task, but nevertheless one that will increase the bill significantly because of the sheer volume of code likely to be involved.

In some projects the decision is taken to implement the operating system and applications software together as one monolithic, real-time system. Rather than designing a separate operating system with a well-defined interface, no distinction is made between operating system and applications functions. This approach, whilst perhaps improving real-time performance by reducing operating system overheads, tends to place all of the software development, both systems and applications, into the complex, high-risk, difficult and thus very expensive, category. Overall, the costs are likely to be even greater.

---

[1] The selection of the hardware for a project should ideally come after the software has been developed when all the required characteristics are known. In practice, because of the difficulties in transporting software from one system to another, the hardware is often selected first.

[2] Some manufacturers of military hardware do provide a vestigial operating system for real-time purposes often known as a 'kernel'.

The Software Crisis

There is thus a real difference in the perceptions of those involved in the procurement and management of non-operational, administrative systems from those responsible for operational, battlefield systems. The problems of the 'software crisis' appear to apply only to the operational community; they are absorbed by the manufacturers in the administrative and commercial field and their costs are amortised across a large user community. This may mean that expensive measures, seen by the operational side as cost effective and essential to combat the crisis, obtain only lukewarm support and sometimes outright rejection from the administrative side. Different branches of the Ministry of Defence may thus be inconsistent in the considered views that they give to industry.

The Development of Real-Time Operational Software

We have now established the need for operating system software and observed that the development of operating systems is a complex, difficult and very expensive process. We note that software to control military, real-time, operational systems is a special case of operating-system software and is perhaps the most complex, most difficult and most expensive of all to develop. We have also seen that, whereas in the commercial sector these development costs are amortised across a large number of users, in military, operational, real-time systems, Defence has to bear the entire cost.

Although we may now recognise that such systems are very complex and costly, we still have not yet determined why their development should cause such severe budget and timescale overruns. After all, we routinely implement equally complex and costly systems in other engineering disciplines without meeting this level of difficulty. What are the factors in real-time software development that result in such apparently unique problems?

It is certain that the real difficulties are often underestimated. Experience in writing applications programs does not necessarily provide sufficient appreciation of the complexities involved in writing systems software. Most application programs are written within and for an operating system environment which deliberately hides the real-world complexities of the hardware from the applications designer. Applications experience cannot simply be scaled up in a linear fashion; development of operating system software for military real-time systems is much more difficult.

The Software Acquisition and Development Working Group

The Working Group Report

Support for this argument comes from the Software Acquisition and Development Working Group (SADWG). This Working Group was set up by the United States Assistant Secretary of Defense for Communications, Command, Control and Intelligence in answer to mounting concern within the Department of Defense

(DoD) over the software crisis. In their final report, dated July 1980, the working Group stated:

> It is common knowledge that software development projects rarely meet cost-benefits originally projected, usually cost more than expected, and are usually late. In addition, the software delivered seldom meets user requirements, often times is not usable, or requires extensive rework.

At the end of the SADWG report, four case histories are presented. They are offered as being representative of the widespread problems that the Working Group found to be associated with software development projects. The case histories cover a range of costs from $100,000 to millions of dollars and demonstrate that beyond a certain project size very similar problems seem to arise.

First Case History

A summary of the facts relating to the first case history is shown in Figure 8.3 and the project is quoted as involving:

> ... the design and implementation of a large data processing system that would automate field station handling of time-sensitive data to include identification, selection, extraction, preparation and dissemination of product and technical information to tactical consumers.

	Estimates at contract award	Actuals at cancellation 2 1/2 years later	New estimates to completion
Cost	$9.2M	$13.0M	$25.0M
Lines of code	30,0000	275,000	540,000
Memory	96K	320K	???

FIG. 8.3   Case History 1

The American Government agency concerned had an initial budget for this work of $10.9 million and eventually awarded the contract at $9.2 million. When the project was cancelled, some 2½ years later, the actual expenditure stood at $13 million and the estimated cost to complete the work was a further $12 million, making a total of $25 million in all.

The initial estimate by the contractor of the amount of software needed for the project was 30,000 lines of code. Lines of code are often used as a measure of the amount of programming effort and thus the cost that a software project might entail. The argument, which regrettably is specious, takes the following form: if the number of lines of code to be written can be estimated, and we have a reasonably good idea of the productivity of our programmers in terms of number of lines of code per year, then we can calculate the number of programmer-years needed for this software and hence its development cost. Given the number of programmer years and the number of programmers available we can also calculate the development time. At least three problems arise: first, any estimate of the number of lines of code for a project of this nature is likely to be little more than guesswork, unless it is based on similar previous experience; secondly, programmer productivity varies considerably between programmers, far more so than in other disciplines and thus is difficult to average; and, thirdly, the assumption that programmer-years may be used as a valid measure of effort is incorrect, as we shall see later.

Nevertheless, 30,000 lines of code was the estimate upon which the contractor initially based his costs. The agency concerned misunderstood this figure from the proposal documentation and was under the impression that the contractor had estimated 60,000 lines of code. Privately it was felt that at least 110,000 lines of code would be needed

When the contract was finally terminated, 275,000 lines of code had actually been written, and it was estimated that a further 265,000 lines would be needed to complete the project making a total well in excess of half a million. It is interesting to try to visualise what half a million lines of code actually looks like. A useful picture is based on a standard box of line printer paper. If every page in a full box is completely printed upon, we estimate that that results in some 50,000 lines of code; so, half a million would require 10 full boxes. Imagine having to read that much code, let alone trying to understand it all.

A similar state of affairs existed with regard to the memory requirements of the proposed system. In the original estimate, the contractor proposed that 96 Kbytes of memory would be needed. Six months into the contract a new estimate was made of 320 Kbytes. Changes of this nature can have significant effects on the feasibility of a project. It may be that space, power, weight and heat factors, say, in an airframe or in a tracked vehicle, do not permit such trebling of the memory requirements for the system. It may also be the case that the hardware configuration cannot be designed to support the proposed increase and that a re-selection of hardware must take place. Under these circumstances, much of the software so far developed will have to be discarded. Problems of this kind were much in evidence in the ill-fated British AEW Nimrod project.

In the event, little, if any of the software for this case history was found to be usable. It is hard to credit such gross errors in estimation: an initial cost estimate of $9.2 million compared with a cost estimate to completion at cancellation of $25 million; an initial estimate of programmer effort of 30,000 lines of code compared with an estimate of programmer effort to completion, $2\frac{1}{2}$ years later, of 540,000 lines of code. Yet, at the time of writing, some 8 years after the publication of the SADWG report, British defence procurement agencies are having to answer to parliamentary criticism over just such issues. We would claim that the problems lie not so much with any inefficiency within the project teams but in the nature of the task that is being undertaken and in the inadequacies of the tools that are currently available. Before we look at these issues, however, we should complete the survey by considering in outline the three remaining case histories which are summarised in Figure 8.4.

	Case 2		Case 3		Case 4	
	Estimate	Actual	Estimate	Actual	Estimate	Actual
Costs	$9.1M	$24.1M	$93K	$124K	$959K	$981K
Status	Completed 3 years late		Completed on time		Cancelled 1/4 complete	

FIG. 8.4   Case Histories 2, 3 and 4

Second Case History

In the second case history, the original contract price was for $9.1 million. Three years late, a working product was delivered at a cost of over $24 million. Again neither the customer nor the supplier had any real idea of the magnitude of the programming task that was being tackled. The entire system was supposed to be implemented in 55,000 lines of code. In the event, one single component, originally estimated at 17,000 lines of code, itself amounted to over 200,000 lines.

Third and Fourth Case Histories

Both of the other two case histories concerned smaller projects. In the first, the system was delivered on time after 28 months work but with an overspend of about 30% on the original contract price of $93,000. In the second, the original estimate was $959,000 over 27 months. After 30 months and an expenditure of $981,000 the project was cancelled, and then estimated to be no more than a quarter complete.

Although these four case histories are in themselves a very small sample, the report claims that they nevertheless are representative of the widespread problems that the Working Group found. With that in mind, it is interesting to note that the most successful project was the third, the smallest and least expensive of them all. Factors associated with costly disasters would seem to include: large size, high complexity, a real-time environment, and a failure to recognise the magnitude of the task that was being undertaken.

The Problems with Programmers

Teamwork

At root, the problems could be said to stem from the programmers. A high-calibre systems programmer capable of thinking through the tortuous code of a real-time operating system is an unusual being. If the task before him is entirely within his own personal scope, then there is little doubt that he will eventually provide a satisfactory and probably very elegant solution to it. If, however, the task is of such a complexity or of such a size as to require more than one individual to deal with it, then difficulties may begin to arise. Teamwork is needed in this case and it is not generally in the nature of such programmers to welcome the close involvement of others. A small university team of three or four people who know one another well is perhaps an exception to this; in general, teamwork is not a natural characteristic of most systems programmers.

Optimism is, however, a frequently met characteristic, and the manager of a software team needs to beware of it. Progress in a software development project is difficult to monitor, as there is little tangible evidence of what has been achieved. Listings of lines of code so far developed are likely to mean little to anyone but their designers. The most obvious way of determining progress is by asking the programmers and here one meets the 90% complete syndrome. The natural enthusiasm and optimism of most programmers can result in a serious under assessment of the effort that is still required to complete a given programming

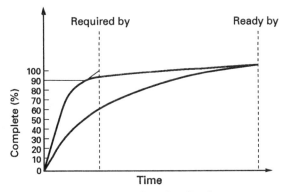

FIG. 8.5   The 90% Complete Syndrome

task; the response is invariably 'it is 90% complete', and Figure 8.5 shows graphically this perceived progress together with the actual progress against time. Those of a cynical disposition have been known to observe that many programs spend 90% of their existence 90% complete.

Partitioning a Problem

One well-tried and proven method for reducing the problems of size and complexity is to partition a given task into smaller and less complex sub-tasks that are that much easier to deal with. Small teams may then be assigned to each of the sub-tasks and these may again be broken down into elements each of which is well within the scope of a single individual. The effects of size and complexity are reduced by applying more people to the problem; and the more people that are applied, the more rapidly the problem should be solved.

Brooks' Mythical Man-Month

This method works well when the project can be truly partitioned into tasks that are not interdependent. Brooks, in his book *The Mythical Man-Month*, demonstrates that a typical software project simply does not fall into this category. He plots curves of required time against number of people for three kinds of project,

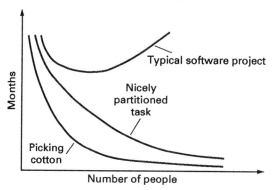

FIG. 8.6   Partitioning of Tasks

shown here as: 'picking cotton', 'a nicely partitioned task' and 'a typical software project' (Figure 8.6).

Given several acres of cotton to be picked, the partitioning of the task into individual activities is simple. Each picker is given a briefing on what to do and allocated an area within which to do it, and there is almost no dependence on what others are doing. Under these circumstances, the more people that are brought in to pick the cotton, the faster the fields are picked, and thus the curve takes the form shown. Similarly for the nicely partitioned task; if the project can be broken down into independent tasks for each individual, then the more individuals made available, the faster the project can be completed.

This is not the case, however, for the typical software project where as more people are brought in so the curve, after initially falling, soon starts to rise again, thus signalling a worsening of overall performance beyond a certain point. It is not difficult to see why this should be so. If the task cannot readily be partitioned, and this tends to be true of most complex software projects, then the work of each individual is not independent of others and a frequent dialogue with those others has to be maintained. This is particularly demanding wherever a high level of intellectual activity is required, as in systems programming work. As more people are added to such a project, so the intellectual lines of communication that are required within the team rise rapidly. A point is soon reached where the addition of a further pair of hands is outweighed by the increase in intercommunication overheads, and thus the curve starts to rise.

Given that we tend to start our projects at a point on the curve somewhat to the right of the minimum[1] shown in Figure 8.6, then this has important consequences for a project manager.

Brooks' Law

The natural course of action when a task is falling behind schedule is to add more resources; in this instance, doing just that will exacerbate the situation. Two

---

[1] It would be preferable, under these circumstances, to buy in a few high calibre systems program-mers to tackle the project rather than, as is normally the case, contract for many more average programmers at lower rates.

useful maxims may be derived from this figure, the first of which is known as 'Brooks' Law':

▶ Adding more people to a late software project will increase costs and make the project later.
▶ Cost does indeed vary as the direct product of the number of people multiplied by the number of months; unfortunately, progress does not.

Brooks' mythical man-month is, of course, highlighting the error in the assumption that the key measure of effort for a software project is the 'man-month'. This is based on the erroneous notion that the product of people and time is a constant for a given project. In other words, the notion that one can refer to a project as requiring, say, 80 man-years of effort. If this were so, then the two situations

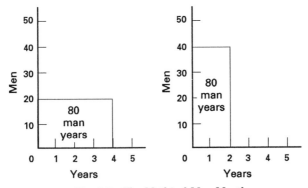

FIG. 8.7   The Mythical Man-Month

shown in Figure 8.7 would be equivalent: the project could be completed in 4 years using 20 programmers or in 2 years using 40 programmers.

This does not work because, as we have already seen, the more people involved, the greater the number of lines of communication needed between them and the less the overall efficiency of the team. Thus attempting to reduce timescale by increasing the team size is a certain recipe for failure. There is a case for stating a minimal time period shorter than which it is simply not possible to complete successfully any given software project. This perhaps also helps to explain why time and cost estimates based on numbers of lines of code can be so grossly in error.

The Engineering Approach

Standards

As we have already discussed, one approach to reducing the problems of size and complexity is to partition the task into smaller, less complex sub-tasks, and a number of software engineering methodologies aim to do just this. Such partitioning is much assisted if there already exist well-defined and well-understood interface standards that can be used to separate out one element of the system from another. Clearly if two designers are working on separate sub-systems that interface with one another only through such well-defined standards, their need for intercommunication is much reduced.

An existing engineering infrastructure tends to provide such standards, and this makes partitioning of a task that much easier. Common training for engineers aids the communication process between designers and thus these critical software problems seem to be encountered much less frequently in the more traditional and better established engineering disciplines.

Components

An engineering infrastructure, however, provides much more than this. A keystone of the engineering approach is the construction of new systems from well-proven and standard components. This permits the new system to be built to a predictable quality, reduces the risk of failure, and utilises the skills and expertise of other engineers, which have been encapsulated in the production versions of well-proven components.

Of course, similar skills and expertise are encapsulated in the well-proven programs of software engineers, and so it should not be impossible to re-use their work as components of some new system. To do this, however, requires portability of software between different systems, and, as we have seen, there is little commercial pressure for this capability; indeed, there is a positive antipathy towards it. Currently, when a new, real-time, military software system is built every part of it has to be redesigned from scratch; every wheel has to be re-invented; every element of it becomes high risk. Dr Edith Martin, Vice-President of the Boeing Corporation, summed it up neatly at the London MILCOMP conference in 1985 when she stated:

> If we built houses in the way in which we build software systems, trees would be taken to the building site and whittled with penknives.

Building Houses

Building houses provides an excellent example of the differences in practice that exist between a long established discipline, such as civil engineering, and the still nascent discipline of software engineering. We would have little difficulty in specifying to an architect our detailed requirements for the building of our new house. The locations of doors and windows, whether or not an outlook should be south facing, the number, sizes and shapes of rooms are all matters that can readily and unambiguously be described by means of sketches and plans, and our architect can then produce a set of drawings to show precisely how these requirements are going to be met. These drawings can then be used by a builder to produce a bill of quantities and, from this, relatively accurate estimates of cost and timescale can be made. We would expect these estimates to be accurate to at least 10% and this works well because of standards: communication standards, such as, for example, the drawings which are well known and understood by everybody concerned and are used to help confirm and specify the requirement; and building block component standards, such as bricks, sizes of timber, mixes of mortar, and so forth. Because these are standard, the builder knows them and knows how much time and effort is required to produce a given construction using them; also he can buy them in as production components to a known quality and does not have to develop them for himself.

Compare this with the situation faced by a software development customer. There is no equivalent to the drawings and the best that one can hope for from the developer are typically some five thick volumes of text that try to describe in words how it is that he intends to meet the operational need. He almost certainly will not be building the system from any standard software components, largely because of the difficulty in re-using existing software and so it is all going to be re-invented yet again. The real user requirements are almost certainly not properly understood nor catered for, but neither party can readily establish this without thoroughly absorbing and interpreting those volumes of probably very indigestible written text.

With all these difficulties besetting the software developer, it is no wonder that real-time projects beyond a certain size and complexity so often run over budget and over time; perhaps it is rather more surprising that such projects are ever brought to a successful conclusion.

The needs for the future of the discipline can, however, be readily determined from this discussion: standards and the re-use of software as 'production' components must play a major part. The 're-use of software as components' requirement can be met only if some agreed mechanism for providing software portability across different hardware systems can also be established, and we shall return to this issue.

Problems with Errors

However, there are yet other problems that need to be resolved. The software development process, as we have already observed, is inherently difficult to manage. The only tangible output from a development process that may extend over many years in a set of paper listings of one form or another, and deficiencies in the developed software may remain undetected even beyond acceptance testing.

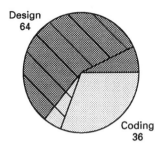

FIG. 8.8 Software Error Categories

The resulting situation is shown graphically in the pie chart of Figure 8.8. Software errors, or defects as they are sometimes called, tend to be placed in one of two categories: design errors and coding errors. Of these, coding errors are the easier and less costly to put right, but they represent only 36% of the total. The remaining 64% are design errors, and the hatched area shows that most of these are still resident in a system when it is delivered into service. The correction of these defects, as they are detected, is a major task in itself and an in-service defect reporting and modification infrastructure needs to be established to manage the process. Significant additional funding also needs to be set aside for this purpose.

Testing

It may be felt, with some justification, that systems should not be delivered into service with such a high proportion of defects. If proper, exhaustive testing had been carried out in the first place the situation would not have arisen. Unfortunately, rigorous exhaustive testing is not a solution to software based systems, as this simple example demonstrates.

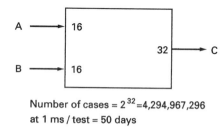

Number of cases = 2^{32}=4,294,967,296
at 1 ms / test = 50 days

FIG. 8.9   Multiplication of Two 16-Bit Numbers

Given, as shown in Figure 8.9, a piece of code that takes two 16-bit binary numbers and produces a 32-bit result (a multiplication function perhaps), then the number of different possible cases that need to be examined for an exhaustive test are the number of different patterns that could be held in the result: 2^{32} or 4,294,967,296. Assuming that with some automated test equipment we could perform a thousand tests per second, an exhaustive test run would still take 50 days. The inevitable conclusion is that exhaustive testing is just not physically possible. Testing strategies have to be applied which limit examination to the most critical areas. With a physical product, such critical areas can often be calculated or spotted intuitively; with an intangible product like software the determination is much more difficult. The best that we can aim for is progressively to reduce the number of errors by tracing and correcting the ones that come to light until a level is reached that is operationally acceptable. As one authority puts it:

> You can never be sure that there are no errors, only that none of the errors that you are looking for has been found.

Recent work on software integrity testing tools does give some hope. Such tools examine the source code of the software for potentially dangerous and incomplete constructs and highlight where programmers have ignored the mandatory codes of practice set up by the project to improve integrity. Such testing does lead to a significantly improved level of assurance, but it is costly in analysis time and is usually employed only for secure or safety-critical systems. It is a sad fact that many of our real-time software based systems will continue to be fielded with a large but unknown number of errors still residing in them.

The Need for Change

When a hardware system is developed, the requirements are usually frozen well before construction starts and the work can proceed from a known, fixed baseline. With operational software-based systems this does not seem to be practicable and indeed may not even be desirable.

The reasons for this are not hard to find. The development process typically extends over a long period of time, possibly many years. Not only is it likely that the users' initial perception of their needs will not have been fully understood by the developers, but also, during the development period, the users as individuals and the methods and working of the users as a group will almost certainly have changed. Acknowledgement of the part that command and control systems play in the conduct of military affairs also suggests a need for continuing change. Command and control and military information systems represent, in software, a model of some part of the doctrine and procedures that the military organisation uses to carry out its function. Military systems, in particular, must adapt quickly and must amend their doctrine and procedures to match potentially hostile changes in the environment. Such adaptations and amendments of doctrine and procedures must also be reflected in the software of a command and control system if that system is to continue to serve its purpose; thus the need for some form of evolutionary software change would seem to be inevitable.

Whole Life Costs

All this implies that software systems must continue to be modified after their introduction into service if they are to retain their value. A detailed analysis carried out on a large number of American military software-based projects supports this conclusion. It can best be summed up by the so-called Raleigh-Norden

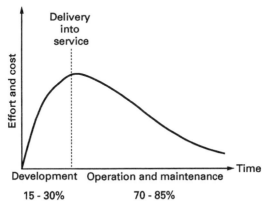

FIG. 8.10   The Raleigh-Norden Curve

curve, shown in Figure 8.10. This demonstrates that over the entire life-cycle of a software development project only 15-30% of the actual software effort and costs are expended in the development phase; the remaining 70–85% are incurred after delivery into service. The operations phase is therefore the most expensive in software terms and may cost the users up to three times the original software development. This is, of course, largely due to the following three factors:

▶ Correcting defects as they are discovered in service.
▶ Meeting the actual requirements, as opposed to those that were perhaps wrongly perceived.
▶ Meeting new requirements and evolutionary change.

It is perhaps of greatest significance to consider the situation that occurs when we eventually reach the right-hand edge of the curve in Figure 8.10. The system has been in service at this point for many years, perhaps 20 or so. The hardware is now dated and becoming increasingly difficult to maintain. Not only is it impossible to obtain replacement parts (the micro-chips have long been out of manufacture and all the maintenance reserve stocks have by now been used up), but finding maintenance staff who are trained in this old technology is no longer feasible. The hardware, therefore, has to be replaced. What, however, of the software? At this stage it is the best that it has ever been. The majority of the defects in it have been found and corrected. It has been modified continuously throughout its in-service life to meet evolutionary needs and it is now precisely what the current users want. Now is the time when we throw it away! It is designed to be executed by a particular hardware configuration and, because the software is not portable, we have no option but to discard it when we replace the hardware. We start the whole development cycle over, re-inventing all the wheels yet once again.

Future Proofing

If we had portable software we could future-proof our not insignificant investment in software by re-using it on the next generation of hardware. The key factors here are: portability and re-useability.

A Way Forward

Software First

If we re-examine the first case history, we note that the hardware was selected before the software was written. Within six months of the project's starting, the hardware requirements were revised by the software developers. This points clearly to the need for hardware independence in software development; the so-called software first approach. Using this technique, software can be written without any specific hardware in mind, and, provided that we have true portability of software, the suites can be transferred to the most up-to-date set of hardware that has the necessary power and memory capacities. Portability is thus essential.

Developing this reasoning further, given true portability, we can be confident that the software, the most expensive part of the system, can outlive the hardware, and be transferred to some future set of equipment when the original system is no longer maintainable. This future-proofs our systems and means that the software, which does not wear out and which becomes more reliable (and thus more valuable) with age as more errors are discovered and removed, can be re-used. Re-useability is essential.

Given true portability, we can invest our expertise and knowledge in software components and start to implement an engineering approach similar to that used by other disciplines. This alone will improve significantly the quality of the product and its reliability, reduce the risks involved and improve our ability to estimate more accurately the costs and timescales needed for the development. Software components and standards are essential.

Ada

It is in order to put in place the basic engineering infrastructure needed to provide these capabilities that the DoD, MoD and NATO have committed themselves to the programming language Ada. This language does indeed provide good mechanisms for portability, re-useability and the production of software components, but the technical mechanisms provided to effect these facilities are of far less importance than the value that the language has as an enforced standard. The concept is one of a programming or project support 'environment'[1] which provides on the input side a constant, standard interface for source code programs (Figure 8.11).

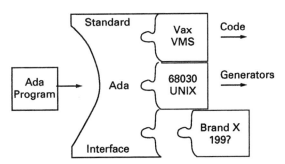

FIG. 8.11   Ada Environment

On the output side, any number of different 'code generators' may be plugged in such that a standard package of source code can be compiled through the system to generate object code for any given hardware and operating-system configuration. When an application needs to be transferred to a different hardware configuration, all that has to be done is for the source code of the application to be recompiled using the relevant code generator. When an entirely new piece of hardware is developed only a new code generator for that hardware need be written.

For this idea to work, the input side of the environment must be a rigidly enforced standard, otherwise source-code components would not be re-useable at a later date when perhaps the environment had been changed.

Ada is such a standard because the name has been trademarked by the DoD and no product may use the name unless it passes some 3,000 tests that have been laid down by the international body responsible for the language. The set of tests

---

[1] For Ada, the environment is called the APSE (Ada programming support environment). More recently the term IPSE (integrated project support environment) has been used.

has to be passed annually and so all products that are to continue to use the name have to be maintained continually up to date. It is in its role as an enforced standard, unlike that of any other programming language, that Ada comes into its own; the technical merits or otherwise of its language structures and performance are of far less importance, and this point is frequently misunderstood.

The real need for the operational defence community if it is to overcome the software crisis is to have put in place an engineering infrastructure that will permit the re-use of software and the development of software-based systems from components. The Ada programming language is but the first of the steps along the road to this goal; it is a necessary but not in itself sufficient condition. Until, however, enough such steps have been taken, the software crisis is going to remain with the defence community.

9.

Interoperability

Introduction

Given the enormous scope of the field across which it is possible to apply communications and information systems in support of command and control, it is perhaps not surprising to find that there is a tradition of piecemeal development to meet individual aspects of the whole requirement. The field is commonly broken down into what have become known as the 'battlefield functional areas', or BFAs, following work in the United States in the 1970s. The five most commonly cited BFAs are:

▶ Manoeuvre control
▶ Intelligence
▶ Fire support
▶ Air defence
▶ Combat support (logistics)

On examining the possible requirements for CIS to support any of the areas listed above, it soon becomes apparent that there is a need to be able to exchange information with one or more of the other areas. For example, users of the fire support system will have a strong interest in knowing where their own forces are deployed, and this is information which one would expect to find in the manoeuvre control system. When the fire support system controls a surface-to-surface artillery mission, the fact that ammunition is expended is of interest to the combat support system, because it must organise the re-supply of it. The intelligence system will have an interest in the location and description of the targets engaged, to add to the picture of the enemy which it is responsible for compiling. One could go on quoting such examples, but instead let us turn our attention to how that need to exchange information might be satisfied.

An approach which would seem to be possible is to avoid the piecemeal development of systems to serve individual areas, and concentrate instead on building one tightly-coupled, monolithic battlefield CIS, which does everything. It need not have all facilities available to all users; one could envisage variants of the system for the distinct functional areas, but all would share a common 'core' of facilities which would ensure the unimpeded passage of information between users on the battlefield. Two major objections to this approach spring to mind. First, as introduced at the beginning of this chapter, the problem is too big to lend itself to a monolithic solution using any of the development techniques hitherto available. Recent history is full of examples of attempts to produce large, general and comprehensive systems which have failed through an inability to manage or even to understand the enormous complexity of the problem. Secondly, there is the simple fact that we no longer have a 'clean sheet of paper'. It may be possible for an 'innocent' in the CIS field, perhaps the army of an 'emerging' state, which has not hitherto had any automated support, to consider taking the monolithic approach, but for most of the armies of NATO that day is long past. There are already a number of individual functional area CIS in existence, and others at different stages of the development process. Given that the approach of scrapping existing systems and starting again is likely to be ruled out on cost grounds, the only option left is to find some suitable 'glue' with which the individual functional area CIS may be bound into an apparently homogeneous system.

So far we have considered only the 'internal' requirement for information exchange, that is, between the different functional areas of the same army. In an alliance such as NATO, where armed forces of different nations are deployed alongside each other, there is a clear need for information to be exchanged between similar functional areas of different armies. If the command structure of the Alliance is to allow, for example, the grouping of divisions of different nations under the command of a particular national corps, then the need for the manoeuvre control systems of the participating nations to be able to exchange information becomes apparent. There would be considerable advantage in the ability of the fire support CIS of one army to be able to control the fire of the guns of another, and it is hard to envisage how an air defence system could operate effectively over an area where the armies of more than one nation were deployed if the air defence CIS of those armies could not exchange information. This would seem to be an even more difficult problem than 'internal' interoperability. In the internal case, one ought at least to gain some advantage from the fact that all the interoperating systems belong ultimately to the same organisation and are subject to the same procurement rules.

Definitions

The 'glue' we are looking for is *interoperability*, for which we offer the following definition: *the ability of one system to exchange data or services or both with another system*.

There are different degrees of interoperability, according to the extent of manual involvement. This is illustrated in Figure 9.1. Degree 5 is the least restricted; it is fully automated and information flows freely between the interconnected systems with no restriction at all. At present, the target within NATO is to achieve Degree 4 interoperability. This does impose some control over the exchange of information, and such control is felt to be essential both for security purposes, and to retain some control over the provenance of information. It can be vitally important to know where a particular item of information has come from, and whilst it would not be impossible in a system with Degree 5 interoperability to tag information

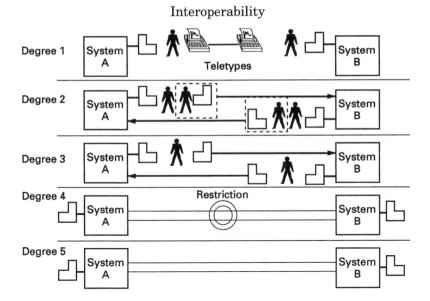

FIG. 9.1   Degrees of Interoperability

with details of its source, the extra control available in the Degree 4 situation is felt to be necessary.

The Layered Approach to Interoperability

A Human Example

Many of the salient features of interoperability may be illustrated by an example from the field of person-to-person communications. Take the case of two business-men, one British and the other Japanese, who need to communicate with one another in the course of their business. One can identify a 'hierarchy of needs' which must be satisfied if they are to accomplish a successful dialogue. In other words, there is a whole series of requirements to be met, and each requirement in the series is a prerequisite for those which follow it.

The starting point, or foundation, is some physical (or possibly electronic) means of allowing a conversation to take place. That is, the two persons must either be both in the same place and able to talk to each other directly, or they must be linked by some telecommunications medium such as the telephone. It is an inter-esting aside to compare the information exchange 'bandwidth' available to the participants between direct, face-to-face conversation, with the full range of facial expression and 'body language' accessible to both parties, and the limited dialogue possible over a long-distance telephone line.

Whatever means is used to convey the words of one man to the other and vice versa, the next important decision to be made is the choice of language. Whilst it is true that special, 'international' languages have been developed to allow communications between persons of different nationalities, it is most unlikely that our businessmen will be speaking, for example, Esperanto. It is about 99% certain that they will be using the *de facto* standard of human business communications in the Western world, the English language.

So far our two protagonists have reached the stage where they can establish communications, using a 'protocol' along the lines of 'Hello Mr Nakamura, John Smith from Acme Widgets here', 'How are you today?', and 'What's the weather like in Tokyo?'. Such small talk forms an essential part of the conversation as a whole, but will not by itself achieve the business aims of the dialogue. Sooner or later the speakers must get down to work.

When they do start to 'talk shop', they will need a knowledge of their subject and its vocabulary in the language being used. It is one thing to know a foreign language at the general purpose, or 'tourist' level, but quite another to be able to hold a technical conversation in it. Our two men are experts in their subject, and are soon deeply involved in discussing the technical parameters of the components made by Mr Nakamura's firm from which Mr Smith's will build its widgets.

A level which comes somewhere between the ability to hold a general conversation and the conduct of technical business is that of culture, or ethos. This is a difficult aspect to define accurately, and has to do with the different ways in which persons of different cultures go about their business. Whilst the difference in cultures between the East–West extremes used in our example may be obvious, less obvious but no less serious differences exist even between cultures which apparently use the same language. There is considerable scope for misunderstanding between, for example, a British person and a North American if due allowance is not made for the cultural differences between them.

The 'hierarchy of needs' governing the dialogue between our two business men

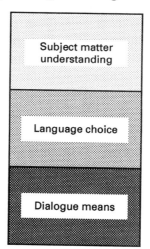

FIG. 9.2   The 'Hierarchy of Needs' in the Human Dialogue

is illustrated in Figure 9.2. This diagram illustrates and introduces the layered approach to interoperability. Each need is seen as a layer which relies on the proper functioning of the other layers beneath it in order to carry out its function. The cumulative dependence of the layers may easily be tested by considering the result of removing any one of them. At the most fundamental level, for example, if the physical connection were to be broken it is obvious that the dialogue would cease. Remove the layer of 'subject matter understanding', and whilst a conversation about the state of the weather or some other trivial matter could continue, the ultimate aim of the dialogue would not be met. A similar approach may be taken to the dialogue between computer systems, but, as one might expect, the layers and their functions are more rigidly defined and interpreted than is the case in our human example.

The Layered Approach Applied to Information Systems: Open Systems Interconnection (OSI)

The model which is used to describe the layered approach to the interconnection of computer systems is the International Standards Organisation (ISO) 7-layer reference model for open systems interconnection (OSI), which was introduced in Chapter 6. ISO document 7498 contains the definitive description of the reference model, a simplified view of which is given in Figure 9.3.

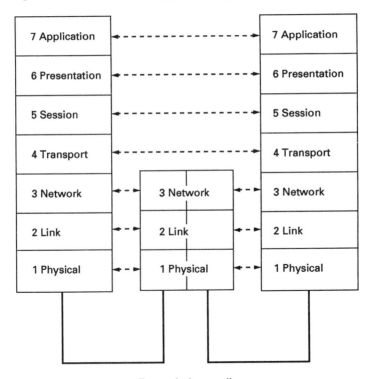

Transmission medium

Fig. 9.3   The ISO 7-Layer Model for Open Systems Interconnection

The concept of the model follows directly from that of the human example given earlier. The layers are arranged in a hierarchy, with cumulative dependence. Each layer accepts services from the layer below and provides services to the layer above.

A concept which is not so clearly illustrated in the human example is that of protocols between the peer layers of co-operating systems. Figure 9.3 shows that, whilst the actual communication is between the layers of one system, across the physical communications medium connecting them, and up the layers of the other system, there is an apparent or virtual connection between a layer in one system and its peer in the other. This virtual dialogue will be conducted in accordance with the protocol established for the layer concerned.

Layers 1 to 3

Layers 1 to 3 have already been described in some detail in Chapter 6, so no more than a summary of their functions is needed here.

Layer 1: The Physical Layer. The physical layer contains the specification for the electrical connection to the communications medium. For instance, it defines the way in which bits are represented, e.g. the voltages used to represent '1's and '0's, and the duration in time of symbols.

Layer 2: The Link Layer. The link layer embodies the mechanisms for the control of communication over a point-to-point link, and normally provides for the transmission of data across the link in groups of bits known as frames.

Layer 3: The Network Layer. The network layer controls the communication of data across a network, assumed to consist of a number of links, each one of which is under the control of a level 2 protocol. The level 3 protocol will contain provisions for flow control across the network and addressing.

Layer 4: The Transport Layer

The transport layer provides a standard interface between the communications network and the higher layers. To do this it must be able to provide a match between the services demanded by the higher layers, and those available from the communications network. One of the features of the level 4 protocol is the provision of facilities to negotiate the class of service required before a connection is established. Five classes of transport protocol are defined by ISO. They are described below, under headings which indicate the types of network for which the transport protocol classes are appropriate.

Reliable Networks. Networks with a low rate of resets and disconnects, and a low rate of unsignalled errors. Most LANs come into this category.

> Class 0 (Simple). This is the basic class of transport protocol. It contains no error-recovery features, and depends instead on the inherent reliability of the network. This class is used where the quality of the network is acceptable for the application, and no multiplexing is required, i.e. there is a one-to-one relationship between application entities and communications connections. Class 2 (Multiplexing). This class provides the basic facilities of class 0, but with multiplexing, i.e. several applications entities may share the same connection through the transport layer to the communications network.

Reliable but Frequently Disrupted Networks. These are networks where the rate of unsignalled errors is low, but the rate of resets or disconnects is high. This would describe the sort of network which is operating over an inherently unreliable medium, but which uses its own protocols to ensure that the service provided to the higher layers, although it may be frequently interrupted, may be trusted to preserve the integrity of data. Such a description could apply to a WAN containing links which are subject to disruption, or a busy CSMA/CD LAN in which frequent collisions are occurring.

Class 1 (Error Recovery). The transport protocol contains a mechanism for recovery from disconnects and network-signalled errors. This class would be used where the network can be relied upon to signal errors, but their rate is too high for the application.

Class 3 (Error Recovery and Multiplexing). This class combines the error recovery facilities of class 1 with the multiplexing features of class 2.

Unreliable Networks. A network is unreliable if it has a high rate of unreported errors. An example would be a packet network in which corrupted packets are simply discarded, with no attempt on the part of the network protocol to recover from this situation, e.g. by requesting a re-transmission of the offending packet(s). In this case the transport layer must compensate for the lack of capability in the network layer.

Class 4 (Error Detection and Recovery). This class provides the facilities of class 3, but also has the capability to detect unsignalled errors and out-of sequence data.

Layer 5: The Session Layer

The session layer provides the facilities to manage and co-ordinate the dialogue between the connected systems. Different types of application have widely differing needs in this category, so the approach to the design of the session layer has been to include a 'toolkit' of facilities whose use may be negotiated at the time of establishing contact. The 'tools' in the 'kit' are known as functional units, and may include some or all of the following:

Kernel. The kernel is the fundamental functional unit of the session layer, and is used to manage the setting up and closing down of the connection.

Transmission Mode. The mode may be duplex or half-duplex. These terms refer to the type of connection established. A duplex connection, allows full two-way transmission, i.e. a system may transmit and receive simultaneously. A half-duplex connection allows two-way transmission, but only in one direction at a time.

Synchronisation. A number of different functional units are associated with the synchronisation of the dialogue. For example, re-synchronisation services allow the dialogue to be restarted from an agreed point following a loss of connection, without loss of data.

Layer 6: The Presentation Layer

The topic of data representation was covered in Chapter 2. What is significant from the interoperability viewpoint is that computer systems from different manufacturers often use different ways of representing information. If they are to interoperate successfully, agreement must be reached on a common representation standard. The OSI term for the common rules for data representation is the 'transfer syntax'. At the beginning of the connection, and if needs should change during the connection, the presentation layer provides the means for the systems to describe to each other the sort of data which is to be exchanged, and to agree a common form of representation. A special language called the abstract syntax notation one (ASN.1) has been defined for the process of describing the data structures to be exchanged. It must be noted that the level of representation dealt with by the presentation layer is that of mapping bit patterns to higher-level symbols, such as alphanumeric characters. It is not concerned with the meaning of the symbols in application terms, that is, the way in which combinations of characters are used to represent entities in the 'real world'. To reinforce this point with an example: agreement will be reached at the presentation layer on which patterns of bits will be used to represent which letters of the alphabet, e.g. 'T', 'A', 'N', 'K', but there will be no association at this stage between those letters and the name of a class of armoured vehicle.

Layer 7: The Application Layer

The OSI model describes a means for achieving interconnection between unlike systems in order that they may co-operate in the execution of some set of functions or applications, on behalf of their users. The model does not describe the functions themselves, but in layer 7 provides an interface between the communications capabilities provided by the lower layers, and the applications which use them. The standards developed for this layer describe the services provided, and the protocols used by what are termed application service elements. These may be regarded as functional building blocks, which may be used flexibly to provide the required services. There is a set of common application service elements, and some application service elements which are specific to particular applications, such as:

FILE TRANSFER ACCESS AND MANAGEMENT (FTAM)

FTAM standards support remote access to files, transfer of files between systems and other aspects of remote file manipulation.

JOB TRANSFER AND MANIPULATION (JTM)

JTM standards are specified for distributed processing. Under these standards, jobs may be initiated on remote systems, with results either passed back to the initiating system, or sent to a third system. Jobs may call upon files held by other systems. This provides the basis for flexible resource sharing, across a community of systems whose extent is limited only by that of the communications network to which they are connected.

VIRTUAL TERMINAL (VT)

The VT standards allow a terminal from one system to access a remote system. The initial standard is for character mode (teletype) terminals only, but will be extended to cover block mode terminals in due course.

ELECTRONIC MAIL

Electronic mail and message handling (EMMHS) is probably the fastest growing and most important OSI application area. Products conforming to the CCITT X.400 series of standards for EMMHS are now becoming available. These standards allow for the transfer of blocks of data between subscribing systems. Initially, the blocks will be interpreted only as text files, but the standards will soon be available to transfer blocks of bits capable of any desired interpretation, such as text, graphics, scanned images or even digitised voice. The EMMHS may interface directly with human users, in which role it is already taking the place of the Telex and other similar text message handling systems, and will soon provide an alternative to facsimile transmission (fax) for the transmission of images. It may also interface automatically with other applications running on the host computer, thereby providing the basis of a resource-sharing facility. The potential flexibility of the services to be provided under the X.400 heading is enormous. It is expected that the X.400 series of standards will become part of the emerging ISO message orientated text interchange system (MOTIS).

Other OSI Features

The ISO is concerned with a number of activities in support of the basic reference model described above, such as:

Naming and Addressing.   This is concerned with the development of ISO standards for the naming of applications (regardless of their location) and the identification of their location. Such information will be accessible through directory services.

Security.   Under this heading such aspects as access control, authentication and data encryption are being addressed. Security is being addressed through the medium of the security addendum to the basic reference model (ISO 7498/2), which is returned to in the next chapter.

Management Framework.   A model for the management of OSI communications resources has been defined, as well as a set of standard management information services.

The Relevance of OSI to Battlefield CIS

Few would now doubt that OSI is the key to interoperability in the civil information system field. It has moved from a concept to a growing reality, with an ever-increasing list of tried and tested products in a relatively short time. In military information systems for use off the battlefield, which have traditionally tended to follow civil standards, OSI is already appearing. For battlefield systems the situation is not so straightforward, and there are some difficulties involved in the application of the OSI approach.

Communications Loading

The reader may already have formed the impression that OSI is a somewhat 'bureaucratic' approach to solving the problem of interoperability. There is a considerable amount of 'overhead' in the communications between systems in the form of elements of information which are present only to implement the different

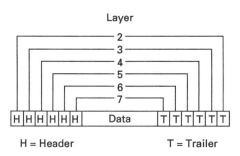

H = Header   T = Trailer

Fig. 9.4 'Envelope' Structure

levels of protocol. Figure 9.4 shows the concept of enclosing the operational information to be exchanged in a number of different protocol 'envelopes' or 'wrappers'. Down at the physical layer, this can represent a significant increase in the amount of data to be transmitted. For short transmissions, such as acknowledgements, the envelope data may outnumber the operational data several times over. OSI was designed primarily for the civil environment, where communications bearers of relatively unrestricted bandwidths are available, operating in a benign environment.

As we have seen in Chapter 6, battlefield communications systems can offer only limited bandwidths and must cope with a hostile electromagnetic environment, which will tend to push available bandwidths down even further. The very general approach of OSI tends to use the limited bandwidth available somewhat inefficiently. To get round this problem, but retain the interoperability advantages of OSI, the concept of minimum functionality has been introduced. As was seen in the detailed description of the layers of the reference model, at most of the layers there are alternative services and protocols, and facilities built-in for the negotiation of the class of service and protocol to be used. This feature allows automatic interoperation between systems without prior arrangement, or 'manual' choice of alternative standards, which is the OSI philosophy. To cut down the overheads involved in order to make more efficient use of battlefield communications, it is possible to define a subset of the standards which has classes of service pre-arranged. In this way, quite a lot of the protocol overhead can be avoided. The penalty is that some of the generality of the approach is lost, and agreements must be reached on the standards to be used.

Other Military Requirements

There are other features of OSI which may not meet the specific military needs. Probably the most significant of these is security, although this topic is now being addressed by ISO as an addendum to the basic reference model. The difficulty has been to find a means by which the ISO can be influenced to take account of military needs. The advantage in so doing is clear: if military needs can be satisfied by techniques, equipments and even whole systems which have been designed and built to widely accepted civil standards, there are considerable savings in cost to be made. The difficulty stems from the difference between the truly international nature of the ISO, and the more limited, political nature of military standardisation bodies such as NATO or ABCA. If a NATO standardisation panel should reach agreement on a particular aspect of OSI, it cannot as a body present that agreement for consideration by ISO. Instead, the national representatives at the NATO panel must return to their nations, and convince their own national ISO representatives to take the case to the ISO. It does not take much imagination to see how long-winded this procedure could be.

Interoperability in Practice

The Application of OSI

One could be forgiven at this stage for believing that all interoperability problems may be solved simply by procuring all future systems to the emerging civil OSI standards, suitably adapted to meet military needs where they differ from those of the civil world. To do so would only get us part of the way there; to return to the analogy of the businessmen: it would get us to the stage of being able to talk about the weather, but would not by itself achieve any operational purpose. To fulfil the operational purpose of interoperability, agreement must be reached on what information and services need to be exchanged between which systems, how the information is to be described, and how the services are to be performed. We are now at the stages of 'technical vocabulary' and 'culture' of our human analogy.

Stating the Interoperability Requirement

The rationale for interoperability, that of binding the CIS serving separate functional areas into an apparently homogeneous system, was set out at the beginning of this chapter. Having now described, through our study of the OSI approach, how the communications problems of interoperability can be solved, we now have to return to the starting point and look in more detail at what it is that needs to be communicated in order to achieve interoperability.

Figure 9.5 illustrates the situation. The information held by CIS serving distinct functional areas is shown as a set of interlocking shapes. It is that information represented by the areas of overlap which needs to be exchanged between the different systems. What this information is can only be determined by an analysis of the operational need; that is, it should follow from an examination of how the

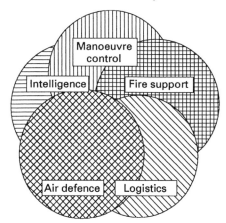

FIG. 9.5   The Interoperability Requirement

different battlefield functions are to be performed and therefore how they interact with other functions. Take the example quoted at the start of the chapter, of a fire support system interacting with a manoeuvre control system. To do its job, the fire support system needs to know where our own forces are located, and it will obtain this information from the manoeuvre control system. This required exchange must be looked at from a number of angles.

The Representation of the Information

The two systems must agree on a way of representing the type of information to be exchanged. In our example, this will call for a standard way of representing map grid references and unit identifications. This goes beyond the symbolic conventions which are covered by the presentation layer of OSI.

Control of the Exchange

Does the fire support system ask the manoeuvre control system for specific items of information as they are required, e.g. when a particular fire mission is to be performed, or does the manoeuvre control system supply to the fire control system those items of information in which it knows the other system has an interest without waiting for a specific request? These are issues which must be addressed during the design stage; their resolution will affect the ultimate shape of the system.

Timeliness

Information has a time value or perishability. The most extreme examples are probably to be found in the air-defence field. If a sensor with a range of 50 km situated some 25 km from a firing unit takes more than about 12 seconds to tell the firing unit that an enemy aircraft flying at 650 km/h is coming its way, it might as well not bother. The information would be 'history' by the time it arrived at the firing unit. The need for timely delivery places a demand on the communications system, but if such delivery is to occur across an interface or interfaces between two or more co-operating systems, it places a demand on the interoperability mechanism.

SECURITY

If systems which are required to interoperate contain information which is at different levels of security classification, the design of the interoperability mechanism is made considerably more difficult. Safeguards are needed to restrict the distribution of information to those parts of the system entitled to receive it. This inevitably imposes an overhead, since processing power and time must be devoted to the task of checking the security classification of information against the entitlement of elements of the system to receive it.

INTEGRITY

Given a suitably designed communications network, that is, one with adequate error detection and/or correction mechanisms, it may be taken for granted that information will be distributed between systems without corruption. There is a higher level aspect of integrity to take account of which was touched on in Chapter 4. This is the consideration of the validity of information received from sources external to the immediate system. Information received, whilst not corrupted in any way, may be out of date, or simply wrong. Care must be taken in the design of a system to ensure that the integrity of the information held by the system is not compromised by the acceptance of information of doubtful validity from external sources.

Summary

This chapter has addressed the need for interoperability between CIS serving different functional areas within the same army, and between the same functional areas of armies of allied nations, in order to effect co-operation on the battlefield. The ISO 7-layer OSI model has been described, but its limitations as the basis of interoperability between battlefield systems have been recognised. Finally, the need to address above the information transfer mechanisms provided by the OSI approach has been outlined.

In conclusion, the following approach to the design of interfaces between CIS is put forward:

1. *Establish the operational requirement.* What is to be achieved by the interface? What is the tactical scenario within which the interface will operate? These are questions to be answered by the operational staff.

2. *Establish the information exchange requirement.* What information needs to be exchanged in order to achieve the operational requirement established above? How is the information to be represented? What are the requirements for timeliness, and for security? Where should the interface(s) be located, and how does their location affect information flow within the system as a whole?

3. *Design the information-exchange mechanism.*   Based on the description of the services required established above, an information exchange mechanism between the interoperating CIS can be defined. This will include details at all the layers of the 7-layer model, down to and including the communications bearer to be used. Where they exist, standard protocols and exchange mechanisms will be specified.

4. *Devise procedures for the use of the interface.*   It is highly unlikely that the interface designed at step 3 will fully satisfy the requirements identified and derived in steps 1 and 2. Many factors, technical, procedural and financial, will combine to make the solution less than ideal. Operating procedures will be required which minimise these shortcomings.

10.

Security

Introduction

Many of the chapters so far have made reference to the need for security in its various forms. Chapter 6 covered the topic of communications security and encryption of data in some detail, and mention was made of radiation security in Chapter 7. Chapter 8 touched on the topic of computer security, and, in the context of interoperability, the subject was mentioned again in Chapter 9. The sum of all of these passing references is not enough to do justice to this important subject. As we shall see, it is the nature of CIS that has raised the importance of security, and until some of the security problems have been solved, our aspiration for widespread, integrated CIS will not be realised.

To see why this should be so, we shall look first at one aspect of security, that is the protection of information against disclosure to those who are not entitled or authorised to have it. Since the dawn of conflict commanders have striven to keep from the enemy information which could be of value to him. This means not only plans, intentions and capabilities, but also weaknesses and vulnerabilities. Some fundamental principles have been applied over the years. The most obvious of these is the 'need to know' principle, on which information is made accessible only to those who need to use it in the performance of the task. Physical security is another obvious requirement; when information is not in use it should be locked away beyond the reach of unauthorised persons. Communications security is also an ancient objective. If one has to expose secret information to the chance of interception, whether by radio eavesdropping or through the ambushing of a horseback messenger, it would be wise to send the message in an enciphered form. Thus the security 'envelope' may be described as a barrier of containment around the minimum number of authorised personnel. Until the introduction of CIS, this type of procedural control was adequate. Its effectiveness depended upon the rigour with which it was applied; the more 'secret' your secrets, the smaller is the population with whom they are shared, and the stronger the locks behind which they are protected.

In CIS there is a major conflict between the design concept of widespread distribution and interconnection, and the demands of security. In the last chapter the open systems interconnection (OSI) approach was described; the very term is at odds with the concept of 'need to know' and containment just introduced. Wide interconnection of different systems is necessary, but if they have different security requirements, their interaction must be strictly controlled.

There is another dimension to the problem of security in CIS. No longer can the concern of security be confined to the protection of the system when in operational use. An attack can be mounted at almost any stage in the system's life cycle. The security procedures are a feature of the system's software, which will almost invariably be written by civilian contractors who may not be subject to the same degree of security control as the uniformed personnel who will use the system in the field. Rather like the sabotage of major civil engineering works through the use of sub-standard materials, the deliberate interference with software during its development can sow the seeds of future disaster.

Definitions

The field of security has a jargon all of its own, and it is a necessary aid to the clarity of what follows to define the specific meanings of some of the terms used.

Security

First of all, the term security itself must be defined: this is the protection of the information system from deliberate actions which would lead to unauthorised disclosure, modification or destruction/loss of data, or the denial of the system's services to its users.

Note that we are concerned here with deliberate actions, that is, actions by persons with malicious intent. Some wider definitions of the term embrace accidental actions which would lead to the undesirable effects listed in our definition, but we have specifically excluded these.

Threat

A threat is a potentially hostile action against the system.

Vulnerability

A vulnerability is a weak point in the system which could be exploited, causing its data and/or services to be compromised or degraded.

Risk

The risk is the quantified assessment of the likely damage which would occur if a threat were to materialise and exploit one or more of the system's vulnerabilities. Hence we see that threat, vulnerability and risk are related:

$$THREAT + VULNERABILITY = RISK$$

Some would argue that the "+" sign should be an "×", or multiplication sign, but we are not trying to state the case with mathematical rigour.

The Scope of Security

Since this book is concerned with computer and communications systems, we would propose to concentrate in this chapter on the specialist, technical aspects of security as they affect that type of system. We cannot do so in isolation, however, because the security of electronic information systems relies on a combination of measures, most of which are as appropriate to the security of paper-based information systems as they are to the computer-based variety. Hence we cannot proceed with an account of the specialist, technical measures without putting them into their full context.

Physical Security

Physical security deals with the traditional containment approach whereby that which is to be protected is put into an environment, access to which is confined to authorised personnel. The environment can be as large as a whole group of buildings, say those comprising a research establishment, or a manufacturer's premises, or the group of vehicles comprising a field headquarters. It could be a single building or vehicle, or it could be as small as a single safe used to store magnetic recording-media holding classified information. This is not the place to detail the wide variety of means which can be used to achieve physical control of access, but it would be worth mentioning one important principle, because the same principle is relevant to certain aspects of computer security. The principle is that of the time-value of security controls. No single, physical security device or means is intended to provide protection indefinitely. Even the best safe will be cracked by someone who is given unlimited and undisturbed access to it and the freedom to use any appropriate means of gaining entry to it. Thus it is usual to combine physical protection with surveillance; if a safe which is believed to be uncrackable in less than 4 hours' undisturbed work on the part of the cracksman is in a room which is visited every 3 hours by a watchman, all is theoretically well. Security measures are applied in combination, and care must be taken to ensure that the combinations hold good under all possible circumstances.

Personnel Security

Personnel security is the most important single aspect of security. In the end, no matter how good the physical and technical measures, it is necessary to trust people. Elaborate procedures exist within government organisations for establishing the trustworthiness of individuals. Such vetting procedures are necessary for the initial and periodic screening of personnel, but are not intended to replace the responsibilities of managers to ensure that their staff are properly supervised and motivated, and to detect signs of disaffection at the earliest stage. Personnel security is relevant and important throughout the lifecycle of a system, from its inception to the time it eventually becomes obsolete, because people are always involved.

Procedural Security

Within large organisations, especially government organisations, many aspects of security depend upon the application of rules and set procedures. At the heart of most security rules is a system for the classification of information according to its degree of secrecy, e.g. 'confidential', 'secret', or 'top secret'. Rules exist for how information in paper form at the various levels of classification should be handled. Access lists are normally drawn up saying who within the organisation is entitled to see which levels of classification. It is common to find restrictions on access beyond the simple security classifications being imposed through the use of special caveats and other security markings. The rules will also lay down procedures for the recording or registration of classified material, so that the organisation knows exactly what information it owns at what levels of classification, knows where it is at any given moment, and also knows where it has been in the past. This last information is of use should the need arise to investigate suspected security compromises. This aspect of security presents the opportunity to introduce two more important principles which are also relevant to computer security. First, security must be manageable. If the prescribed security procedures are over-elaborate and time-consuming in their application, they will obviously reduce the time available for productive work. In the worst case, people may be tempted to take short-cuts which may negate the security value altogether. The amount of effort or overhead involved in the application of security measures must be in proportion to the risk, and the strongest measures must therefore be reserved for the highest risks. Over-classification is to be avoided, if the proportion of information requiring the highest security protection is to be kept to the minimum. The second of these principles is that we are trying to protect the system particularly against undetected access. If an enemy agent manages to break into the headquarters, blow open a safe and get out with files containing the general deployment plan, the resulting situation will be inconvenient to say the least, but not necessarily disastrous. If we know that the other side knows our plans, they can be changed. It is the covert attack which poses the most serious threat.

Radiation Security

The concept of radiation security (the phenomenon known as TEMPEST) was introduced in Chapter 7. It represents a potential, unseen breach through even the strongest physical security by the transmission beyond the secure perimeter of information-bearing signals. The transmission may be via free-space radiation, or via conductors which penetrate the perimeter. The factors which cause unwanted emissions, and the technical countermeasures were described in Chapter 7. In the context of overall security, such TEMPEST precautions at the equipment level are combined with physical protective measures. The wider the three-dimensional perimeter within which it is possible to guarantee that no unauthorised personnel could approach undetected, the less stringent the need for protection at the equipment and installation level.

Communications Security (COMSEC)

COMSEC has already been introduced in the chapter on communications. There is an obvious need to afford protection to information when it is in transit through the outside world, where it is not possible to guarantee that it will not fall into unauthorised hands. The difference between link-by-link encryption and end-to-end encryption across a network of many links has been identified, and is of great significance to the security of computer-based information systems. Link encryption is a relatively straightforward process, normally involving the encryption of the entire traffic stream between the two ends of the link. The traffic may be a single digital channel, or many such channels multiplexed together into a composite bit stream. End-to-end encryption needs to be much more selective; for example, in a packet-switched system, only the contents of the packet must be encrypted and not the information in the 'envelope' surrounding the packet, because this information is used by intermediate switches in the network to determine the routing of the packet. The control of cryptographic keys between the two ends of a link is a simple enough task compared with that of key management between end users who may wish to be interconnected in an arbitrary manner. We shall find it difficult, as we proceed, to make as clear a distinction between computer security and COMSEC as is possible between it and the other forms of security summarised above.

The Balance of Trust

All the aspects of security described above rely ultimately on trust; trust that the security measures, whether they are based on machines or people, will work properly and provide an adequate degree of protection. In computer security we are trying to shift the emphasis of our trust away from people towards machines, that is, computer hardware and software. This principle is illustrated in Figure 10.1.

As the security functionality of a system increases, so does the relative amount of trust which must be placed on the machine rather than the man. The shape of the final part of the curve is significant, since it implies that there is a residual level of trust which must continue forever to be placed on the man; no matter how comprehensive the security features of a computer system, it will still be necessary to trust people to do their jobs correctly.

The Key Risks

Before going on to examine the techniques of computer security, we shall restate the key risks against which the information system is to be protected.

Unauthorised Access to Information

The obvious risk under this heading is unauthorised 'read' access, through which information is divulged to those who are outside the 'need to know' category. We must also consider unauthorised 'write' access, through which the information

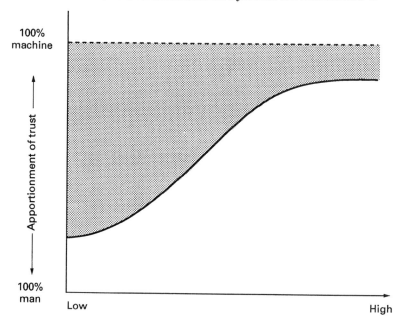

FIG. 10.1   The Balance of Trust

could be corrupted. Such corruption could take an obvious or destructive form, in that the information is overwritten by 'garbage', or it could take a more subtle, deceptive form in which entries are falsified in a plausible manner which may be difficult to detect until serious damage has been done to the system (or to the system's credibility, which comes to the same thing in the end). An example of this type of risk in the commercial world is the fraudulent attack, in which information is changed in order to bring some financial benefit to the attacker.

Loss of Information

Information is a resource which has a finite value to the organisation which owns it, and therefore any loss of information through interference with the system carries a measurable penalty. If adequate back-up precautions have been taken such a loss is unlikely to be total, but the time lost in restoring the information from back-up and the re-entry of lost data will impose a degree of inconvenience and may deny the services of the system to its users for a period of time.

Denial of Service

Once an organisation comes to rely upon its computer-based information system to support its vital activities, denial of the services of that system obviously has serious consequences. There is a close parallel between the forms of risk, or attack on the information system and those which can be mounted on a communications system, as described in Chapter 6 under the heading of electronic warfare (EW).

In EW the enemy has the choice of either trying to extract information from signals, or to jam them and cause disruption of the friendly command and control processes. The same applies to the computer system, but the methods he may use to disrupt it may be much more subtle than radio jamming, and may be applied at very long range, in time as well as space.

A Computer Security Model

The simple diagram of a computer system in Figure 10.2 shows the system as being encapsulated within a perimeter. Inside the perimeter reside the infor-

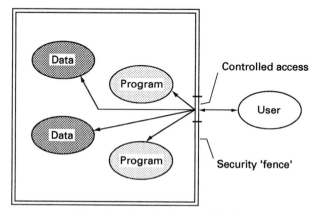

FIG. 10.2   Simple Security Model

mation held by the system and the programs which implement the processes to be performed. Outside the perimeter are the system's users. All these three elements, information, processes and users, are entities known to the system. The security model will define rules for the way in which those entities are allowed to relate to one another. We can break down the types of control required into two categories: access control and distribution control.

Access Control

Access control is concerned with the control of access by users through the system's perimeter to the entities within it. In most of the literature on computer security, the entities are distinguished as either 'subjects', i.e. active entities which wish to do things to other entities, or 'objects', i.e. passive entities which have things done to them. Human users are obviously classed as subjects. A program may be an object (e.g. when a subject such as a human user wishes to execute it), or it may be a subject (e.g. when it wishes to access data during the course of its execution). The purpose of access control is to convince the system that the subject is valid and authorised, and the usual way of doing so in the case of human users is by using a password. A password is some combination of symbols which is known only to the user and to the system. It is normally associated with a name by which the system knows the user. So, a user wishing to gain access to a system will first have to tell the system who he is, and then, if he is recognised as a user, to enter a password. The password is rather like the lock on a physical security device; it is not an absolute guarantee of security, but a means of guaranteeing security for a period of time. Clearly the more symbols in the password the more difficult will it be for an intruder to 'crack' it by exhaustive search, but on the other hand it will be more difficult for the user to remember it without writing it down somewhere, which could obviously lead to a security breach. The degree of pass-word protection must be commensurate with the security level of the system. It is worth noting a few key facts about passwords:

▶ Passwords are never 'echoed' on to the screen when entered by the user to prevent their interception by someone looking over the user's shoulder.

▶ Passwords are normally stored in the system in an encrypted form, so that someone who succeeds in breaking into the password file cannot retrieve all the passwords and hence gain unrestricted access to the sys-tem. The encryption process is carried out by what is known as 'one-way algorithm', i.e. a series of transformations carried out on the password which would require a great deal of time and computational power to reverse (again, time and power which are commensurate with the security level of the system). If one imagines the password to be on the end of one of the branches of a large, bushy tree, it is easy to find one's way to the trunk. Starting at the trunk and going the other way, the location of any individual twig is a much more difficult process. Each time the password is entered the encryption process is performed on it and the result is compared with the stored, encrypted password.

▶ Passwords may be generated by the system and offered to the user for selection, or they may be invented by the user. Some systems have a facility for generating passwords which are pronounceable combinations of letters, i.e. nonsense words, which are relatively easy to remember but still difficult to guess or to obtain by exhaustive search.

▶ Passwords are normally valid for a set period of time only. The time period is determined by the system administrator, and will once again be a compromise between the extra security afforded by frequent password changes and the burden on the user of having to remember too many random combinations of characters.

▶ Sometimes, especially in the case of remote access, it may be necessary for the user to ask the system to authenticate itself. A remote user needs reassurance that he is connected to a legitimate recipient for any classified information which he may enter during his session.

▶ Most systems make some provision for a remote terminal to be automatic-ally 'logged-out' after some pre-set period of inactivity, so that, if a user should leave his terminal logged-in and unattended, the period of time dur-ing which it is vulnerable to use by an unauthorised person is limited.

▶ The password may be used in conjunction with some other form of user authentication, such as an electronic badge or card reader, or some physio-logical identification system, such as a voice-print analyser, a finger-print recogniser or a retina scanner. A device which has appeared recently uses the challenge-and-reply authentication technique: the system challenges the user by displaying some sequence of characters on the screen which the user then enters into a hand-held device resembling a pocket calculator; this displays the reply to be entered by the user via the terminal keyboard. Challenge-and-reply pairs may be valid for a very short period of time only, which further increases the security value of the system.

Distribution Control

Once users have been authenticated by the use of a password or other means, they become a trusted subject within the system for as long as their connection remains valid. The distribution control aspect of the system's security lays down a set of rules governing which subjects may do what with which objects. Categories of access include: read only, read/write, write only, and execute, in the case of program files. Each user will be accorded certain rights of access to facilities within the system and within these categories. Likewise, processes within the system may be accorded rights of access to data and to other processes. Data files, and possibly individual records within files or even fields within records, may be labelled to indicate their security classification or sensitivity. The level down to which security markings may be applied and implemented is often referred to as the security 'granularity' of a system. Below a certain level, the 'grains' of information have little security value in their own right. For example, it would be meaningless to assign a security classification to a single bit or a single character. However, that bit or character within certain contexts could convey meanings which are very security sensitive.

Two basic rules governing the interaction of entities within the system from a security point of view are taken from what is known as the Bell–Lapadula security model, named after the authors of a paper on the subject published by the MITRE Corporation in the USA in 1976:

▶ *The simple security property.* A subject is allowed only read access to an object if the subject's security level is higher than or equal to that of the object.
▶ *The star property.* This property states that a subject is allowed write access to an object only if the security level of the object is higher than or equal to that of the subject. This would prevent a user with security level 'secret' from writing data to a file with security level 'confidential', which could then be legitimately read by a user or process with security level 'confidential', thus breaching the security rules.

Another way to describe the security rules of a system is in a matrix form, as shown in Figure 10.3. Here the allowable relationships between entities are shown in the cells of the matrix. There is a significant difference between this approach to security and the security-labelling approach described previously. In the matrix approach, sometimes called the access control list (ACL) approach, the rights of access of users and, by implication, the degrees of sensitivity of information are embodied in the matrix. The matrix will itself be a file on the computer, which may or may not be organised on the storage medium as an actual matrix or two-

Objects / Subjects	A	B	C	D	E	F	G	H
A	R, W	R, W, E		R	R, W	R		R, W
B	R, W	R, W, E		R, W	R, W		R, W	E
C	R	E	R	R	R	E	R	R
D			R, W	R, W	R, W	E		R
E	R	E	R	R	R	E	R	R
F		E	R	R				
G	R, W	E	R	R, W	R	E	R, W	R
H	R, W	E	R	R				

R = Read

W = Write (including over-write, or modify, often treated as a separate category.)

E = Execute

FIG. 10.3   Security Rule Matrix

dimensional array. Attempted accesses must be referred by the security mechanism to the access matrix. In the example in Figure 10.2, for instance, if user A requested write access to file F, the system would tell him that access was not allowed, since the matrix only allows user A read access to file F. The drawback to this technique is that the data file itself does not necessarily carry any security markings. If the file were to be exported to another system, it would be entirely a matter for procedural control to ensure that the file was given the same degree of protection as it was afforded by the access matrix in the original system. In the labelling approach all files and in some cases entities below the file level, such as records or fields, may be labelled with a security level. Objects in the system are all accorded rights of access at defined security levels, and the security control mechanism is essentially one of comparing the levels of 'subject' and 'object' to determine whether or not the requested access obeys the two principles defined above. No actual access matrix exists, although it is still possible to think of the relationship between subjects and objects within the system in general in these terms. Any data which are exported from the system carry their security markings, so that they may be properly handled by other systems which follow the same security procedures.

The two approaches are not mutually exclusive; the security labelling technique may be used to enforce the security rules of the organisation, whilst the matrix approach may be applied by the system administrator to keep separate the different users and groups of users on a large, multi-user system.

The type of system outlined above, which holds information at different security levels and permits access by users with different security clearances yet prevents users from gaining information for which they are not authorised, is described as being multilevel secure. There is a much simpler approach to distribution control, in which the system treats all information as being at the same security level. This means that all the information in the system must be accorded the protection appropriate to the highest security level of any information held by the system. Access control is still required, but is simplified by having only one class of authorised user. The term 'system high' has been coined to describe this approach, which has a number of serious drawbacks. First, it positively encourages over-classification. In a system which has been classified as, say, 'System high SECRET', quite a high proportion of the individual items of data will have a real security level which is lower than SECRET. However, they must be protected as if they were SECRET. Any magnetic recording medium which is used on the system automatically attracts the SECRET classification, which must remain forever, until the disc, tape, etc. is destroyed. Serious problems arise if it should be required to interconnect two systems which have different 'system high' levels. The absurd situation could arise where System A, which has a lower level than System B, could pass an item of data to System B, but would not be allowed to take that item of data back, since it would then carry the higher classification. The 'system high' approach has been used in practice only because, in the absence of acceptable multilevel security techniques, it was the only way to provide an adequate measure of protection.

A More Complex Model

The model introduced above treats the computer system as a collection of data and program entities, to which users gain access through the secure perimeter via access control mechanisms. It is essentially a model of a single, monolithic, albeit multi-user and multi-tasking, computer system. The security controls are assumed to be exercised by one 'authority' within the system, normally the operating-system software. This simple model can seldom be applied directly to CIS, which are far more likely to consist of many computer systems connected together by a communications network. A model is therefore needed which can describe the security mechanisms of a networked, multi-computer system. There are two ways to look at this. In the first, one can simply expand the secure perimeter to encompass all the elements of the system, with users in the outside world being granted access via control mechanisms as before. This is shown in Figure 10.4.

The model of Figure 10.4 suffers from a lack of generality; it assumes that the only entities which need to be vetted are users. The individual computer systems within the network appear to trust one another implicity. Whilst such a system is conceivable, a more general model is that of Figure 10.5. This makes no assumptions about the trustworthiness of the network components; to each computer in the system all the other computers, and the users lie in the 'outside world'. They must be vetted by the access-control mechanism before being allowed access. Figure 10.5 is essentially the simple model of Figure 10.2 repeated once for every computer installation in the network. Each computer treats connections to other computers in just the same way as they treat users; they must both be recognised and authenticated before being granted access.

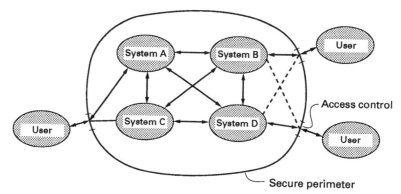

FIG. 10.4   Network Security Model: 1

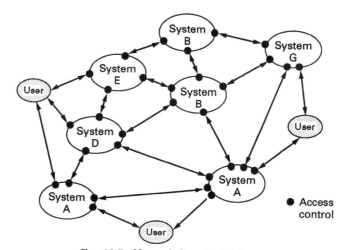

FIG. 10.5   Network Security Model: 2

The Security Models Applied to Battlefield CIS

It will be an advantage once again to start from the simplest system configuration and work up to the more complicated (and more realistic) systems. We shall start therefore by looking at a computer installation serving users within a field head-quarters, for example at divisional level. We shall at first ignore its communications with other installations at other headquarters, without which it cannot really be considered to be CIS but merely some sort of tactical office automation system. Figure 10.6 illustrates the divisional headquarters system.

As introduced at the start of this chapter, we must look at the computer security aspects of the system along with all the other protective measures. When we do so, we see that the system is relatively well protected, compared with a system of similar scope in a commercial office, or even an exactly similar system serving the same headquarters in its barracks. Physical security is tight; the system's components are all housed in vehicle containers (some of which are armoured), which are manned round the clock. The vehicles are located within a secure perimeter. Personnel security is even tighter; there are relatively few users, all of

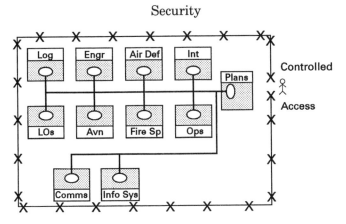

FIG. 10.6 Divisional Headquarters

whom are known to one another, so the chances of an unauthorised person gaining access to one of the system's terminals are small. In a system as simple as this there is probably little to lose from adopting a system high approach to security.

Unfortunately, the situation is not so straightforward, even for the most simple system. What we see in Figure 10.6 is a snapshot of the system in operation in its operational environment. As we have seen, in this environment a high level of security protection is relatively easy to provide. If we were to look at the system throughout its lifecycle, we would see a very different picture. Extending the security envelope to protect the system during the development of its software, during the predeployment preparation of its database, and during the perform- ance of software support tasks to correct faults or incorporate modifications, imposes a far higher degree of difficulty than the protection of the operational system. It is worth looking at these phases in some detail, reminding ourselves as we do that the key risks against which we are protecting the system are the unauthorised access to information and the denial of services.

Protection During Development

There are two aspects to consider here. First, it is obvious that during the development phase of the project the security features which will protect it once in service are developed, along with the things the system must do to perform its primary function. It goes without saying that these security features must be well specified, designed and executed, and we shall be looking later at some of the ways of ensuring that this is so. Second, there is a need to ensure that all the software of the system, not only the directly security-related elements, performs only those tasks which it is designed to do, and does not contain any deliberately created features which may cause it to malfunction once it is deployed operationally. Some of the ways in which software may be attacked during development are described below.

TROJAN HORSES

Readers will no doubt remember the story of the great wooden horse of Troy, in which were hidden soldiers who crept out of the horse once darkness had fallen and unlocked the gates of the city from the inside. A software 'Trojan horse' does exactly that. It is a section of program code which has some outwardly innocent function to perform, but which contains instructions which can bypass the system's security features and 'let in' an unauthorised user.

SLEEPERS

A 'sleeper' is some hidden section of code which, under normal operating conditions, performs no function at all, i.e. it resides somewhere in the computer's memory and is not executed. On receipt of some outside stimulus the sleeper is 'woken up', i.e. executed, normally causing some form of disruption to the system. The stimulus may be deliberate, that is, a set of conditions which are input specifically to activate the sleeper, or it may be triggered by some random occurrence, such as the appearance of a particular data value in some variable within the program. Several examples of sleepers which have been detected in recent years used specific dates as the trigger.

VIRUSES

The software virus is a relatively recent phenomenon. It is essentially a form of sleeper, with the vital difference that it possesses the ability to 'reproduce' itself. The typical software virus is a section of code which resides somewhere in the bootstrap area of a PC program floppy disc. When the disc is inserted into a machine and 'booted up', the virus transfers itself into main memory. Once there, it performs two jobs. One is to copy itself on to any other disc that is inserted into the machine, thus ensuring its 'survival' by propagation. The other is to count itself down to destruction. The virus code contains a counter which counts the number of times it is called upon to reproduce itself. Once this reaches a preset limit, the virus sets off a process which overwrites all the mass store on-line to the machine. Theories about the origins of viruses differ (just as they do over their biological counterparts). One 'strain' is believed to have been designed by students at an American university as a joke; so prevalent was the swapping of unlicenced copies of software at that establishment that the virus spread at an enormous rate, doing a staggering amount of damage in the process. Another virus is believed to have been created by professional software developers as a means of discouraging the 'promiscuous' exchange of software in contravention of the copyright laws.

The prevention of these forms of attack is no easy matter. Clearly, the software developer must rely heavily upon traditional means of security, especially personnel security, but this alone cannot provide the answer. The manual checking of code to ensure that it contains nothing untoward is simply not feasible. The software for a system of realistic size when output in printed form would be a stack several feet high. People with a similar level of skill to those who wrote the programs would be needed to do the checking, and such people are in short supply.

Automated code analysis techniques offer some hope. A code analyser is designed to work on a section of program code and produce a description of the function of that code. It should be able to detect sleepers as areas of code which have no apparent function or whose function does not appear to have anything to do with the specified task of the program module. The most promising route is the use of formal methods for the high-level specification of system function, from which the program code is derived, and against which it is possible to check the code to ensure that it does only what was specified and nothing else.

Protection Post-Development

Having produced software which has been checked using the best methods available and is as 'correct' as it is practicable to make it, the system authorities must then exercise strict control to ensure that it stays correct. For example, it would be most unusual for the military users of a battlefield CIS to have any means of altering software in the operational environment. The subject of system support is raised in the next chapter, but it is enough here to say that the task of changing software will be confined to a support organisation and carried out in an environment where it is possible to exercise full control over the process, and over the distribution of new issues of software.

In-Barracks Use of the System

If the system is to be of use once deployed for war or for exercises, it must be prepared in barracks. The database must be maintained between periods of deployment, so that the system is ready for deployment at any time. The current trend towards the integration of so-called general purpose CIS used in barracks with those systems used in the field will help in this respect, but contains dangers from a security point of view. We have already seen how self-contained a purely tactical, battlefield system can be. As soon as it is used in barracks, or connected to static systems, the risks that this containment will be breached increase enormously. The environment is inherently less secure, because physical and personnel security levels are invariably lower. The use of standard, commercial software, both operating systems and applications, whilst it certainly can reduce costs and enhance the integration of systems, can cause severe vulnerabilities if there is any possibility of users introducing 'unvetted' software to the system. Procedural controls could, of course, be applied, that is, rules forbidding the use of unauthorised software on the system, but the potential damage which could be caused by the introduction of just one disc containing a virus should persuade any responsible system authority that such controls can never be adequate by themselves.

Once we apply the more complex model of Figure 10.6 to the battlefield CIS, we see that we can no longer rely upon the simplicity and tight physical control of the battlefield environment to provide a significant proportion of our security protection. Interoperation across the battlefield, between functional areas, and up and down the chain of command produces a complex system which demands a high degree of in-built security protection. The system high approach is no longer adequate, since across the totality of the system created by the wide interconnection and interoperation there is bound to be a great number of different 'need-to-know' categories as well as the formal levels of security.

Practical Approaches to Computer Security

The DoD Orange Book

In 1983 the American Department of Defense published its book *Trusted Computer System Evaluation Criteria* which has become universally known as the *Orange Book*. This was a most significant development in the computer security field, and the criteria of the *Orange Book* have become more or less *de facto* industry standards for secure computer systems. The *Orange Book* sets out a number of different categories of secure computer system from D (the least secure) to A (the most secure). The categories A to C are further subdivided into classes, e.g. B1 and B2, where the higher the number, the higher the security protection of the system. The categories and classes are listed and described later; it would be useful first to examine the rationale on which they are based.

Fundamental Requirements of a Secure Computer System

The *Orange Book* identifies and describes six fundamental requirements:

Security Policy

The security features of the system must be based on, and be an implementation of the security policy of the organisation. In the case of an official or government organisation, such as a military establishment, such a policy is likely to have some legal backing, that is, it will be based on the laws governing the handling of classified information. A distinction is made between mandatory security policy, and discretionary security policy. The former is based on a comparison of the access rights of individuals against the security classification of the material held by the system, and reflects the 'laws, regulations and general policies from which it is derived.' Discretionary security policy control access by individuals on a 'need to know' basis.

Security Marking

Information to be held by the system must carry markings to indicate its security level. As previously indicated, such markings could apply at the file level, or below it at the record and the field level. The different levels of classification will be defined in the security policy.

Identification

Individual subjects must be both identified and authenticated by the system so that their actions are accountable. In this context a 'subject' is a process within the system which has a requirement to access 'objects' within the system. One class of subjects will be the processes which relate directly to human users of the system, but such a direct relationship does not necessarily exist for all subjects.

ACCOUNTABILITY

The system must keep a record of transactions so that it is possible to determine which users have accessed which information. This is required so that suspected security breaches may be investigated, and has a strong parallel with the manual accounting procedures used to control the distribution of classified paper documents.

ASSURANCE

The mechanisms in the computer system which implement the features listed above must be capable of independent evaluation to provide assurance that they can provide an adequate level of protection. One would normally expect the features to be embedded in the hardware or in the operating system software. This requirement calls for the features to be identified as such in system document-ation, and to be separable from other functions of the hardware or the operating system.

CONTINUOUS PROTECTION

There is a requirement for the mechanisms which implement the security policy to be protected against unauthorised changes, so that the level of protection which they afford can be guaranteed throughout the lifetime of the system. This is particularly important during the performance of system support tasks, to correct faults or incorporate modifications. Care must be taken to ensure that such changes do not threaten the integrity of the security mechanisms, and after the performance of such tasks it will be necessary to revalidate the system to the original level of assurance.

The Divisions

The divisions and classes are described in ascending order of security protection. A principle followed is that each higher division or class contains all the features of the lower classes, as well as additional features; in other words, the security features of the ascending classes are applied in a cumulative manner. The term trusted computing base (TCB) is used to describe 'the totality of the protection mechanisms within the computer system', that is, all the hardware, firmware and software used to implement and enforce the security policy. It is the TCB which is the subject of evaluation against the criteria laid down in the *Orange Book*.

DIVISION D: MINIMAL PROTECTION

This is the lowest division, and contains only one class, which applies to systems which have been evaluated and have failed to meet the criteria for any higher division. Note that it applies only to systems which have been evaluated.

DIVISION C: DISCRETIONARY PROTECTION

Systems in this division are designed to provide need-to-know protection and accountability, through audit. There are two classes, CI and C2.

> Class CI. The TCB of a CI system provides the means for separating users and data, i.e. it allows users to create areas of data which may be private to the individual user or to groups of users. The information within a CI system will normally be at one security level (i.e. system high).
>
> Class C2. The C2 Class builds on to the discretionary protection afforded by CI by strengthening access control, e.g. through the use of passwords, and provides audit facilities for security accounting purposes.

DIVISION B: MANDATORY PROTECTION

The concept of security labelling and the enforcement of mandatory security rules, i.e. those relating to the formal security classification of information and the clearance of users, is introduced within this division. There are three classes: BI, B2 and B3.

> Class BI: Labelled Security Protection. Following the cumulative protection principle outlined above, systems in class BI contain all the features required by class C2. The significant addition is that of security labelling, and a mandatory requirement for all accesses to be controlled by the checking of the security label of the object against the security clearance of the subject. Information exported from the system must retain its security labels. This includes information output in man-readable form, e.g. on paper. Designers of a system put forward for evaluation at BI level must provide a description (which need not necessarily be a formal description) of the security policy on which the TCB design is based, and demonstrate that the TCB mechanisms comply with the policy.
>
> Class B2: Structured Protection. The key difference between B2 and BI is that the design of the TCB must be based on a formal model of the security policy. Authentication requirements are also strengthened. The designer must show that the TCB is tamperproof, cannot be by-passed, and is correctly implemented. An important functional requirement introduced at this level is the need to control covert channels. A covert channel is a communications channel which breaches the security protection of the system. These may be created within the storage media used by the system, for example, an area of disc may be used by two processes at different security levels, thereby

creating a means of communication between the processes which is outside the control of the TCB. Another form of covert channel is that created by the modulation of some aspect of the system's resources in a way which conveys information to an observer who is outside the system's security perimeter. For example, the running of a secure process may cause modifications in the response time of the system to other, non-secure users in such a way that they could extract information from the secure system. In the analysis of systems offered for B2 evaluation, covert channels must be identified and their information bandwidth assessed. If the bandwidth is of the order of that available to a legitimate terminal user, i.e. a few hundred bits per second, the covert channel would pose an unacceptable security threat to the system.

Class B3: This class requires that the TCB must satisfy the requirements of a reference monitor, i.e. it must control all accesses of subjects to objects, it must be tamperproof, and it must be small enough to be subjected to anlaysis and tests. Its complexity must be minimised, and it will contain only code which is essential to the implementation of the security policy. It has a higher requirement for discretionary (i.e. need-to-know) access control than B2, and a more demanding security audit requirement. The system designer is required to produce a descriptive top-level specification (DTLS) of the security policy, and to show informally that the design of the TCB is consistent with this specification.

DIVISION A: VERIFIED PROTECTION

There is no essential difference in functionality between systems at B3 level and those at AI. The difference is that the AI system must be shown by formal verification to be a true and correct implementation of the security policy. The assurance starts with a formal model of the security policy, which must be mathematically provable to be consistent with the security rules. On this model is based a formal top level specification (FTLS), which can be formally proved to be consistent with the model. Likewise, the actual design of the TCB must be formally proved to be consistent with the FTLS. Formal methods are also used for the analysis of covert channels. The very strictest configuration control procedures are called for to maintain the integrity of the system. It follows that the amount of time and effort, and therefore cost involved in the production and evaluation of a system to the division A is much higher than that required for B3.

The *Orange Book* had the advantage of being the first, and for a long time the only written guidance to manufacturers on computer security features. It has achieved wide recognition and acceptance, and many of the major manufacturers have invested effort in producing systems which have been designed to and ultimately accredited within a particular class of the *Orange Book*. The book does have a number of disadvantages, however. Some of its critics point out that as the required degree of assurance goes up through the classes from D to A, the functionality of the system also increases. There is an inherent contradiction in this situation since the higher the functionality, the higher the complexity and therefore the more difficult it is to reach a given level of assurance. In the security field, 'small and simple is beautiful'; the lower the level of functionality, the easier is it to reach a high level of assurance that the system will perform correctly.

A second criticism of the *Orange Book* is that it deals with single computers, and makes no provision for the situation where computers are interconnected in a network. As this is increasingly the situation most commonly encountered in practice, it is a serious drawback.

Network Security: the Raspberry Book

The deficiency noted above was recognised by the Department of Defense, and has been overcome to a large extent through the issuing of the *Raspberry Book*— The American National Computer Security Center's *Trusted Network Interpretation* of the *Orange Book*, published in 1987. The *Raspberry Book* recognises two views of a network, which are not unlike those taken in Figures 10.4 and 10.5 earlier. In the first view, the network is composed of a number of individual trusted, accredited computers. This is the general situation of Figure 10.5, where the network is a loose 'federation' of systems developed separately, and under separate management. Their second view of the network is more like Figure 10.4, in that the whole network is regarded as a trusted system, and accredited as such. This is only ever likely to be possible in a system under common management, with a much higher degree of control than the loose federation concept of Figure 10.5. The network has a single network trusted computing base (NTCB) which is partitioned amongst the components of the network. The NTCB enforces the network security policy on the network as a whole, by implementing the mandatory and discretionary access controls, and audit measures. The *Raspberry Book* sets out a number of classes of security protection for NTCBs which are aligned with the TCB classes of the *Orange Book*, i.e. C1, C2, etc. In particular, it gives rules governing the transfer of information at a given security classification between components of the system which may have different security levels. In so doing it is applying at network level the kinds of rule which the *Orange Book* laid down for the exchange of information between different entities within the same computer. It also introduces the concept of trusted communication paths between elements of the network.

Most of the *Raspberry Book* is devoted to the accredited network concept, i.e. the NTCB. It does, however, provide some guidance on the ways in which individual trusted systems may be interconnected so as to ensure that the mandatory security policies are not violated. Each component of this type of system is regarded as a device with which the other components may exchange information. Individual devices may be accredited to handle information at a single level or over a range of levels. The guidance is based on what is termed the interconnection rule, which says that any individual device in the network need only be aware of the security level of other devices to which it is directly connected. Over that direct connection information will only be transmitted if the security level of the receiving end is appropriate. Figure 10.7 illustrates a simple network with multilevel secure devices spanning different security levels, and shows the logical connections which are permitted between them. A problem associated with this approach is the

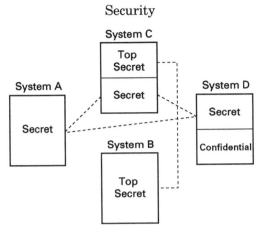

FIG. 10.7   The Cascade Problem

'cascade' effect. Consider devices C and D of Figure 10.7. C spans the levels 'secret' and 'top secret', whilst D covers 'confidential' and 'secret'. A user of C overcomes the security protection mechanism of that system and downgrades some 'top secret' information to 'secret'. He then causes this information to be sent over the link to D, and somehow overcomes the protection mechanism of D and downgrades the information to 'confidential'. Thus the potential damage which is caused by the compromise of C's security mechanism is magnified through the connection to the system at a lower level of security. There is a rule which can be applied to test whether the cascade problem exists between two systems, but in many cases where it does theoretically exist the security management may judge that it does not represent a serious risk and allow it to exist. The rule is that the levels of adjacent systems should either be disjoint, i.e. have no level in common, or they must be nested, i.e. the range of one is included within the other.

The Security Gateway Approach

Both of the approaches outlined in the *Raspberry Book* place the onus for implementing the security procedures on the component systems of the network. Another approach to interconnection of unlike systems is to use gateways between elements of the network, or possibly between communities which are operating at different security levels. This is illustrated in Figure 10.8. The advantage of this approach is that it confines the security measures to the gateways, which 'police' the traffic flowing between network elements, rather than have the procedures embedded within the systems themselves. The merit of this lies in it simplicity; only the gateway hardware and software need to be subjected to the full range of security scrutiny, and a high level of assurance can be achieved that these components do their job correctly. A security monitor is used in conjunction with the security gateways. Its main function is to keep a record of security activity in the form of a log or audit trail, which meets the requirement for accountability within the system.

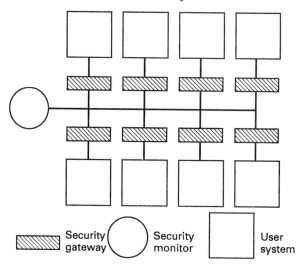

FIG. 10.8   Network with Security Gateways

Security and the ISO OSI 7-Layer Reference Model

The 7-layer model was described in some detail in Chapter 9. As we said in the introduction to this chapter, there seems to be a fundamental conflict between 'openness', as embodied in the OSI model, and security. Although it has to be admitted that the issue of security has come relatively late in the day to the OSI concept, the conflict is not as serious as it might at first sight appear. Openness, in the OSI sense, implies that the capability exists for systems to interoperate, if such a need exists to satisfy the operational/commercial goals of the system's owners. An OSI-compliant system is 'open' only to those other systems to which it is connected. It is admittedly not a simple matter to know exactly what other systems are connected in a large network, since every station in theory has the capability of establishing a logical connection to any other station. Consider the case of the network in Figure 10.7. System A may have a requirement to be connected to System B, and likewise System B to System C. However, System A may not need, and may positively wish to exclude, any connection with System C. In a totally 'open' network, the inhibition of any logical connection between A and C would have to be treated as an exception. Current ISO/OSI work in the security field is based on the security addendum to the open systems reference model (ISO 7489/2), in which security features are built into the protocols at the different layers. Thus access control between systems will be a feature of the open system protocols, and need not be handled as an exception. Security at the application layer, i.e. layer 7 of the OSI model is the subject of current work with the European Computer Manufacturers' Association (ECMA), which has produced a draft set of standards based on a subject—object model not unlike that discussed earlier in this chapter.

Role of System Components in Security

Hardware

As was seen in Chapter 3, the modern microprocessor is a very complex device indeed. From a security point of view, complexity is usually a disadvantage. It is likely that the majority of designers working with these devices do not have a full understanding of all the devices' features, but only of those which are most relevant to the application in hand. The scope may exist therefore for the more obscure features to be exploited to the detriment of system security. It may even be the case that the device contains features which have not been publicly declared by the manufacturer; these could be features which are intended to be implemented in a later version of the device. They may exist in the silicon of earlier versions, without official 'support'. This may also create the scope for exploitation in a way which weakens the overall system security. The overwhelming advantages in cost and development time of building systems from commercially available components mean that it will only be considered worthwhile developing special hardware for applications with the highest security requirements. Devices which are specifically concerned with the implementation of the security policy, such as trusted gateways, will certainly come into this category. The designer of secure hardware implements in silicon a design which can be proved to meet the security specifications.

A further consideration in the selection of hardware for secure applications is that some hardware contains features which are of positive benefit in the design of secure systems. Processors which offer memory protection are an example of this. In such processors checks are performed at the hardware level to ensure that programs do not access areas of memory to which they are not authorised.

Software

The operating system has a critical role to play in implementing the security policy. Most of the functions already mentioned in this chapter, such as access control, authentication, and distribution control, are features which will be implemented by the operating system. An operating system, such as was described in Chapter 3 and again in Chapter 8, is a vastly complex collection of software, and we have already seen that complexity and security do not go well together. It is important that all features of the operating system are visible and understandable, and the UNIX operating system has been designed and developed with that feature as one of its goals. Where the level of security demands that the operating system be verified from a security viewpoint, the usual practice is to define a core, or kernel of the operating system which is responsible for implementing the security policy. All security accesses will be checked by the kernel, which will be isolated so that its code cannot be modified by any other program. The kernel is of a manageable size, with a precisely specified role so that it is amenable to formal verification. It may be possible in some systems to embody some or all of the kernel's features in firmware, thereby increasing the strength of its isolation from outside interference, and simplifying the task of controlling the issue of new versions.

Conclusions

Security and openness appear to be in direct conflict. Resolution of the conflict is bound to involve expense in development, and some form of overhead in operation. In other words, computer security, as with all other forms of security, has a price, and a balance must be drawn between the cost of the security and its value to the organisation. This chapter has necessarily concentrated on computer security, but this aspect cannot be viewed in isolation. Computer security has to take its place alongside the other forms of security, especially personnel and physical security, and its application must be subject to the same general rules as any other form of security. In computer security we are striving to reach the situation where the maximum amount of the trust which it is necessary to place in the overall system can be placed upon machines rather than men, but most authorities would recognise that it will never be possible to exclude man completely. People are responsible for the design, implementation and application of security procedures. Much scope exists and continues to exist for these people to get things wrong, either through carelessness or through malicious intent. Hence the importance of personnel security is unlikely to decline. From the point of view of personnel security, probably the most important feature of the computer system is the provision it makes for accounting for users' actions, so that it is extremely difficult for anyone to mount an undetected attack on the system.

At the time of writing, the availability of acceptable security measures is lagging behind our ability to provide other system features, especially wide interconnection and interoperation. It is inherent in the nature of things that this will always be the case. Security is about the management of risk, and as systems become more complicated, the business of assessing their potential vulnerabilities and hence the risk, undergoes a form of 'combinatorial explosion'. This enormous increase in complexity has called for new techniques of security evaluation, but the basic approach to security remains the same as it ever was.

If one were to ask representatives of the various agencies involved in bringing a computer-based information system to the field to list their three most serious areas of concern, it is likely that security would feature in all the lists, and be the top of many of them. It is likely to continue to be a constraint on the development of widely interconnected information systems. Before the availability of acceptable techniques for multi-level secure working across networks, severe working limitations will have to be accepted and some capabilities which are technically feasible will not be usable until adequate security procedures have been developed. Even when such procedures are available, their use will impose an overhead and some limitation on operations. Security has always had a price, and this situation is unlikely to change.

11.

The Impact of CIS on the Organisation

Introduction

A War Office spokesman was once quoted as saying that there was 'No future for more than a very few telephones in the [British] Army . . . .' Few 'War Office Spokesmen' of today would go as far as that in describing the application of CIS, but it is surprising how many people are apparently unconvinced that the introduction of information technology will have more than a minor impact on the way in which the Army organises itself and goes about its business. In the short term, it has to be admitted that such sceptics do have history on their side. The Army is a conservative organisation, not given to rushing into radical changes. It could be argued that, despite enormous changes in the capabilities and characteristics of battlefield communications systems, the Army's command and control organisation is really not much different to that which was in place at the end of World War II, more than 40 years ago. It is only since the widespread introduction of secure voice radio, and the very recent introduction of area communications systems such as Ptarmigan that we have started to detect the stirrings of change. It is our contention in this chapter that the successful introduction of automated CIS will accelerate that change, and that in the closing years of the 20th century we are likely to see more radical changes in the command and control organisation of the Army than have taken place at any previous time.

Influences on the Organisation

Our contention that CIS must bring about change lies in the nature of the organisation, and a good starting point would be to identify the influences which act on an organisation and determine its shape and character. First of all we must define the scope of the word 'organisation' in the present context. By organisation we mean both the composition of the force—the 'force structure', and the command and control arrangements, that is, the grouping of the force into senior–subordinate relationships, and the composition of the command and control elements: the headquarters.

Taking a broad, general view, it may be said that three groups of influences determine the organisation's size, shape and method of operation. They are the task of the organisation; the environment in which the task must be performed; and the resources available to the organisation to perform the task. In a very real sense the resources are the organisation, arranged in a way which is appropriate to the performance of the task in the prevailing environment. In a military organisation it may be assumed that the environment is hostile to some degree or another, and hence the main influence of the environment is to create a need for the organisation to be able to survive its hostility.

To see how this influence model works in practice, we may look at the organisation of forces on the battlefield today. The example chosen is one of an Army Group within the NATO military command structure, since we have determined

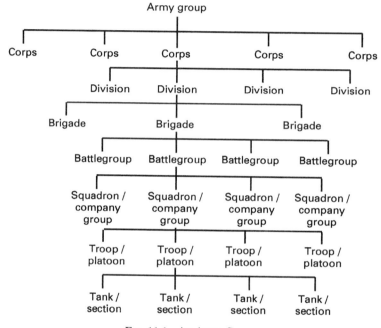

FIG. 11.1   An Army Group

this to be the highest 'battlefield' level of command. The diagram at Figure 11.1 shows a vertical slice from Army Group headquarters down to and including an infantry section. It is clearly a simplified view, since the many supporting Arms and Service units are not shown.

The first thing which strikes one about the shape of the diagram is that it is a simple tree structure, or hierarchy, and that no node has more than five branches, i.e. no level has more than five immediate subordinate levels; most have less than five. This factor is the span of command. It has been found through long experience that, given the nature of the task and the environment, commanders cannot cope efficiently with more than this number of direct subordinates. Historians might argue that Napoleon broke this rule to good effect by having eight corps directly under his Imperial Headquarters. To be sure, he handled these corps most effectively during the strategic manoeuvrings prior to their commitment to battle, but once battle was joined, their direct control by one commander proved to be impossible, as was clearly demonstrated at Jena in 1806. The missions undertaken seldom break down into more than three major concurrent activities. To break them down further would take the commander down to a level of detail where he would be in danger of losing sight of the overall task. This has much in common with the layered approach we took earlier to the design of computer hardware and software and communications protocols. Operating at a given layer, one needs to know the capabilities of the next layer down, and the procedures involved in tasking it, but one is less concerned with the way in which the lower layer carries out the task. Of course, in the military model the layering is not applied so strictly. Indeed, it is a well-accepted principle that commanders should 'think two down'. For example, a battalion commander will take a direct interest in the deployment of platoons; this is a form of 'quality assurance' checking on his part, and also gives him a more complete picture of the deployment of his force. Commanders are also encouraged to think 'two up', to be aware of how their dispositions and action fit into the higher plan.

The task of the force depicted in Figure 11.1, given that it represents a NATO Army Group, is essentially defensive. This is not to say that the counter-attack and counter-stroke will not have a role in the tactical repertoire, but the main significance of the defensive posture is that the force must be reactive. This in turn calls for a great degree of flexibility. At the organisational level, flexibility is achieved by creating scope for varying the composition and grouping of the force elements. The lowest level at which this normally operates is the squadron or company group—formerly known in the British Army as the combat team. This is a grouping of mechanised (or armoured) infantry platoons and tank troops under the command of a squadron or company headquarters. The battlegroup is a similar concept at the next level up, i.e. squadrons and companies under the command of an armoured regimental headquarters, or infantry battalion headquarters. At this level there is a need for a careful balance to be struck between flexibility, on the one hand, and, on the other, the penalty of breaking up a group which has trained together probably over a long period. This is felt to be less of a problem the higher up the hierarchy one goes. There is a much stronger and more intimate bond between the elements of a battlegroup than between brigades in a division, or divisions in a corps. Standard procedures and interoperable equipment should allow the rapid regrouping of brigades between divisions, of divisions between corps, and even of corps between army groups. It also has to be borne in mind that in the NATO structure the corps is the highest national organisation in the battlefield hierarchy; army group headquarters are part of the NATO unified command structure. Hence the movement of divisions and possibly brigades between corps involves the binding into a command relationship of the forces of more than one nation, and calls for all the interoperability measures discussed in Chapter 9.

The role of the environment in shaping this organisation is seen more in the headquarters and command structure than in the bare branches of the 'tree' diagram. The environment is hostile by definition, and the organisation's response is to arrange itself to ensure the survival of the command and control functions. Thus we see headquarters broken down into more than one element, with a degree of in-built redundancy to provide resilience in the face of attack and damage. This point is picked up later under the discussion of headquarters organisation.

The resources, as we indicated above, are the organisation. Of importance under this heading are the weapons, vehicles and other equipment with which the force is equipped. The range and effectiveness of the weapons, the mobility, protection and firepower of the fighting vehicles, and the capabilities of supporting vehicles will all have their effect in determining tactics, and, via tactics, the organisation of the force. In our context, though, we are specifically concerned with the resources for command and control. Thus, on transferring the bare 'tree' diagram of Figure 11.1 on to a map, to show how the force is geographically organised in its area of operation, we would see that the relative positions of the headquarters at the different levels of command are strongly influenced by the capabilities of the available communications equipment. It is, of course, influenced by the environment, particularly the nature of the terrain, but this in turn is a key influence on the performance of the communications links. Below brigade level, VHF combat net radio is the primary means of communication for command and control, and although a limited amount of re-broadcast equipment may be available to extend the range of such communications, it is often the range of a single VHF link in the prevailing terrain which confines the deployment of headquarters. It is a headquarters' traditional role to place itself in a position where it can communicate with its subordinates. This follows obviously from the task influence; the subordinates' task is to carry out their tactical mission and they will be located accordingly. Their superior headquarters' task is to exercise command and control over its subordinates. This relationship recurs through the different layers of the command structure, in that each superior headquarters is also a subordinate of its superior headquarters. At the lowest level the location of the forces is determined strictly by their combat role, that is, they are located where they are needed to fight the battle. Precisely where that is depends upon the weapons and equipment and therefore the tactics employed.

Headquarters Organisation

It is now time to focus on the headquarters. Having spent some time looking at the whole army group hierarchy, it is clear that we cannot take a headquarters in isolation; it must be looked at in the framework of the whole organisation. The task aspect of the headquarters is fairly clear, as introduced above, which is to exercise command and control over its subordinates. In the days of Marlborough, the siting of the 'headquarters' was a straightforward enough task. The requirement was a hilltop with a view over the battlefield, preferably out of range of musket fire but accessible to messengers on horseback. Nowadays the influences are of the same nature but of a totally different order. There is certainly a need to protect the headquarters from enemy action, and the measures taken, as we shall see, have a considerable influence on its shape and size. The 'view' of the battlefield, provided by automated sensors as well as the more traditional faculties of the troops in contact, is conveyed to the headquarters electronically, as are the despatches to the troops previously carried by messengers.

MOBILITY: CONTINUITY OF COMMAND AND CONTROL

Modern warfare is expected to be a fast-moving affair. In order to keep up with a mobile battle, the headquarters must be mobile, or at least the ability must exist for the command and control function to keep pace with the movement of the battle. Only at the lowest levels is it practicable to exercise the basic command function from a headquarters while it is actually moving, and even a battlegroup headquarters prefers to be in one place whilst operating. Thus to maintain continuity of the command and control function during rapidly moving operations, a procedure must exist, backed up by the necessary staff and equipment, to allow the working element of the headquarters to be static whilst another element is moving to a location from which it can take over. This moving element of the headquarters is usually termed the 'step-up', and it may consist of anything up to a full mirror-image of the main headquarters. Once in location, the step-up headquarters will be activated by a party of staff officers from the main headquarters. It has the same communications as the main headquarters and is therefore able to keep fully up-to-date on the progress of the battle. At the appropriate moment, control is passed to the step-up, which becomes at that instant the new main headquarters. The old main then becomes the step-up and is free to move to a new location to continue the process. Note that we said *control* is passed from one headquarters element to the other; *command* resides with the commander, who may remain at the main headquarters until control has passed, and then move to the new main headquarters.

Under some circumstances, the commander may be exercising command from his tactical headquarters throughout the process of change of control. Tactical headquarters is yet another element, consisting of the commander's vehicle and those of his immediate staff and advisers. Its purpose is to allow the commander to be in closer contact with some particular aspect of the battle. The commander can best influence the situation by being where the problems are greatest, but he is best served by being where his information is. CIS should help to reconcile these two often conflicting needs by allowing the commander to move around the battlefield yet stay in complete touch with his staff and the progress of operations.

The process of splitting the headquarters into a number of elements is taken a step further by the logistic commander of a formation and his staff who form a separate logistic, or rear headquarters to command and control the logistic assets of the formation. This subdivision serves two purposes. First, it places the logistic headquarters nearer to the resources it controls, normally towards the rear of the formation's area of responsibility. Secondly, it reduces the size of the main headquarters, thus making it easier to conceal and defend.

SURVIVABILITY

Reducing the size of the individual headquarters elements is one way to improve their survivability. It is an aid to concealment, which is the first line of defence for headquarters at brigade level and above. Detection from the air by visual or infrared sensors and position-finding through the interception of radio transmissions are the greatest threats. Thus great efforts must be made to reduce the visual, thermal and radio 'signatures' of the headquarters. Dispersion of the headquarters' component parts can help with this, but current CIS cannot yet compensate for the loss of operational effectiveness incurred through dispersion. This is a point which is returned to later.

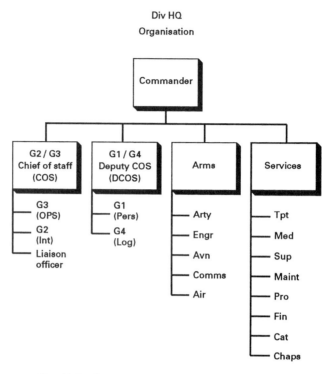

FIG. 11.2   Organisation of Divisional Headquarters

Headquarters Internal Organisation and Procedures

The organisation of a divisional main headquarters is shown in Figure 11.2. The staff is organised into functional branches, which are given the NATO standard designations of G1 for personnel, G2 for intelligence, G3 for operations, and G4 for logistics. Clearly, as the diagram shows a main headquarters, the G2 and the G3 branch will be the principal components; G1 and G4 are represented at rear headquarters. The other functions represented at main headquarters are fire support (including close air-support), air defence, engineers, aviation and communications. The staff system binds the different functional cells into a closely coupled team, under the direction of the chief of staff. Each cell will have a need to communicate both outside the headquarters, in order to perform its specialised function, and with the other cells. In the absence of automated CIS, the information storage and display means which tie together the activities of the cells is the paper map, with its perspex or plastic film overlay showing the tactical situation. Plastic covered stateboards, maintained with chinagraph pencils, display tabular information, such as details of each unit's readiness, states of reserve demolitions or stocks of ammunition. Each cell must have the same view of the general situation, but will have its own record of information relating to its specialised function.

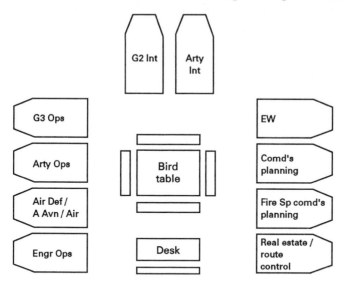

FIG. 11.3   Headquarters Operating Environment

To many commanders and staff officers, the ideal operating environment is the arrangement shown in Figure 11.3. There is one central mapboard (the 'bird table') showing the main tactical information, which is updated by the G3 operations staff and the G2 intelligence staff. Specialist cells, such as artillery and engineers, have their own maps and displays, with the key tactical information being drawn from the central map, and 'private' information relating to the cell's function displayed. The ease of direct 'eyeball' contact between staff officers and the immediate sharing of information are arguments in favour of this form of head-quarters organisation. The central map is a valuable feature, and the arrange-ment has psychological advantages; it is strong on team spirit, the importance of which should not be underestimated. Sadly, it is not very practicable under most realistic, operational circumstances. It can be difficult to find suitable covered accommodation in which to set up the headquarters. Setting up and taking down, involving the installation and recovery of communications and power cables, as well as the furniture, map boards and other fittings, is both time consuming and labour intensive. The 'big office' headquarters is extremely vulnerable to attack; one high explosive missile or bomb could destroy it all.

It is tempting to believe that dispersion of the individual headquarters' cells is the only way to survive, but this too has its drawbacks. Dispersion certainly reduces the chance of detection, and the effects of attack by missile or aerially delivered bomb. Against a ground attack of the type which could be mounted by special forces infiltrated into the rear areas, it may, however, offer the opportunity for the enemy to pick off the individual cells one by one. After all, not many American wagon train leaders seemed to think that dispersion was a reasonable course of action when the Cherokees attacked! The survival measures obviously have to be related to the prevailing threat, but it does seem to be the case that the

Fig. 11.4   Headquarters Operating Environment (© *M. Rice*)

requirements of survivability are in conflict with the way in which commanders and staffs would like to run the headquarters. This is certainly an area where CIS can help.

Before we leave the subject of headquarters organisation and procedures, it is worth looking in more detail at the mechanics of staff work. There is still a lot of paperwork involved. Written operation orders (OpOs) are widely used, although the map-based 'overlay OpO' has found favour in many headquarters. The production of an operation order is a team effort. The commander will state the mission, and possibly the general outline of how the operation is to be executed; the G3 staff will supply the details of the execution. The paragraphs on enemy strengths and intentions will be supplied by G2, and the aspects of fire and other support will be contributed by the appropriate specialist branches of the headquarters. There is thus a physical collation and co-ordination task to be carried out by the G3 staff who are responsible for the production and issue of the complete OpO. As many G3 staff officers have discovered to their cost, this process can take an inordinately long time. The end result, produced by a combination of handwriting and typing, by cut-and-paste and photocopying, is often far from satisfactory. This area of routine operational staff work can be revolutionised by nothing more complicated than the introduction of standard, commercial office automation equipments and techniques to the field headquarters.

Impact of CIS

Force Structure and Organisation

At the organisational level, the introduction of CIS should produce the degree of flexibility required to achieve rapid regrouping of forces. Thus we might expect to see formations being organised to suit the prevailing circumstances. It probably has to be accepted that the tried-and-tested hierarchical force organisation will remain, but commanders will have much more freedom to adjust the components of the hierarchy.

This is probably a good place in which to introduce the concept of CIS as a force multiplier. This term, coined in the USA, implies that a characteristic of CIS is to multiply the effectiveness of one's own forces. This is easier to say than it is to prove with any degree of rigour. The argument suggests that having the right resources in men and *matériel* positioned at just the right place and at just the right time, to counter some specific enemy action is, of itself, equivalent to having additional units under command, and that CIS has the potential to effect the timely positioning of those resources.

Perhaps a better way to look at it is to consider that the perfect, timely application of a given element of the force equates to a force multiplication factor of 1, i.e. 100% efficiency. This is hardly ever achieved in practice. The application of force at the right time, in the right place and in the right relative strength to bring success in battle demands timely and accurate information on which the right decisions can be made, and a means of passing on the results of the decisions in the form of orders. This whole process must take place faster than the enemy's decision-making process; after all, if he can change his mind and change the action of his force whilst you are still trying to react to his original plan, he will have something of a competitive advantage. To use the jargon, we are trying to operate 'inside the enemy's control loop'. The major delay in that loop is the time taken to deploy troops on the ground into a particular posture. It is the commander's key objective to force his opponent to commit his forces into a particular deployment, and to attack him before he can react to what is actually going on. Reliable and effective CIS can provide the means to do this, and thereby achieve the full potential of the force. The 'force multiplication factor' we are seeking is 1, and without the benefit of CIS, it is likely most of the time to be considerably less than 1.

Another concept which is relevant here is the 'time value of information'. Perfect, total information is useless to the commander if it is received too late for him to act on it. Commanders need to be aware of this fact and know how much information they need and by when in order to take effective decisions. Knowing when to accept an approximation and when to demand more precise information is a matter of fine judgement, based on experience. An example of this principle at work, supported by CIS, is that of the divisional commander who asked his engineer whether or not a minefield could be constructed in a particular gap by a certain time. The engineer's staff consulted information held by the CIS, and he was able to reply in a few minutes that the task was indeed feasible. When asked about the accuracy of the information in the automated system, the engineer replied that it was probably just as accurate a picture as his staff could have obtained by calling all the units and asking for up-to-the-minute information specific to the requested task, but by the time they had done that, the chances of meeting the deadline for the minefield's construction would have been greatly reduced.

To refer the improvements which can be brought about by CIS to the command and control model of Chapter 1, consider first the information gathering sub-system. Here, the use of more sensors of greater capability, backed up by suitable communications, can greatly improve the quantity and quality of information available to the commander. In the decision-making sub-system, the vast quantities of information will be made manageable and meaningful by improved techniques of data fusion. Improvements in display techniques will assist commanders and staffs to assimilate the information presented. They will have a much better 'view' of what is going on than that available to the Napoleonic commander on his horse on a hill top. It is an interpreted view of reality, which can 'see through' the fog of war, created not so much by the black-powder smoke from musket and cannon as by the enormous complexity, scope and variety of modern warfare.

Headquarters Organisation

As already outlined above, the introduction of office automation to the field headquarters would revolutionise its working at a stroke. This has been tried by a number of formations, notably the 9th Infantry Division of the United States Army, and the 3rd Armoured Division of the British Army. Standard, commercially available software packages, provided that they are used on hardware which is appropriate to the field environment, offer a perfectly satisfactory solution to most of the problems of routine field staff-work. For example, to produce an operation order, no longer does each cell have to produce its contribution on paper to be cut and pasted, or even retyped under the co-ordination of the G3 staff. Contributing staffs compose their sections of the order on their terminals using the standard word-processing package, and pass them via the local area network to the G3 cell, where they can be electronically cut-and-pasted into the complete order. When the order is ready, electronic mail can be used to distribute it. This approach can dramatically reduce the time needed to produce and distribute a complex operation order, time which it is vital to save if we are to work 'inside the enemy's loop'.

Recent analysis has shown that the most survivable headquarters' configuration in the environment likely to be encountered in a central region war is that of dispersed staff cells in armoured vehicles. However, as suggested earlier, dispersion reduces the effectiveness of the headquarters. The application of CIS can give the headquarters the ability to disperse with minimum loss of effectiveness, when the threat demands it. By using very short-range radio links, a form of 'cordless' headquarters LAN can be created, which allows the headquarters to be sited with maximum flexibility. It also allows a great degree of flexibility in the composition of the headquarters, which might be needed to reflect the composition of the forces under command. For example, when a divisional headquarters takes under command a brigade from another corps (i.e. by implication, a brigade of a different nationality), an operations/liaison team could join the headquarters and be integrated into it immediately through connection to the LAN. Another example, this time from operations at army group level, is the concept of an army group rover headquarters, which could establish itself within the headquarters of the corps which is, at a given period of the battle, responsible for the most crucial element of the army group's operation, requiring closer than normal liaison with army group headquarters and with other corps. The organisation suggested here would allow elements of army group headquarters to become an integral part of any corps headquarters as soon as they arrive in location. This type of headquarters does not preclude the face-to-face meeting of commanders and staffs when the conditions allow it. One might see the use, for example, of a central briefing area in a suitable covered location. The important feature is that the headquarters has the capability to work without this sort of contact when conditions demand it, as would be the case when working in a chemically-contaminated area. The use of CIS, and especially the interconnection of the headquarters' vehicles by LAN, makes possible a sharing of information which is even more effective than that achievable in the 'big office' concept. Also, routine staff work through the use of office automation techniques will work perfectly well under dispersed, closed-down conditions where the old paper cut-and-paste approach would fail badly.

Command vs Control

The distinction between command and control was made in Chapter 1, and touched upon again earlier in this chapter. Essentially, commanders command and staff control. Most of what has gone before in this chapter was concerned with how CIS can help the staff in their control functions; does CIS have a direct role to play in support of the command function? As has already been said, command is a very personal business and style plays quite an important part in it. The commander needs to have his subordinates inside his mind. The required closeness of thinking and understanding cannot be achieved instantly and without effort. It must first of all be built on a firm foundation, provided by a common understanding of the concept of operations. This process starts long before operations commence; the concept of operations is the basis of doctrine, taught in staff colleges and arms schools.

On to this solid foundation must next be built a common understanding or perception of the prevailing situation. This will depend largely on the availability of information; generally speaking, a common understanding of the situation demands access to common information. Next, there is a need to interpret and apply the concept of operations to the current situation. This calls for a recognition of the situation as a set of circumstances which is covered in the concept of operations, and taking appropriate action. Of course, the concept of operations cannot explicitly cover all possible situations, but it should at least give some guidance on how to react to the unexpected.

The final requirement which underpins all the others is for reliable communications between the commander and his subordinates. This obviously includes telecommunications, but must also encompass face-to-face contact which will often be appropriate and desirable, but, unfortunately, not always physically possible.

CIS can assist at every stage, but its most telling contribution will be in the assembling and presenting of information in order that a common view of the situation may prevail, and in ensuring the quality of commander-to-commander communications. Information is the common bond, and in this context information is almost invariably terrain related, that is, it can be presented in the form of symbols on a map. If a commander can be sure, when giving out his orders, that his subordinates are all looking at the same map display, he will be more than halfway to achieving a common understanding of the situation. If it is physically possible to bring all the subordinates together and group them round a map display, so much the better. At the lower levels of command, say battlegroup and below, it is important at some stage to get the subordinate commanders together where they can see the actual ground over which the battle will be fought. Should circumstances prevent the achievement of these ideals, as will all too often be the case, CIS should provide the electronic substitute. For many senior commanders, the ideal CIS would be one which provided the electronic equivalent of a face-to-face 'orders group', i.e. a common map display of adequate resolution and an all-informed voice net.

All the foregoing has been aimed at providing the commander with the necessary degree of contact with his subordinates. What has not yet been addressed is any means of direct support for the commander's own decision-making process. Again, this is an aspect of command which will vary considerably from one commander to another. Some commanders are content to have their staff present a number of options to them, with a recommended preferred option, and select a course of action accordingly. At the other extreme is the commander who prefers to rely on his personal analysis of the situation, and have his staff evaluate options which he himself has generated. Given this wide range of command styles, it is not surprising to find that decision-support systems are so hard to design. The most obvious common denominator in such systems is the need to give the commander the clearest possible view of the situation, and this is really no different from the requirement seen above for a common display to be available to the commander and his subordinates. How far one can go in building on this common base, by adding such refinements as situation modelling, or artificial intelligence based option generation techniques is for debate.

Situation modelling gives the commander the means to visualise future situations, so that he can try out his options on the (computer-generated) map display. Using the information describing the current situation as a starting point, the commander can input certain assumptions or assertions concerning the future deployment of both his own forces and the enemy's and see the effect 'on the ground'. Such modelling could show up previously unforeseen details, such as gaps in defences, or unexpected points of vulnerability on either side. This sort of technique is really no more than a convenient, electronic means of displaying and analysing information which is already known, or is postulated by the system's users. The approach based on artificial intelligence takes things a step further, in that the system is allowed to make postulations of its own, based on its 'knowledge' of the situation, of the concept of operations, and the commander's current priorities. This is a subject which is raised again in the final chapter, when we look further into the future. Automated decision-making assistance is not something which is likely to find much favour with the present generation of senior commanders, but, as we shall see later when we discuss the introduction of CIS, there are grounds for believing that future generations of commanders may have fewer technological inhibitions and, indeed, come to take such support for granted.

Introducing CIS

The introduction of any new equipments, techniques or procedures into an established organisation is something which is bound to cause a measure of disruption. Ever since the industrial revolution, the business of management has largely been concerned with the management of change, and to this day the majority of industrial news stories have at their heart some aspect of change. All too often, it is the inability of one party or another to come to terms with that change which brings the situation into the headlines. 'Automation' has always been a particularly emotive term in this context, all the way from Hargreaves's 'spinning-jenny' in 1764 to the *The Times's* 'new technology' at Wapping over two centuries later. Probably the most important element to be considered during the introduction of a system is the people who are to use it, or perceive that their lives will be affected by it.

Some of the people problems we may meet can result from poor systems design and we must be particularly wary of this. One staff officer's perception of a CIS system at a higher formation headquarters might be that of a benevolent genie that provides him with much of the timely information he needs to brief his commander. A subordinate staff's view of the same system at unit level might be that of a time-wasting tyrant that provides nothing of value but which has to be fed with routine information at all too frequent intervals. If our CIS system is to make demands of a staff at some level, then it must be designed to give something of value in return.

We need to be careful, too, that we do not put the man in the position of a machine-minder. It is tempting for some designers to use an office analogy with CIS; messages come in to an in-tray, are processed by the man and then placed in an out-tray. The machine acts as the in- and out-trays and drives the man as a machine-minder. This is a very different design concept from the one that sees the machine as providing a continually updated source of information which the man uses as and when he needs to perform his real task. All the 'housekeeping' tasks associated with providing that source of information are the responsibility of the machine.

It would be tempting to think that in the Army we have a technically aware, fully-co-operative population which will accept with eagerness all the technological assistance offered to it, and adapt rapidly to its use. As we shall see, that is a situation which cannot be taken for granted.

The introduction of any new system, especially a military CIS, will carry with it a degree of technical risk. As we saw in the two previous chapters, it is the scale of CIS and the uncertainty of the battlefield environment which are likely to be the most significant areas of risk. It is impossible to be totally confident that a system which has performed well in the clinical conditions of the manufacturer's premises will perform correctly in the field. There are ways of simulating the environment before deployment and other techniques are available to increase confidence that the system will work well under realistic conditions, but the first setting up of the system in the field will always show up problems which had not been anticipated during its development. This factor is related to the previous one concerning personnel; poor performance by the system on a first fielding can cause its users to lose confidence, which may be difficult to regain later. It is therefore doubly vital that new systems be introduced following a well-thought out strategy, which takes due account of personnel, technical and all the other factors which lie in wait for the unwary project manager.

Personnel Factors

THE USER POPULATION

The days are now long past when automated CIS could be introduced to a population which was totally unversed in the ways of the computer. This was close to being the case in the mid 1970s, when the first field CIS were introduced, although the situation was a mixed blessing. On the plus side, users were relatively easily impressed by technical wizardry and therefore readily convinced of the need for automated CIS. On the minus side, their lack of familiarity with the technology and its applications made it difficult for them to specify their requirements with enough precision, or to make the best use of systems when they were fielded. To someone who has grown up with computers, the use of a screen and keyboard is as much second nature as pencil and paper. It is therefore somewhat paradoxical to find that with today's 'computerate' commanders and staff officers, the introduction of CIS can be just as difficult as it ever was. The problem is now the other way around: for all the many reasons discussed in the last two chapters, the full range of automated support available off the shelf in the civil field cannot yet be reliably provided on the battlefield. The term 'de-appetisation' has been coined in the USA to describe this unfortunate need to curb users' understandable wishes to transfer all their peacetime office automation on to the battlefield.

It is dangerous to generalise about people; in any survey it is as important to know who is being asked the questions as it is to know the questions and answers. In this case there is likely to be a difference of outlook between senior commanders and junior staff officers, brought about as much by their different ages, and hence exposure to computer culture, as by their different perspectives of the job in hand. The chart at Figure 11.5 attempts to put the population situation into perspective. Its main message is that it would be unwise to attempt to introduce advanced, integrated CIS until the first products of the 'computer generation' have attained positions of senior command. We have somewhat loosely defined the start of the 'computer generation' to be around the mid 1970s, when time-sharing computer terminals first started to be used widely in schools. A more pessimistic view would be that it did not start in earnest until the arrival of the home computer, in the late 1970s or early 1980s.

However, by our definition, it would seem, by some happy coincidence, that the introduction of fully integrated CIS for use in peace and war, on and off the battlefield, is unlikely to occur until the first member of the 'computer generation' has reached two-star rank. It will take that long before, to paraphrase Martin van

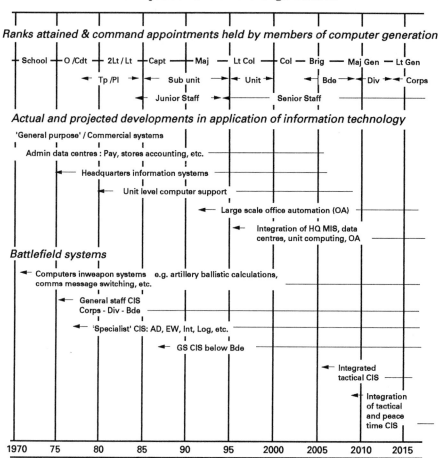

Ranks attained & command appointments held by members of computer generation

School — O /Cdt — 2Lt / Lt — Capt — Maj — Lt Col — Col — Brig — Maj Gen — Lt Gen

Tp /Pl — Sub unit — Unit — Bde — Div — Corps

Junior Staff — Senior Staff

Actual and projected developments in application of information technology

'General purpose' / Commercial systems

Admin data centres : Pay, stores accounting, etc.

Headquarters information systems

Unit level computer support

Large scale office automation (OA)

Integration of HQ MIS, data centres, unit computing, OA

Battlefield systems

Computers in weapon systems e.g. artillery ballistic calculations, comms message switching, etc.

General staff CIS Corps - Div - Bde

'Specialist' CIS: AD, EW, Int, Log, etc.

GS CIS below Bde

Integrated tactical CIS

Integration of tactical and peace time CIS

1970   75   80   85   90   95   2000   2005   2010   2015

FIG. 11.5   User Population vs Advances in Technology

Creveld's observation on the development of telegraphy in the mid 19th century, CIS has 'reached the stage of maturity where the basic rules governing the employment of a new technology, and its effects, are no longer the subject of debate.'

To be effective and accepted, CIS must actually be taken for granted, as the successive means of command and control have been over the ages. We must accept that it is within the capability of current and emerging technology to make the incredibly fast processing of unimaginably large volumes of information from an enormous variety of sources seem to be an easily achieved and everyday matter. In so doing it may be putting obstacles in the way of its own continuing success. Whilst it is important for commanders and staffs to be able to use their systems easily and to take them for granted, if they do not have a true appreciation of the systems' real complexities, it may be hard to persuade them to allocate the required degree of priority to providing the resources which are necessary to keep the systems running.

Training in the use of CIS will ease the task of introducing systems into service, especially if the training can start well before the system has to be used in earnest. There is great merit in the introduction of CIS at general training establishments, such as staff colleges, especially if they bear more than a passing resemblance to the systems used in the field. It can be argued that such training systems do not have to be exact replicas of operational systems in order to teach the basic principles, but there is considerable advantage to be gained from the use of a common style of MMI in both systems. There is even more advantage to be gained from having an MMI style which is common to both the operational system and those used in barracks, as was suggested in Chapter 5.

Introduction Strategies

The introduction into service of a system or equipment is but one, albeit very important, stage in the process of procurement. In the case of a particularly novel or complex system the need to manage its introduction may dictate the strategy of the whole procurement. Chapter 8 stressed the difficulty of requirement specification; a procurement/development strategy which seeks to overcome this difficulty is prototyping, in which the requirement is refined through the development and introduction to service of prototypes. The prototypes embody an interim implementation of the solution, possibly based on off-the-shelf hardware. Experience of using the prototype equipment is used to refine the requirement and guide the development of the next generation of equipment. The prototype will probably be limited in its deployment; for a system which is ultimately intended to serve a corps, the prototype may be issued to one division only. A potential problem with this approach is that, through financial and other pressures, the prototype may come to be regarded as an operational system and be retained in service far longer than was originally intended. With this likelihood in mind, it is important that any prototype which is introduced to the field has been designed to survive the field environment. Whilst there is certainly scope for the modelling of tactical system characteristics on completely non-rugged, commercial hardware, such systems should never be deployed to the field. To do so would be to encourage users to become reliant upon systems which would probably not be usable in wartime.

An introduction strategy to be avoided is the 'big bang', or introduction all at once of one or even more large and complex systems. Of course, there are occasions when this style of introduction is inevitable; for example, who would contemplate the phased introduction of a change in the law requiring drivers to switch from one to the other side of the road? Even when the introduction of such large-scale changes must be synchronised, it is frequently physically impossible to carry out the change at once. In that case, the introduction is complicated by the need to establish interfaces between the old system and the growing population of the new. Further complications are introduced if more than one system is introduced at the same time, especially if the systems need to interact in any way. At a stage in their introduction when the support staffs will not be familiar with either system, it will be difficult to know which is at fault when things go wrong—as they inevitably will. Such situations are best avoided, but all too often good technical planning will be thwarted by financial, operational and other pressures beyond the control of the project manager.

Fallback

Even those systems which have been designed and built to withstand the rigours of the battlefield environment will suffer the occasional failure. The important thing is that no catastrophic failure should occur. The system as a whole should have a degree of built-in redundancy, to give it resilience in the event of failure. 'Graceful degradation' is a term often employed to describe the ability of a system to reduce its level of service in proportion to the amount of damage it has sustained, rather than fail completely the first time it is hit. There are those who believe that the ultimate level of fallback in the total command and control system is the resort to manual methods and procedures, and that, no matter how sophisticated the automated system may be, the staff should always be able to revert to map, china-graph and 'steam' radio. This may be an extreme position, but it would be foolish to move too quickly to total dependence on the automated system. The new system has to prove itself, and be seen to have its own built-in degrees of resilience. The more complex the automated system becomes, and the more the users come to depend on it, the more difficult will it be for them to do without it. It also goes without saying that any fallback mode, whether partially automated or fully manual, will represent a considerable reduction in capability. What must also be recognised is that the more effective is the CIS, and the more its users depend on it, the greater is its vulnerability to enemy action. It becomes a more attractive target, and 'counter C3' measures now feature in most tactical repertoires.

Management and Support

If we have given the impression up to now that CIS is something which, once installed and taken into service, can be left to manage itself, now is the time to redress the situation. To be sure, there was a belief a few years ago, when some of the first generation of tactical CIS were being introduced, that such systems could be 'self-managing'. In other words, there should be very little need for any operator intervention to make the system's facilities available to its users. It would seem that, in the light of recent experience, this was an unwarranted assumption. The dynamic, constantly changing nature of the system, where communications links may come and go with little warning and users frequently change their locations and means of access to the system, calls for a strong, 'hands-on' approach to system management. As was brought out in Chapter 8, CIS software is extremely complex and we are some way from being able to guarantee its total 'correctness'. There will also be complex interactions between software and hardware components and with other systems. Furthermore, the requirement will seldom be static; systems will be the subject to modifications throughout their in-service life to take on new capabilities and features. The management and control of these complex activities are normally grouped under the heading of system support and demand considerable resources.

System Management

The demands of system management call for facilities within the system itself and a management organisation. In a situation where there may be a number of interoperating CIS serving both the commanders and general staff and specialist users, such as artillery and engineers, it will be normal for the overall system management to be co-ordinated by the communications network provider. The communications network is the common factor which binds together the different information systems into an integrated CIS. Some of the tasks to be carried out by this management organisation are described below.

Communications Network Management

DEPLOYMENT OF NETWORK RESOURCES

The nodes of the trunk network and the mobile subscriber access-points must be located to provide the coverage required by the subscribers. Sufficient uncommitted reserves and spare capacity must exist so that the network can survive enemy action, and be able to react quickly to changing requirements.

CONNECTIVITY MANAGEMENT

Connections between trunk nodes and from access nodes into the trunk network will need to change as elements of the network move; throughout this change the network must remain resilient and coherent.

REAL ESTATE MANAGEMENT

Communications resources must compete with other resources for the use of real estate on the battlefield. The control and allocation of real estate is an operational staff function, and the communications system managers must liaise closely with those who exercise it. Similarly, road movement will be tightly controlled in wartime especially on the main supply routes, so the movement of communications resources must be carefully planned.

FREQUENCY MANAGEMENT

The issue and the control of use of radio frequencies in an extremely congested electromagnetic environment is a major problem for communications managers. The limited numbers of frequencies in all bands from HF to SHF must be allocated by sharing between users, taking into account the effects of terrain and equipment characteristics.

Information Service Management

The term 'information service management' is used to cover the actions needed to maintain the reliable provision of the information system's facilities to its users.

It covers the provision of the terminals on the users' desks and the provision and operation of any central processing and storage resources in the system. The information service manager is responsible for maintaining the integrity of the database(s) in which the information is held, and by applying security measures to ensure that the information is seen only by those who have the right to do so. The maintenance of adequate interconnection between system elements via the communications network is also an information service management task, which obviously calls for close liaison with the network managers. In many organisations the information services and communications network management responsibilities are held by the same branch, thereby recognising the integrated nature of CIS.

Information Managers

We may distinguish between the type of 'services management' described above and the need for information management. Information is a resource which calls for a degree of husbandry to preserve its value. Particularly where databases are distributed or replicated (see Chapter 7), there is a need for some positive management intervention to ensure the integrity and currency of the information held. Again, this activity must be supported by 'tools', or features built into the system, and by an organisation of information managers at different levels of the command hierarchy. Its also calls for a close liaison between the services manager and the information manager. Information managers must be drawn from the staff users of the system, that is, they must be in a position to understand and make judgements on the meaning of the information.

System Support

The Requirement

It has been learned through hard experience that the support of software-based systems demands a totally different approach to that which was applied to traditional hardware-based equipments. Even a fairly complex item of electronic equipment, such as a radio set, is not more than a single, individual piece of equipment. Should it fail to operate correctly, a well-established procedure may be applied to discover what is wrong with the equipment and to repair it. In the case of a software-driven system, the situation is vastly more complicated. First, in a distributed system, as opposed to an individual equipment, a fault in one part of the system may manifest itself somewhere else. Secondly, faults in software may be transient, caused by combinations of conditions which occur extremely rarely and which therefore are very hard to replicate when investigating the fault. In a software system of any realistic size, the number of combinations of conditions or states in which the system can be at any given instant is for all practical purposes infinite. Although a well-specified and designed system may be very reliable and fail infrequently, when it does fail it can be extremely difficult to diagnose the cause of failure. It should be possible to identify most pure hardware faults by using built-in test equipment (BITE) and hardware self-test routines, but even these do not always exercise the hardware in every possible mode, and some of the more obscure faults are caused by the interaction of hardware and software.

When a software-based system is modified, the effect of the modification on the whole system must be considered. Modifying elements of the system in isolation, or introducing modifications on a piecemeal basis, may lead to unplanned inter-actions and system failure. It is also vital for the modification state of the whole system to be kept under strict control. So-called configuration control measures are essential to keep track of which versions of both hardware and software have been issued.

To carry out the tasks of fault investigation and rectification and the investiga-tion, development, introduction and control of modifications, a system-support organisation is required.

The System-Support Organisation

A typical system support organisation is shown in Figure 11.6. This recognises that there are two main aspects to its role. First, it must act in direct support of

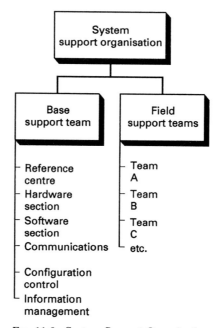

FIG. 11.6   System Support Organisation

the information services managers in the field, and be on call to them to investigate faults as and when they occur. Secondly, it must have the capability to investigate faults and requests for changes to the system away from the operational system. In this latter aspect it may have a development capability in its own right, or it may act through contractors.

The first part of the role is the task of the field support teams (FST). Where a number of interoperating CIS exist, serving different battlefield functional areas, each one may have its own FST(s). The FSTs will be called in when problems arise which are beyond the capability of the 'first line' system managers to put right. The FSTs' ability to rectify faults in the field will be strictly limited. In particular, it would be most unusual for an FST to become involved in software modification in the field. Their normal *modus operandi* would be to record the circumstances of a fault in as much detail as possible, and to pass these details back to the base support team (BST). They may devise and recommend a 'procedural work-round', that is, a temporary change to operating procedures which avoids the conditions which are believed to have caused the fault. When software changes have been devised and tested by the BST, they will be issued for installation in the field by the FSTs. In urgent cases, this process may be carried out very quickly, with new issues of software being released and installed as quickly as it is possible to identify the fault and devise a solution to it. It is impossible to give a general time estimate for this sort of operation, but it would not be unusual to find 'fixes' for urgent but relatively simple faults being delivered to the field with 48–72 hours of the initial investigation of the faults by the FST. It would be more usual for the rectification of less urgent faults and for minor modifications to be grouped together into one new issue of software over a much longer timescale. Major modifications may require a software, and possibly a hardware issue in their own right.

The BST's role has already been introduced. It will be staffed by a combination of military and civilian personnel, and will usually have the support of contractors. Its other main resource is a set of reference systems, that is, collections of hardware and software which are representative of the systems deployed in the field, including the communications systems. It will seldom be possible to reproduce in the reference system the full physical scale of the field system, and computer simulation techniques may be used to increase the apparent size of the reference systems. The reference systems serve a number of purposes. First, there is the investigation of faults and requests for change reported from the field, and the testing of the software modifications in response to these demands. Secondly, the reference systems will be used to test new, interoperating systems before their issue to the field, to ascertain that they can interoperate as required with existing systems and do not cause any unforeseen interactions anywhere in the system as a whole.

The BST will exercise configuration control over the systems for which it is responsible. It will maintain records of the software and hardware modification states, and strictly control the issues of new software and hardware to the field. In the case of major modifications which must be introduced system-wide, considerable co-ordination is called for. In a system which may have several hundred distributed elements, all of which need to be modified before the system can regain its operational status, this is not a trivial task. As each element is modified, a set of internal tests must be performed to check that the modification has been correctly carried out, and then when all elements have been modified, the whole system must be connected and tested.

The BST will also contain an element of information management, just as the system management organisation did. There is a need for centralised management of a data dictionary, which is the definitive list of data elements and their symbolic representations used throughout the organisation. The information managers are also concerned with the information exchange requirements (IERs) between different functional areas. They will need considerable computer support, for their task is effectively that of building and maintaining a data 'model' of the organisation and its activities.

Summary

In this chapter we have made the assertion that the introduction of CIS will have a profound impact on the organisation. By increasing its responsiveness and allowing it to operate more flexibly, CIS will open the way to changes in the composition and structure of the organisation, so that the advantages can be exploited to the full. The impact will be felt most strongly in headquarters' organisation. The rapid distribution of information and its effective display will allow greater dispersion of the command and control functions, which should increase their chances of survival. It will also allow a greater degree of flexibility in the composition of headquarters, so that they may be responsive to changes in tasking.

To achieve the potential benefits of CIS, its introduction must be carefully managed. We cannot take for granted that the future users of CIS are all 'computer literate' and convinced a priori of the effectiveness of automated methods. If gradual, evolutionary deployment is possible, it is normally to be preferred to the revolutionary, or all-at-once 'big bang' approach.

Finally, the introduction of CIS will not save manpower. The dramatic increase in capability which CIS can bring about must be paid for. To maintain its functions in the field, staff and resources are needed for system management. For the longer term maintenance and development of the system's capabilities, a system support organisation is needed, which must be appropriately staffed and equipped with reference and other equipment. The information in the system must itself be managed; information managers are required in the field, backed by a central authority responsible for ensuring the consistent representation of information throughout the organisation, and its development to meet the changing—and invariably growing—need.

12.

The Future

Introduction

Any attempt to predict the future in the information technology arena is almost certainly doomed to failure and all who attempt to do so run the risk of seeing, in the twenty-twenty vision of hindsight, their wise words held up to public ridicule.

In his book *Using Computers*,[1] Raymond Nickerson quotes a story told by Lord Vivian Bowden who, in 1950, was asked to determine whether it would be possible for commercial firms to manufacture computing machines and sell them at a profit. Bowden said:

> I went to see Professor Douglas Hartree, who had built the first differential analysers in England and had more experience in using these very specialised computers than anyone else. He told me that, in his opinion, all the calculations that would ever be needed in this country could be done on the three digital computers that were then being built—one in Cambridge, one in Teddington, and one in Manchester. No one else, he said, would ever need machines of their own, or would be able to afford to buy them.[2]

That that prediction should be so wrong—in 1984 the number of personal computers in homes in the United States was estimated at six or seven million—is really not so surprising. The rate of technological advance in this field is without precedent. Toong and Gupta suggest that if the aircraft industry:

> ... had evolved as spectacularly as the computer industry over the past 25 years, a Boeing 767 would cost $500 today and it would circle the globe in 20 minutes on five gallons of fuel.[3]

We proffer this chapter, therefore, with some trepidation, and hope to avoid falling into the same trap as others have by trying to point to trends rather than by making any dogmatic prediction about the future. A major technological breakthrough, as was the case with the development of the micro chip, can so radically alter the baseline of possibilities as to make any such predictions valueless. It would seem from recent history that the range of possibilities is often not even perceptible until well after exploitation of the breakthrough has begun.

We start by examining where the existing information technology might be further applied to our command and control model of Chapter 1, and we note, in passing, requirements that we cannot yet see how to meet without significant advances being achieved. We then look at where current research activity and trends seem to be taking us and, finally, we examine what improvements might be brought about by the application of these ideas to this field. Again, however, we must stress that a major breakthrough in the technology could radically alter these trends and make feasible applications that today have not yet been conceived.

Further Applications of the Existing Technology

Sensors

Returning once more to our original model of Chapter 1, shown here as Figure 12.1, we start our review with the sensors. We can clearly continue to apply the existing technology to an increasing range of automated and semi-automated sensors: imagery from satellites and drones; signal intelligence (SIGINT) from

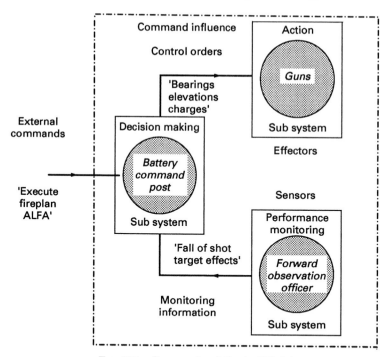

FIG. 12.1   Command and Control Model

electronic warfare (EW) systems; electronic intelligence (ELINT) from radars and sonars, and so forth. The computer programs that need to be written to control these kinds of system tend to be about where to look and when to look, and such programs are relatively straightforward, at least in concept, to develop. Concerns here are mainly associated with speed of response, sensitivity and area of interest; and the use of faster microprocessors together with an increased parallelism of system components (which does, of course, complicate the software) are the likely trends. The physical characteristics of the devices tend to determine the nature of what is found; although the information produced by such sensors invariably requires considerable human interpretation, and therein lies a significant problem. As was outlined in Chapters 1 and 2, improvements in sensor performance and in the numbers deployed rapidly give rise to raw information data rates that threaten to swamp the human agencies responsible for the interpretation and correlation of information into the desired product: namely timely intelligence. This is the problem of data fusion.

Raw information from one or more sources may be interpreted and correlated with processed information from a number of different sources before an overall picture is passed back. This data fusion process is very manpower intensive and demands high skills. It is an applications area where we cannot yet see clearly how to write computer programs that will effectively tackle these kinds of problem and thus permit us to use the information technology to its fullest advantage. Data fusion is a vital part of the command and control process, and there is an increasingly urgent need to solve the information-processing problems associated with it. This is one of the major areas for future development and provides much of the basis for the current military interest in artificial intelligence and parallel processing. It is a theme that we shall return to later.

Communications Networks

The communications networks are also obvious candidates for the technology. It is relatively straightforward, at least in principle, to write computer programs specifying how information should be routed round the network, which systems should be switched in, when, and so forth; the new British Ptarmigan system is a good example of all these working in practice. Two points, however, are worthy of note. One limiting factor in the performance of these communications systems will, we believe, arise from a lack of communications manpower rather than from insufficient application of the technology. It is an unfortunate fact of life that, whilst the technology can certainly improve overall performance, it tends not to save manpower. In practice, a worsening of the situation occurs in that new and higher-grade skills tend to be needed to manage and maintain the automated systems and these force upon us inevitable organisational and operational changes. The second point concerns the issue of interoperability, discussed in some detail in Chapter 9. The rate at which the necessary standards can be agreed and implemented will be a further limiting factor in the improvement of these systems. The clear need for the future is integrated communications networks and this is another theme that we shall pick up later on.

Decision Support

Field support for the staff who serve the decision maker is typified by systems such as Wavell, and what these really provide is a co-ordinated and consistent information-handling and distribution network, not just within the one decision-making sub-system but also between it and all others in the larger system. The computer programs for such systems should again be, at least in principle, within the current state of the art; although the development of software to perform reliable management of distributed databases in a battlefield environment comes into the very difficult category. More of these systems are planned and will continue to be introduced; and, as they are, so the urgent need for system interoperability and the integration of their associated communications networks will become ever more apparent.

In addition, the increasing application of office-automation techniques to the staff cell functions both in the field and in barracks also makes sense: word processing, spreadsheets, database file management and storage can all assist in improving efficiency and performance and in relieving the staff officer of much of the routine work within the decision-making sub-system.

For the decision maker, however, there is today very little direct assistance. Decision support systems can be expected, in the future, increasingly to aid the staff, and to a lesser extent the commander, in the functions of situation assessment and resource allocation, and these issues are discussed in a later section together with the data-fusion problems mentioned previously. Improved presentational facilities would certainly assist in briefing the commander and in providing him with a better visual picture of the overall situation, but, as we saw in Chapter 5, the search for a large flat screen display for presenting graphic information related to a map is still continuing, and the quite significant unit costs and practical disadvantages of present systems tend to outweigh what may be seen currently as only marginal benefits.

Effectors

Though not strictly part of command and control, the technology can equally well be applied to weapon systems. Fire-and-forget smart weapons are with us already, and we shall see these increasingly being integrated into complete target-acquisition and fire-control systems where speed of response is the crucial factor.

Looking somewhat further to the future, what might be called task-and-forget systems, such as the autonomous battlefield vehicle, are under serious consideration and investigation. Improbable as it may seem, in a paper presented by a British research and development establishment to a conference on intelligent knowledge based systems (IKBS) in 1984, it was stated that:

> it has been suggested that widespread use of unmanned vehicles could have an impact on warfare comparable with that of the tank . . [4]

It is important to recognise what an autonomous battlefield vehicle is and what it is not. It is not a remotely piloted vehicle (RPV), for there are no external controls; the system is autonomous. One example might be an armoured vehicle that has no driver, no observer, no gunner, no human presence within it at all. It is not remotely controlled by some distant human operator, but instead contains within itself a number of computers each of which is running some kind of advanced rule-based expert system. It is these advanced expert systems that are making the moment to moment decisions that control every aspect of the vehicle's behaviour. One system might control the driving, another the weapons, a third the navigation, and in overall control we might expect some kind of goal-seeking mechanism. Many difficult problems remain to be solved, not least of all those associated with vision, pattern-recognition and route following.

From the military standpoint, it is not too difficult to visualise a situation where a tasking agency gives general direction to the goal-seeking element of the autonomous battlefield vehicle in the form of a mission; perhaps to carry out a reconnaissance patrol in this area, or seek out and destroy this enemy

FIG. 12.2   Autonomous Land Vehicle Test Bed (DARPA)

facility, or, even, deny access to this particular piece of ground. Then having been given its mission, all the other expert systems in the vehicle co-operate with the goal-seeking expert system in attempting to fulfil the mission. Practical implementations of such systems are a long way off and we consider what advances in the technology still need to be made in a a subsequent section of this chapter. Nevertheless, significant research efforts are in progress and Figure 12.2 shows a photograph of the autonomous land vehicle test bed which is being funded by DARPA.

Current Research Activity and Trends

Expert Systems

Having mentioned expert systems in the context of the autonomous land vehicle it is perhaps not inappropriate now to consider the concepts underlying their operation.

As shown in Figure 12.3, an expert system is usually considered to consist of an inference engine and a knowledge base, the latter being sometimes shown as further divided into a rule base and a fact base. The knowledge base is a collection of information that relates to the domain of expertise within which the expert system has been devised to solve problems. Given a problem, via some suitable form of user interface, it operates by repeatedly applying its rules of inference to the knowledge base until either the problem is solved or no further inferences can be drawn. The knowledge base is created from information that has been elicited from human experts in the field and is usually structured so that it can be easily updated and expanded in use. This updating process allows further expertise to be added to the system as experience in its use is gained.

The process of knowledge elicitation, that is, the obtaining of expertise from a human expert, is a very difficult task, not least of all because most human experts are not consciously aware of their decision-making activities. Further, the ways in which the knowledge is represented in the system have a significant effect on the performance and capabilities of the system. Facts in a knowledge domain rarely stand alone, but are related, often in very complex ways, with other facts in the domain and these relationships need also to be represented. This area of endeavour is increasingly being known as 'knowledge engineering'.

One representation of knowledge that is most usually found in current expert systems is the rule-based paradigm. Knowledge is specified in the form of IF <condition> THEN <consequence> rules, that are sometimes referred to as productions. Given a set of facts or assertions and a set of rules each of the form:

	ANTECEDENT		CONSEQUENT
IF	<assertion 1 is true>	THEN	<assertion x is true>
	<assertion 2 is true>		<assertion y is true>
	:		:
	:		:
	<assertion N is true>		<assertion z is true>

then, a forward-chaining expert-system problem solver might carry out the following process:

> For each rule in the rule base attempt to match all the antecedent assertions in the rule, in their order of appearance with existing assertions in the fact base. If a match is found for all the antecedent assertions, the rule is said to have fired and the consequent assertions of the rule are then added to the

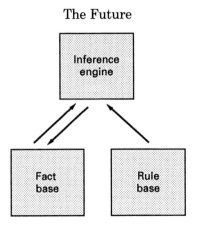

FIG. 12.3   Basis of an Expert System

knowledge of the system. This process is repeated continuously until no more rules fire.

As a very simple example, consider the following rule and set of initial assertions:

IF	<name-of-animal x> is a <type-of-animal y>
	<name-of-animal z> is offspring of <name-of-animal x>
THEN	<name-of-animal z> is a <type-of-animal y>

> FIDO is a DOG
> TIDDLES is a CAT
> PATCH is offspring of FIDO

Applying the forward-chaining mechanism, the first antecedent assertion '<name-of-animal x> is a <type-of-animal y>' is matched by the assertions from the fact base: 'FIDO is a DOG' and TIDDLES is a CAT'. The second antecedent assertion '<name-of-animal z> is offspring of <name-of-animal x>' however is matched only by 'PATCH is offspring of FIDO' and hence the sole consequent assertion '<name-of-animal z> is a <type-of-animal y>' that can be inferred and thus added to the fact base is: 'PATCH is a DOG'.

The forward-chaining approach works from known facts to new, deduced facts. It is possible, however, to put forward a hypothesis and use the antecedent/consequent rules to work backwards seeking supporting evidence for the hypothesis. For example: we may hypothesise that 'PATCH is a DOG'. For this to be true, the sole production rule that we have in this simple example tells us that we must find evidence that 'PATCH is the offspring of FIDO' and that 'FIDO is a DOG'. We can now search the fact base for such supporting evidence or, as in more realistic cases, apply further rules until the hypothesis is reduced to evidence that exists in the fact base. This approach is called backward chaining and is at the very heart of many goal-seeking systems.

One essential feature of an expert system is the facility for the user to question its reasoning. We might wish to say, for example:

WHY do you assert PATCH is a DOG?

and would expect an explanation that was based on the assertions in the fact base and the rules that had been fired: perhaps something as follows:

> IF   FIDO is a DOG
> AND   PATCH is offspring of FIDO
> THEN   PATCH is a DOG   . . .rule x

In practical systems one can expect rule bases of some hundreds to thousands of rules, and real-time performance can then become a limitation. This is of particular concern, of course, in the command and control field. A term that has recently come into use to indicate a measure of performance for expert systems is that of logical inferences per second or LIPs, and much effort is going into the Japanese fifth generation project to develop inference engines which have performances of many megalips. This is again an area where parallel processing and new computer architectures are being investigated in order to increase significantly the inference-engine performance. It is, however, often very difficult to see how knowledge bases for a particular application can be simply partitioned between a number of separate inference engines operating in parallel.

Expert systems may be written in one of the traditional programming languages such as Pascal or FORTRAN, or one of the artificial intelligence (AI) languages such as LISP (LISt Processing) or PROLOG (PROgramming in LOGic). Often, however, an expert system shell may be provided by a software developer which is, as it were, an empty expert system. The mechanisms which are needed to implement the inference engine are already built into the software as are the knowledge representation structures. All the designer of a specific expert system has to do is add the knowledge that is relevant to the required problem domain in the appropriate predefined format. This, of course, is the most difficult part of the whole construction.

So far in this discussion, we have been dealing with what Szolovits and Pauker have called categorical reasoning systems;[5] that is systems with rules of the form: IF X THEN Y. However, the real world of decision making is seldom like that; we can rarely be so categorically certain that X is the case and hence Y must be so. More often we may consider that X might be the case and that there is hence a good chance that Y may be too. There is thus a need to be able to incorporate uncertainty into practical decision support-systems in order to handle judgmental rules and incomplete evidence. These are sometimes called probabilistic reasoning systems and the rules may contain numerical factors (usually between 0 and 1) which represent the degree of certainty associated with the assertions. Although such certainty factors may represent genuine probability values, often there is no mathematical basis for them and they may have been determined by little more than intuitive guesswork.

Such certainty factors may be associated with the antecedent assertions, the consequent assertions or with both, and the inference-engine procedures for combining certainty factors have to take into account: how the certainties associated with the antecedents of a rule are to be combined into the overall input certainty for the rule; how the rule is to translate input certainty into output certainty; and, how the multi-argued certainty of an assertion is to be determined when several antecedent/consequent rules argue for it. The use of Bayesian probability theory to represent uncertainty under these circumstances has not been found entirely satisfactory and several possibility theories have been proposed, no single one of which appears to be significantly better than any of the others.[6] This, too, is an area of continuing and active research.

Intelligent Knowledge Based Systems (IKBS)

We have considered so far only systems where the knowledge of the expert is represented by a collection of IF THEN rules; the so-called expert system. This approach is adequate where the problem domain is very narrow and highly specific. When we wish to deal with a broader domain the rule-based representation becomes unsatisfactory and this is particularly true when we wish to represent and utilise what we understand as common sense knowledge.

FIG. 12.4 Human Pattern Recognition Example

As an example of the way in which the human mind applies common sense knowledge, it is instructive to try to interpret the probable meaning of the pattern enclosed by the goose-egg in Figure 12.4.

We suggest that most English-speaking people will arrive at an unequivocal interpretation within a fraction of a second; they will rapidly form the view that it is most likely to be the word 'Yours'.

Now it is interesting to note that no identifiable symbols nor words are present in the figure to assist one in making that interpretation. The pattern simply consists of a series of squiggles. The pattern of the squiggles, however, vaguely suggests the structure of a personal letter and it is the recognition of this structure that is essential before any inferences can be drawn. The common sense or experiential knowledge base that is needed to enable this pattern recognition process to take place without any other relevant context seems to be very large indeed. It is necessary, for example, to understand the concept of writing; to 'know' that humans communicate with one another by the written word; that documents carrying the written word have a formal structure; that this pattern of squiggles slightly resembles one such formal structure; that within that particular structure, the squiggle within the oval would be part of the final salutation; and that the first part of such salutations is invariably the sequence of letters 'Yours'. This is a gross over-simplification of the processing that needs to be done, and all within a fraction of a second.

Although this is typical of the kind of problem which a human is very good at solving, even when presented with incomplete or inconsistent information, we have little idea of how it is done. If we follow the knowledge-base approach, we certainly do not yet know how to represent or process so quickly in an automated system what must be a very large, complex, and highly interrelated knowledge base. In order to be able to exercise 'judgement' in decision making, it does seem that we require such a common sense, experiential knowledge base and this does seem to take many years even for a human to acquire. Some workers believe that were we ever to devise an effective computer model of the process with adequate representation of the knowledge, it still might take 40 years or so to teach the system enough common sense before it started to become useful!

Nevertheless, the most profitable route to more effective expert systems, perhaps leading eventually to useful decision support-systems that directly assist the commander, seems to lie in better knowledge-representation approaches. It has been found impracticable to try to incorporate common sense knowledge simply through the addition of further rules to the current expert-system rule-based model, and so we need to examine other more useful knowledge-representation mechanisms. This field of endeavour tends to go under the generic title of intelligent knowledge based systems or IKBS, of which current rule-based expert-systems are often considered to be a sub-class.

One popular approach to more complex knowledge representation is the semantic net which denotes objects by labelled circles (called nodes) and describes relations between them by means of labelled arrows (called links). An example is shown in Figure 12.5.

Here we see, in a fairly self-evident manner, that: FIDO IS-A DOG, that FIDO is of COLOUR BROWN, and that PATCH is the OFFSPRING-OF FIDO and thus also that PATCH IS-A DOG. A semantic net is a graphical way of associating intuitive meanings with objects.

Object nodes, such as FIDO, are often implemented in knowledge-base systems as frames which have slots that may hold many link pointers, such as IS-A, to other

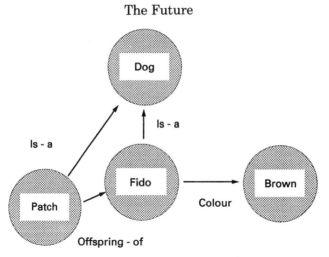

FIG. 12.5   Semantic Net Example

frames, such as DOG. The frame concept is very powerful and permits complex semantic relationships to be represented. Associated with it are such ideas as classes (DOG could be a class), instances (FIDO and PATCH could be specific instances of the class DOG) and inheritance (FIDO and PATCH could both expect to inherit some of the characteristics of the class DOG, whilst, in addition, having some specific instance characteristics of their own). This approach is not limited to objects but can equally well be applied to events. Many modern artificial-intelligence systems utilise the frame approach and a clear and concise introduction to the subject can be found in Winston.[7]

Neural Networks

Since about the beginning of 1987 there has been much excitement in the popular technical press over the discovery of the 'new' field of neurocomputing; a field that is concerned with the use of neural networks to assist in the solution of some of the traditionally hard artificial-intelligence problems of speech and vision systems and of learning and pattern recognition. We have deliberately placed in quotes the adjective 'new' here because, in fact, the field has been around for a long time; at least as long, that is, as the much better known Von Neumann concepts that form the basis for the modern digital computer. The key starting point for modern research in this area is probably the classic paper by McCulloch and Pitts published in 1943,[8] and it is likely that this work also influenced Von Neumann in the development of his ideas.

McCulloch and Pitts devised a model for an artificial neuron which consists of a node with a number of separate inputs and a single but possibly branching output (Figure 12.6). The work formed the basis for what are now known as binary neural networks. Each node in a network of nodes has an activation value which appears on its branched outputs. Associated with each of the inputs (*i*) to the node are weighting values (*w*) which modify the effect of the inputs on the node. In a network of nodes, connections, which are analogous to synapses in the biological model, connect the outputs of some nodes to the inputs of others. Each node sums

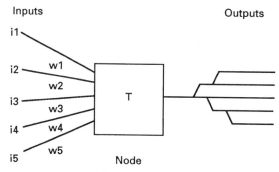

FIG. 12.6   The Artificial Neuron

the weighted activation values that it receives from the other nodes in the system and produces an output value in accordance with some internal transfer function T, sometimes called the activation function.

In the binary neural network model, the output activation value is 1 if the weighted sum exceeds some threshold value and 0 otherwise. Other activation functions have been investigated and a paper by Grossberg gives an excellent overview of the subject field.[9]

The activation values are often called short term memory (STM) traces, and if procedures are introduced to change the value of the weighting factors (w), the resulting adaptive weights are called long-term memory traces. This provides an important learning mechanism, as all the accumulated knowledge of the network is then represented by the total set of weights. Various learning algorithms have been investigated: perhaps the most famous being that due to Hebb[10] who suggested that:

> . . . when an axon of cell A is near enough to excite a cell B, and repeatedly or persistently takes part in firing it, some growth process or metabolic change takes place in one or both cells, such that A's efficiency, as one of the cells firing B, is increased.

This has given rise to an algorithm which ensures that each time an input contributes to the activation of a node, its associated weight is increased, and each time it fails to cause stimulation, its weight is decreased. In this way, patterns of information that repeat are reinforced and patterns that do not repeat, are 'forgotten'. This makes neural networks inherently sensitive to patterns in data and permits them to be 'taught' to recognise particular regularities.

Artificial neural networks have been defined by Kohonen as:

> . . . massively parallel interconnected networks of simple (usually adaptive) elements and their hierarchical organisations which are intended to interact with the objects of the real world in the same way as biological systems do.[11]

In the biological model, the nodes are neurons, the outgoing branches are axons and these make variable connections or synapses with other neurons, or perhaps muscles and glands. An important point to note about biological neural networks is their size: the whole human central nervous system contains of the order of some hundred thousand million neurons and the number of interconnections is estimated at some ten thousand times this. Current artificial neural networks are orders of magnitude smaller than this, with typical systems at the time of writing having perhaps thousands of nodes with tens to hundreds of thousands of interconnections.

The implementation of artificial neural networks may be direct or virtual. In the direct case, each neural node is implemented in hardware as an individual processing element with some appropriate interconnection architecture. The hardware implementation may be electronic, optical or electro-optical and may involve very large scale integration (VLSI) of many identical nodes on a single chip. Whilst providing the fastest possible operational form of implementation, such hard-wired networks are very difficult to modify and for research purposes the virtual approach is more popular. In this the neural network is partially or fully emulated by one or more conventional digital computers, and thus the algorithms associated with activation and learning can more readily be modified. Interest in neural networks has thus helped to stimulate work on parallel processing architectures with a view to obtaining the required improvements in performance.

In use, neural networks are not programmed but are 'trained'. Since the basic mechanism adapts itself to the given stimuli by adjusting its weightings, a process of learning, the networks tend to have two modes of operation. In the training mode the network is given repeated examples of, say, a noisy signal together with the expected outputs, and, over a number of cycles, it adjusts its weightings and develops the necessary algorithms to transform correctly input to output. Subsequently the network may be used operationally to identify some other partial, noisy signal, having learned the necessary transformation algorithms for itself.

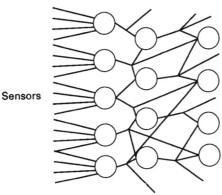

Sensors

FIG. 12.7   Multi-Layered Neural Network

Another useful characteristic of neural networks is their inherent resilience to damage. Since the total knowledge of the network is distributed amongst the entire set of the weightings, damage to part of the network is rarely catastrophic. Even severe disruption of many components seems to be reversible, as the undamaged portion of the network tends to remember sufficient fragments of the whole to guide the retraining needed to regain the lost capability.

Practical neural networks are often multi-layered with each layer specialising in some part of the overall process (Figure 12.7). The first layer may be dealing with raw input from sensors; the second layer perhaps specialising in seeking particular pattern groupings from the processed outputs of the first layer with, say, a third layer organising those groupings into higher-level abstractions. Different activation function strategies may well be used for different layers, and quite complex pattern recognition devices can be built in this manner.

One disadvantage of these systems is their inherent inability to explain their decisions. Since the information is not represented explicitly but is distributed throughout the network in the form of adaptive weightings, it does not seem feasible to be able to question the system.

Application to Future Systems

Decision Support Systems

A hybrid approach might be used to overcome this fundamental disadvantage of neural networks. An effective operational decision support-system could be made up of a neural network paired with a rule-based expert system. By its nature, the neural network would arrive at solutions very rapidly, but it would be unable to explain itself and the solutions it put forward might not be optimal. The expert system, which would operate much more slowly than the neural network, could then be used to examine the solutions suggested by the neural network in order to gauge the extent to which they approached the optimal, and could, in addition, explain its reasoning. This seems to parallel the human approach to problem solving, whereby insight and intuition based on experience are used to obtain a solution, and logic to explain and justify it. There seems much potential value in pursuing this general approach to decision support.

Data Fusion, Situation Assessment and Resource Allocation

The problems of data fusion have been touched upon in Chapters 1 and 2 and earlier in this chapter. The need to interpret and correlate very high flow rates of raw information from multiple sensors in real time in order to provide timely tactical intelligence to the commander is clearly of paramount importance. The use of multi-level neural networks to assist in the initial pattern-recognition process would appear to be an obvious application area, although some authorities are not convinced that the neural network technology is yet sufficiently mature for them to be used in operational environments.

Where correlation between several different sensor sources is required, such as sonar, radar and ESM, then a combination of neural networks for the initial recognition of patterns and rule-based analytical expert-systems for situation assessment could provide a powerful tool for command and control. It is also likely that rule-based systems will be used to assist in resource allocation, that is, in the assignment of weapons to targets, and in the planning of operations. Recent work at the Admiralty Research Establishment as reported by Miles[12] gives an excellent overview of the use of rule-based systems for naval command and control.

Evolutionary Change in Command and Control Systems

We identified in Chapter 8 the need for evolutionary change in command and control systems, particularly where the software implements part of current doctrine which may, in turn, have to be adapted to meet changes in the military environment and the political climate. Where the software has been developed in the normal manner as a suite of particular purpose applications-programs, such changes can be very costly and difficult to implement.

There is a school of thought that proposes the development of a command and control system as a set of common generic functions, such as, perhaps, message handling and database update, that are controlled in detail by one or more rule-based expert systems. The rules implemented by the rule-based controller at the highest level are what might properly be called standing operating procedures (SOPs) or rules of engagement (ROEs). By loading the appropriate set of rules the system can be adjusted for a specific kind of operation. The commander, or more likely his staff, could also modify the rules, or SOPs, to tailor the system to their exact requirements, and these could be allowed to change throughout the various phases of an operation.[13]

There seems to be some reluctance to adopt this approach, perhaps because it is felt by procurement staff that systems should not be capable of modification in the field. However, controlled modification of this form may be the only way of dealing with the evolutionary modification requirement, and, anyway, most would agree that the SOPs adopted by a unit are very much a matter for the commander on the spot and not for some distant developer. This will be a matter for some debate, but it is perhaps interesting to note that such systems are already under trial in the United States Navy.

A Note of Caution

Although there can be little doubt that trained neural networks and improved knowledge-based systems are likely to make significant contributions to the field of command and control, we do need to be cautious. It is perhaps not entirely coincidental that we should see the worst stock market crash in recent years shortly after the 'big bang' computerisation of the London Stock Exchange. A year before that saw reports that heavy selling on Wall Street had been attributed to computerised dealing with systems failing to read the market properly and marking down shares in far too mechanical a manner. As we write this, dealers on Wall Street have again been asked to stop using their automated systems because of wild swings in the market.

Clearly we are not yet able to capture all the domain knowledge of a human expert, and, even if we could, that would still be insufficient, as the decision making of a human expert is tempered with sound common sense.

A further concern in the military environment is the possible predictability of decisions recommended by automated systems. Knowledge of the rules and inference procedures used by a decision support-system may give an opponent an advantage in determining likely courses of action. The final decision will always be a matter for the commander, but he needs to be aware that some options could be predictable through knowledge of his systems.

Despite such cautions, the way ahead seems to lie clearly with neural networks and knowledge-based systems, requiring ever more powerful inference engines, parallel processing and artificial intelligence techniques.

The Future—The Integrated Battlefield Communications System

The different types of battlefield communication system described thus far have tended to be regarded as separate and serving different needs. The need for increased flexibility and speed of response on the battlefield, and the development

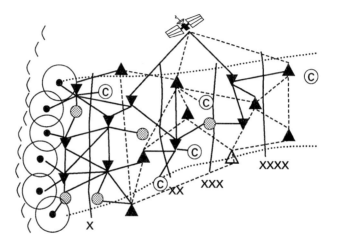

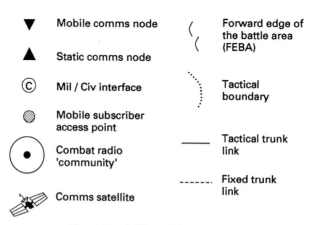

FIG. 12.8   A View of the Future

of information systems which promise to serve those needs is influencing the development of a more integrated approach to battlefield communications.

Although the different components use techniques which stem from the existing, separate classes of communications system, the overall aim is to produce a communications network for the battlefield which can interconnect distributed information system elements wherever they may be, via a standard interface using standard protocols. Such integration will extend vertically up the chain of command, well beyond what is accepted nowadays as the boundary of the 'tactical' area, and horizontally to allow interoperation between adjacent formations of different nationalities. The topic of interoperability, which goes further into some of the problems which must be solved before such a degree of integration can be achieved, has been covered in Chapter 9. A possible view of the integrated battlefield communications system of the future is shown in Figure 12.8.

Bibliography and Notes

General

BATES, W. *The Computer Cookbook 83/84*, Prentice-Hall, 1983.
HARRIS, C. J. (Ed.) *Advances in C³I*, Peter Peregrinus, 1987.

Chapter 1

COYLE, R. G. Management System Dynamics, Wiley, 1977.
VAN CREVELD, M. *Command in War,* Harvard, 1985.

Chapter 2

BISHOP, P. *Fifth Generation Computers: Concepts, Implementation and Uses*, Ellis Horwood/Wiley, 1986.
MOTO-OKA, T. and KITSUREGAWA, M. *The Fifth Generation Computer*, Wiley, 1985.

Chapters 3 & 4

BROOKSHEAR, J. G. *Computing Science: An Overview*, Benjamin/Cummings, 1985.
FREER, J. *Systems Design with Advanced Microprocessors*, Pitman, 1987.
LIPPIAT and WRIGHT, *The Architecture of Small Computer Systems*, Prentice-Hall, 1985.
MITCHELL, H. J. (Ed.) *32 Bit Microprocessors*, Collins, 1986.
TOWNSEND, R. *Digital Computer Structure and Design*, Butterworths, 1982.
WHITWORTH, I. R. *16-Bit Microprocessors*, Granada, 1984.

Chapter 4

PARADAENS, J. (Ed.) *Databases*, Academic Press, 1987.
SMITH and BARNES. *Files and Databases*, Addison-Wesley, 1987.

Chapter 5

HEARN, D. and BAKER, M. P. *Computer Graphics*, Prentice-Hall, 1986.
SHERR, S. *Electronic Displays*, Wiley, 1979.
System Design for Human Interaction, IEEE Press, 1987.

Chapter 6

CLARE, C. P. *A Guide To Data Communications*, Longmans, 1984.
MARSHALL, G. J. *Principles of Digital Communications*, McGraw-Hill, 1980.
MORRIS, D. J. *Communication for Command and Control Systems*, Pergamon, 1983.
TANNENBAUM. *Principles of Computer Networks*, Prentice-Hall, 1981.
TORRIERI, D. J. *Principles of Military Communication Systems*, Artech, 1981.

Chapter 7

BELL LABORATORIES. *EMP Engineering and Design Principles*, 1975.
MINISTRY OF DEFENCE. *Environmental Handbook for Defence Matériel: 00-35, Issue 1, Part 4: The Natural Environment.*

Chapter 8

ABELSON, H. and SUSSMAN, G. J. *Structure and Interpretation of Computer Programs*, MIT Press, 1985.
BROOKS, F. P. *The Mythical Man-Month*, Addison-Wesley, 1979.
FAWLEY, R. E. *Software Engineering Concepts*, McGraw-Hill, 1985.
UNITED STATES, DEPARTMENT OF DEFENSE. *Final Report of the Software Acquisition and Development Working Group*, 1980.
The IECCA Guide to the Management of Software-Based Systems, HMSO, 3rd Edn., 1985.

Chapter 11

Van Creveld M. *Command in War*, Harvard, 1985.

Chapter 12

1. NICKERSON, R. S. *Using Computers. Human Factors in Information Systems*, Bradford Books, MIT Press, 1986.
2. BOWDEN, V. 'The language of computers', *American Scientist*, 1970, **58**(1), pp. 43–53.
3. TOONG, H. D. and GUPTA, A. 'Personal computers', *Scientific American*, 1982, 247(6), pp. 86–107.
4. MARKS, A. J. 'Applications of intelligent knowledge based systems in unmanned land vehicles', *Proceedings of the Third Seminar on Applications of Machine Intelligence to Defence Systems*, 1984.
5. SZOLOVITS, P. and PAUKER, S. G. 'Categorical and probabilistic reasoning in medical diagnosis', *Artificial Intelligence*, 1978, U(11), pp. 115–44.
6. COX, I. J. 'Expert systems', *Electronics & Power*, March 1984, pp. 237–40.
7. WINSTON, P. H. *Artificial Intelligence*, Addison-Wesley, 2nd edn, 1984.
8. McCULLOCH, W. S. and PITTS, W. 'A logical calculus of the ideas immanent in nervous activity', *Bulletin of Mathematical Biophysics*, 1943, **5**, pp. 115–33.
9. GROSSBERG, S. 'Nonlinear neural networks: principles, mechanisms, and architectures', *Neural Networks*, 1988, 1(1), pp. 17–61.
10. HEBB, D. O. *Organisation of Behaviour*, Wiley, New York, 1949.
11. KOHONEN, T. 'An introduction to neural computing', *Neural Networks*, 1988, **1**(1), pp. 1–16.
12. MILES, J. A. H. *Artificial Intelligence Applied to Data Fusion and Situation Assessment for Command and Control*, PhD Thesis, Southampton University, Faculty of Engineering and Science, 1988.
13. CHARNIAK, E. and McDERMOTT, D. *Introduction to Artificial Intelligence*, Addison-Wesley, 1985.

Glossary of Technical Terms

ABCA
America, Britain, Canada and Australia. The quadripartite treaty organisation between these four nations.

Ada
A high order language (HOL), developed in the early 1980s as an American Department of Defense (DoD) program, and subsequently adopted as the DoD standard HOL to be used for all 'mission critical' (i.e. mainly real time) applications. Also adopted as a mandatory standard by the British Ministry of Defence (MOD). Named after Augusta Ada Byron, Lord Byron's daughter who was for a time assistant to Charles Babbage, and is regarded as the world's first computer programmer.

Alvey
A British government five-year program which ended in 1987, aimed at channelling investment in information technology, largely as a response to the Japanese fifth generation computer initiative. Formed part of a pan-European initiative named Esprit.

Address
A group of symbols which identifies a register, a particular part of storage, or some other data source or destination.

Address space
The range of addresses directly accessible to the processor.

Address size
The maximum number of digits used to form the address of directly addressable memory.

Amplitude modulation (AM)
A process of modulation in which the amplitude of the carrier signal is varied in sympathy with the amplitude of the information signal.

ASCII
American Standard Code for Information Interchange. A standard code for the representation of alphanumeric and graphical symbols, consisting of 7-bit (plus one parity bit), or 8-bit (ASCII-8) coded characters.

Assembly language
A computer language in which there is usually a one-to-one correspondence between its instructions and the instruction set of the hardware.

Asynchronous transmission
A data transmission in which the group of bits representing each information character is individually synchronised, usually through the use of start and stop elements.

Automatic channel selection (ACS)
A combat radio transmission mode where the radio frequency used for each transmission is determined by selecting a free channel from a number of frequencies allocated to the link. Also known as free channel search.

Backing store
Store used to support the main memory. Also referred to as secondary store, or mass store.

Bandwidth
A measure of the frequency response of a channel which governs the rate at which data units can be sent down the channel.

Baseband
Baseband transmission involves the transmission of data signals over a channel at the frequencies at which they are generated. The term is used in local area network (LAN) technology to distinguish this approach from broadband transmission, in which frequencies of different groups of signal are changed through a process of modulation so that the groups may be sent over the same physical channel without mutual interference.

BASIC
Beginners' All-purpose Symbolic Instruction Code. A programming language devised in the USA- for use in educational establishments for interactive program development on multi-user, time-sharing computer systems. In most implementations it is an interpreted language (although it can be compiled). BASIC is probably the most widely used programming language through its adoption by manufacturers of home computers. Many home computers are delivered with BASIC 'built-in' i.e. resident in ROM and available for use as soon as the machine is switched on. The original BASIC is a simple language which falls short of most people's definition of a high order language (HOL), but more recent versions have most of the features associated with HOLs, such as block structuring through the use of procedures, and control structures such as WHILE . . . DO, and CASE.

Batch processing
This term is normally used to describe the method of operation whereby batches of data accumulated at the computer centre over a period of time are processed serially, frequently according to a reguar schedule. The term is sometimes used to imply the opposite of 'on-line' or transaction processing.

Bit error rate (BER)
The ratio of the number of bits received in error to the total number of bits transmitted. This is the basic measure of the quality of a communications channel.

Block check character (BCC)
The BCC is used in error detection and correction (EDC) schemes such as the cyclic redundancy check (CRC) method. It is sent at the end of a block of data transmitted over a data-transmission link and compared with a BCC computed by the receiver (from the characters in the whole received block) to determine whether or not the block has been correctly received.

Bootstrap
This term is derived from the expression 'to pull oneself up by the bootstraps.' It describes a simple initialisation program which is used when starting up a computer system to load and run more complex programs.

Bubble memory
A computer data storage device which relies on the property of a thin film of certain magnetic materials to form microscopic magnetic domains or 'bubbles' when subjected to a magnetic field. The binary '1' and '0' symbols are represented by the presence or otherwise of a bubble. Storage densities for bubble memories are approaching those of semiconductor memory devices. Access speeds are much greater than those for mass-memory devices, such as magnetic discs, but considerably slower than for semiconductor memories. Bubble memories have the advantages of being non-volatile and more rugged than electromechanical devices, such as discs and tapes, and have therefore found a use in military applications.

Byte
A group of binary digits (bits) operated on as a unit and usually shorter than a computer word. In the majority of modern computers a byte consists of 8 bits and is used to represent one character.

Carrier sense multiple access (CSMA)
A local area network (LAN) access mode in which a station having data to transmit senses the network to see if any other station is sending before starting its transmission.

Carrier wave
An electromagnetic signal which can be made to convey information through the process of modulation.

CCITT
Comite Consultatif des Telegraphes et Telephones. An international body established, under the aegis of the United Nations, through the International Telecommunications Union (ITU) for the formulation and recommendation of standards in the field of telecommunications, including data communications. Most widely known and applied sets of standards include the V series, for transmission of data over speech circuits using modems, and the X series for digital transmission.

CIS

Command and control, communications and information systems. The combination of communications systems and (computer-based) information systems used to support the processes of command and control.

Circuit switching

A method of switching in which a physical circuit is established between source and destination, and held until it is broken by one or other of the users, whether information is passing or not.

COBOL

Common Business Oriented Language. A programming language for business applications.

Combat net radio (CNR)

Single channel radio, normally in the VHF or the HF bands used as the primary means of communication by combat troops. The primary mode of operation is normally voice, although CNR can be adapted for data transmission. Equipment may be man-portable or mounted in fighting vehicles. An important characteristic of traditional voice CNR is its 'all-informed' nature, i.e. when one station transmits on the net, all others in contact hear the transmission. The word 'net' is frequently omitted nowadays, implying that configurations other than the all-informed net, such as packet radio, may be used.

Compiler

A program which converts programs written in a high level language into the machine code for a specified computer, ready for execution by that computer. The computer on which the compiled program is to be run may be the same as that which is used to perform the compilation, in which case the process is known as host–host compilation. If the program is compiled to run on a different machine (the 'target' computer, the process is called host-target compilation.

Complex instruction set computer (CISC)

The term is used to distinguish between what would formerly have been regarded as 'conventional' CPU architectures, with a rich and varied repertoire of machine instructions, and the reduced instruction set computer (RISC) architecture, in which instruction sets have been pared down to the bare essentials in the interests of improved processing speed.

COMSEC

Communications security.

Concurrency

A term is used to describe the performance by a computer of more than one task at the same time. In conventional Von Neumann-architecture computers such concurrency is an illusion, since the computer is capable only of performing operations one at a time. However, through the use of an operating system which shares the time of the CPU between a number of different tasks, the user can be given the impression that the tasks are being performed simultaneously. True concurrency is only possible in multi-processor configurations.

Database

A collection of interrelated data items stored together without unnecessary redundancy to serve one or more applications.

Database administrator

The person or organisation responsible for the design, development, use, integrity and security of a database.

Database management system (DBMS)

A software system allowing the creation and maintenance of a database, and the execution of computer programs using the database.

Data fusion

The combination of data captured at different places at different times in order to create a coherent picture of a particular event or series of events.

Directory

The 'table of contents' of a data store, such as a magnetic disc, or of a portion of such a store. In some operating systems, such as the Microsoft Disc Operating System (MSDOS), the term is used to describe a section of a hierarchically organised file store.

Disc/disk

When used by itself the term is usually taken to imply a magnetic disc, used for data storage.

Disc drive

The physical device in which a (magnetic) disc is mounted.

Disc handler

The software used to control access and data transfer to and from a disc drive or drives.

Dynamic random access memory (DRAM)
A form of semiconductor random access memory which uses the inherent stray capacitance of transistor cells to hold electrical charges representing digital data. The charges leak away over a few milliseconds and hence the cells must periodically be refreshed in order to preserve their data content.

Electromagnetic compatibility (EMC)
An item of electronic equipment is said to be electronically compatible if it can operate within a specified proximity of other electronic equipment(s) without either suffering from or causing malfunction through electromagnetic interference.

Electromagnetic environment (EME)
The term EME is used to describe the electromagnetic spectrum within which an equipment or system must operate and its occupancy by other users.

Electromagnetic pulse (EMP)
The EMP is an intense electromagnetic field of very short duration generated as a side-effect of a nuclear explosion. The EMP induces short pulses of very high current in conductors within the range of influence of the field. Such current pulses may cause damage to unprotected equipment.

Electronic counter measures (ECM)
Measures taken by one side in a conflict to hinder or disrupt the other side's use of the electromagnetic spectrum. Measures include jamming, i.e. the radiation of deliberate interference, and deception, or the transmission of signals purporting to come from a friendly source.

Electronic intelligence (ELINT)
Intelligence extracted from the interception of non-information bearing electromagnetic radiations, i.e. principally radar signals.

Electronic mail
Electronic mail (EM) is a service made available to computer network users, whereby messages may be forwarded to other users. EM is a component of office automation (OA). 'Messages' may be just that, i.e. the electronic equivalent of inter-office memos from one sender to one or more recipients, or they may be any arbitrary assembly of symbols representing text, graphics, or even speech.

Electronic smog
A term coined to describe the spectral pollution resulting from the operation of computers and other electronic equipments in close proximity to one another. Unpredictable effects occur as emanations from some equipments are received by others.

Electronic warfare (EW)
EW is the term used to describe the battle for control of the electromagnetic spectrum. It includes measures taken to hinder or disrupt the enemy's use of the spectrum, to obtain intelligence from his use of it, and to protect and preserve friendly use of the spectrum.

Encryption
The coding of data to render its meaning unreadable to unauthorised recipient(s) must normally be in possession of the same encryption key as was used to code the data on transmission.

Error detection and correction (EDC)
Measures taken to protect transmitted data from corruption by errors resulting from noise and other unwanted effects in the transmission path. EDC schemes rely upon the addition of redundant data to the transmitted data. Low level schemes permit the detection of the fact that errors have occurred, i.e. the received data differ from those which were transmitted, in which case a repeat transmission can be requested. This process is called ARQ—standing for automatic request repeat. Full error detection and correction schemes can, for a limited number of incorrect bits in a given block of data, identify the actual bits and hence correct the errors.

Expert system
A computer system which attempts to provide solutions to problems by a process of reasoning, based on a description of the problem and on stored facts about the subject area which have been provided by a human expert.

Expert system shell
A computer program which contains the mechanism for asking the questions and carrying out the reasoning of an expert system, but which does not yet hold the knowledge to be supplied by the expert.

File
A set of related records treated as a unit.

File server
A computer with associated mass storage, connected to a local area network whose principal task is to hold files of data for other computers on the LAN.

Filestore

The files of an operating system.

Floppy disc

A magnetic disc storage-medium, consisting of a thin, non-rigid plastic disc coated with magnetic oxide normally on both sides, housed within a cardboard or plastic sleeve. The sleeve has a central aperture for the disc drive spindle, and an aperture slot via which the read/write heads gain access to the magnetic surface. Floppy discs are available in a number of sizes. The largest is the 8-inch diameter disc, which is now uncommon in modern equipment. The most common size is now the 5¼-inch diameter used with the first personal computers, but the 3½-inch diameter device is rapidly gaining popularity, Also known as a 'diskette'.

FLOPS

Floating point operations per second. A measure of processing speed. Floating point operations are operations on floating point, i.e. real numbers with a whole, or integer part and a fractional part.

Free channel search

see Automatic channel selection.

Frequency division multiplex (FDM)

The process of passing more than one signal channel over the same transmission medium, by separating the channels in frequency through the process of modulation with different carrier frequencies. Originally developed for passing analogue speech channels over wideband cable or radio links, it is now used for separating channels in wideband local area networks using coaxial cables.

Frequency modulation (FM)

A process of modulation in which the frequency of the carrier signal is varied in sympathy with the amplitude of the information signal.

Frequency shift keying (FSK)

A process of digital modulation in which the frequency of the carrier signal is shifted up by a fixed amount to represent one binary state, and down by the same amount to represent the other state.

Gigabyte

A thousand million bytes.

Gigaflop

A thousand million floating point operations per second.

Group delay

The delay suffered by signals of different frequencies when propagated down a communications channel.

Handler

A computer program, normally part of the operating system, which is concerned with the transfer of data to and from an external device such as a disc drive.

Hierarchical model database.

A database in which the dominant structure is a tree structure, comprising a number of one-to-many relationships.

High level data link control (HDLC)

HDLC is a protocol for the exchange of blocks of data over a transmission link. In terms of the ISO 7 layer model for open systems interconnection (OSI), HDLC is a layer 2 (link layer) protocol.

High order language (HOL)

Also known as a high level language. A HOL is a computer programming language in which the statements and constructs are optimised for the solution of problems rather than being constrained by the characteristics of the computer hardware on which they run. A HOL program may be compiled, by different compilers, to run on a number of different machines. During the compilation process each HOL statement will be converted into a number of instructions for the target machine for which the program is being compiled.

IEEE

Institution of Electrical and Electronics Engineers; an American professional institution which has sponsored a number of important standards in the information-technology field. Amongst these are IEEE 488, which is concerned with general purpose digital interface buses, and IEEE 802, concerned with local area networks.

IKBS

Intelligent knowledge based system. A generic term for a type of processing system, of which expert systems are an example. The system produces solutions by a process of inference based on knowledge of the problem domain (i.e. facts) and rules which describe the characteristics and behaviour of entities in the problem domain.

Indexed sequential access method (ISAM)
A method of organising data on disc storage where the main records are stored sequentially and accessed via separate index files which hold the key fields and pointers to the location of the main records.

Inference engine
The processing element of an intelligent knowledge based system.

Information exchange requirements (IERs)
IERs are statements of the requirement for information to be exchanged between battlefield users, normally expressed in terms of the nature of the information, the frequency of the transfer, the required speed of exchange, and security requirements.

Information management
Information management is the treatment of information as a resource. It is concerned with ensuring that the meaning and interpretation of information held by the organisation is valid and consistent throughout the organisation, and accurately reflects the needs of the organisation.

Information service management
Information service management is concerned with the capture, storage, and distribution of information, and with maintaining its security, integrity and availability for use.

Instruction cache
In some processor designs, instructions are called from memory before they are required for use and held in interim storage known variously as an instruction cache or instruction pipeline. The object of the technique is to speed up the workings of the processor.

Instruction set
The instruction set of a computer is that set of machine code instructions which are 'built-in' to the machine's hardware.

International Standards Organisation (ISO)
The ISO is an international body which is responsible for publishing standards in a wide range of fields. Of particular interest in the IT field is the ISO seven layer reference model for open systems interconnection (OSI).

Intersymbol interference
Intersymbol interference occurs in a digital pulse-stream during transmission when the time and frequency characteristics of the channel distort the pulses so that they spread in time beyond the confines of the pulse sampling time, i.e. a given sample may contain energy which originates from adjacent pulses as well as the pulse which was generated at that time. The effect is to reduce the detection threshold and increase the likelihood of erroneous reception.

Kernel
The term kernel is generally used to describe the central, essential part of a computer system.

Kilobyte
Nominally, one thousand bytes, but because of the binary nature of computer storage, it is usual to use the term to denote the nearest whole number power of 2, i.e. 1024.

Knowledge base
That element of an IKBS which holds the knowledge or facts about the problem domain.

Knowledge based system
see IKBS.

Knowledge engineering
The process of gathering and representing knowledge about a problem area in such a way that it can be used in an IKBS.

Local area network (LAN)
A data communications network, used to interconnect elements of a computer system within 'local' confines, normally taken to mean within a site (factory or campus), a building, a ship, or tactical headquarters.

Logical inferences per second (LIPs)
A measure of the speed of operation of an IKBS.

Magnetic bubble memory
see Bubble memory.

Magnetic surface memory
Memory devices which make use of the property of thin films of ferromagnetic material, laid on a plastic or metal substrate, to hold information in the form of magnetised domains. Varieties of magnetic surface memory devices include discs, tapes, drums and strips.

Main memory

The working store of a computer which is directly addressed by machine-code programs. In most modern computers the main memory is composed of semiconductor random access memory (RAM), whilst in an earlier generation of machines ferromagnetic core memory was used, which is why one still occasionally hears main memory referred to as 'core store'.

Mass store

A term normally employed to describe storage used to support the computer's main memory. Most commonly used mass storage medium is magnetic disc, but magnetic bubble memory is used in some applications, and magnetic drum storage is still occasionally encountered.

Megabyte

One million bytes (actually 2^{20} or 1,048,576 bytes).

Megalips

A million logical inferences per second.

Message switching

A switching technique based on the transmission, storage and forwarding of whole transactions or messages between subscribers to a network.

Microprocessor

A processor fabricated as a single integrated circuit. The circuit may or may not include some main memory and interface circuitry.

MIPS

Million instructions per second. A measure of processor speed. Unlike flops (qv), the type of instruction is not specified. MIPS ratings alone are not a reliable indicator of the power of a computer. It is important to know the architecture of the machine concerned, and the conditions under which the MIPS were measured. In some circumstances, the time taken to perform certain benchmark tests, i.e. standard tasks, is a more meaningful and useful indicator. Hence the term MIPS is sometimes facetiously translated as 'Meaningless indicator of processor speed'.

Modem

MODulator-DEModulator; a device used to convert digital data signals into a form suitable for transmission over a voice telephone circuit, and vice versa.

MSDOS

MicroSoft Disc Operating System: the operating system used by the IBM Personal Computer, and other compatible machines (sometimes called IBM PC 'clones') MSDOS is a trademark of the Micro-Soft Company.

Network model database

A database whose structure is based on the use of pointers between related records.

Neurocomputing

A form of parallel processing which imitates the operation of neural networks in the human brain. Implementations may be pseudo-parallel, i.e. implemented in software on a conventional single-processor computer, or they may be truly parallel and use purpose-built arrays of processors.

Object code

The result of the compilation process; instructions in the machine code of an 'object' or target computer, produced as a result of compiling source code, written in a high level language.

Open systems interconnection (OSI)

The OSI concept describes the mechanisms by which computer systems made by different manufacturers may be interconnected to exchange data and services. The concept is embodied in the International Standardisation Organisation's 7-layer OSI reference model.

Operating system

The software used to manage the resources of a computer system. The term 'resources' is used here to cover a wide variety of things, from the hardware of the system, e.g. memory (both main memory and mass storage) and input/output peripherals, such as visual display units, printers and communications devices, to other items of software, such as applications programs. In a multi-user system it is the operating system which shares the resources between the users.

Optical memory

Optical memory devices store binary information in the form of microscopic pits in a metallised, light-reflecting surface. The information is read by a narrow, precise beam of laser light which is reflected by the surface into a photodetector. When a pit is encountered, the beam is scattered, and hence the presence or otherwise of a pit in a given location can be used to signify the two binary conditions. The most common form of optical memory device is the rotating disc, developed from the discs used in the audio and video entertainment industry, but optical tape storage is also under development.

Packet radio

A form of single channel radio system in which data are transmitted across the network using the packet switching principle described below. Each radio station maintains a table of those other stations with which it is in direct contact, used in conjunction with a routing algorithm to relay data packets which it receives.

Packet switching

A communications-switching technique in which data to be transmitted from one station to another are broken down into small segments, known as packets. Each packet may be routed through the network independently of the others comprising the same transmission, and the packets are reassembled at the receiving end. This technique makes efficient use of the available channel capacity, because any given channel in the system is occupied only for the time it takes to transmit a packet; during the remainder of the time it is available to accept packets forming part of other transmissions. Contrast this with the circuit switching mode, where a physical connection exists between sender and receiver and is dedicated to those two users whether they are sending or not.

Parallel processing

A parallel-processing system permits the simultaneous processing of more than one data stream, through the use of a number of interconnected processors. Parallel processing systems can take three basic forms. In a multiple instruction, single data (MISD) system, the same data stream is subjected to a number of different processes simultaneously by different processors. A single instruction, multiple data (SIMD) configuration executes the same sequence of instructions simultaneously on a number of different data streams. In the multiple instruction, multiple data (MIMD) approach, different data streams are processed simultaneously by different instruction sequences. According to this classification, the 'conventional' single processor architecture would be referred to as single instruction, single data (SISD).

Parallel transmission

The simultaneous transmission of groups of bits (normally whole bytes or words), which implies the existence of a multi-path connection or highway, i.e. one 'path' per bit. Used only within the confines of the computer system and to connect local peripherals, such as disc drives and printers.

Pascal

A high level language, named after Blaise Pascal, who built a calculating machine in 1642. Pascal is one of the many languages derived from ALGOL, and it emphasises the structured approach to programming.

Pipeline

A temporary storage area in which 'pre-fetched' instructions are held until required for execution by the processor. The 'pipelining' of instructions saves processor time by reducing the need for the processor to wait for instructions to be fetched from main memory. Obviously the greatest saving is achieved during the execution of a sequence of instructions; once a jump instruction is encountered, the pipeline has to be flushed and refilled, starting with the instruction at the jump destination.

Pixel

Picture element; the smallest addressable element of a display.

Portability

When used in the context of software, portability describes the capability of a programme developed in one environment to run in a different environment. Portability can apply at a number of different levels; if two machines are compatible at the instruction set and address structure level, it may be possible to transfer object code between them, but this will be unusual. It is more usual to be able to 'port' software at the source code level, i.e. as high level language instructions which can be compiled into the object code of the 'target' machine. Difficulties with software portability frequently arise from the use by the source machine of non-standard features of the high level language, which are not supported by the target machine.

Prolog

Programming in logic; a non-procedural computer language, designed for expert systems/IKBS applications. The basic elements of the language express logical relationships between entities, and it has a built-in inference mechanism.

Prototyping

A form of system development where an early form of the system, lacking many of the features of the final product, is used to confirm and refine the requirement. For example, in a battlefield system, the prototype may be software which performs the main functions of the final system, but running on commercial hardware.

Radiation security (TEMPEST)

The prevention of unintended radiation of information-bearing electromagnetic emanations beyond the confines of an equipment or installation.

Radio frequency interference (RFI)

The generation of electromagnetic radiations within the passband of radio receiving equipment. RFI can be caused by computers and other digital processing equipment through the handling of electrical pulses with high repetition rates and fast rise times, and also by rotating electrical machinery.

Radio relay

Point-to-point multi-channel radio communications system, using relays (or repeaters) to extend the range of links or to overcome difficult terrain. Military, tactical radio relay systems tend to have relatively low channel capacities (typically 16–32 speech channels or their equivalent), and use frequencies in the VHF and the UHF band for the main longer distance links, and in the SHF band for local distribution. Link lengths are highly dependent upon the nature of the terrain, especially at the ends of the links, but in 'typical' north-west European terrain average link lengths around 25–30 Km are achieved.

Random access memory (RAM)

Literally, memory in which any address can be accessed at random with equal speed (as opposed to a memory where the time to access an address depends on its physical location). In practice the term is used to distinguish read/write computer main memory from read only memory (ROM).

Real time system

A computer system which carries out processing in response to stimuli from the 'outside world' in accordance with time constraints imposed by the outside stimuli. The term can be applied to multi-user, general purpose systems, which must respond to the demands of users in what the users consider to be an acceptable time, just as well as to missile-control systems which must respond to the input from sensors in time to intercept their targets.

Reduced instruction set computer (RISC)

A processor whose instruction set has been reduced to the bare minimum, in the interests of attaining maximum processing speed.

Relational database

A database in which the relationships between entities are expressed in the same form as the entities themselves, that is, in the form of tables or 'flat files'.

Ruggedised hardware

The term 'ruggedisation' is normally used to imply that the hardware has been built (or modified) to a higher physical specification than the normal commercial level, but falling short of the full military specification (MILSPEC).

Scheduler

That element of an operating system responsible for allocating processor time to software modules or processes, according to the rules prescribed by its scheduling algorithm.

Secondary storage

Term sometimes used synonymously with mass storage, or auxiliary storage.

Seek Time

In a magnetic disc drive the seek time is the time taken for the reading/writing head to be placed over the right track on the disc. It is one component of the overall access time for such a device, the other major component being the latency or rotational delay to position the wanted sector under the head(s).

Semiconductor memory

Computer memory built from semiconductor components, normally fabricated *en masse* as integrated circuits. *See* also RAM, DRAM and SRAM.

Sequence control register

That element of a processor responsible for monitoring the step-by-step execution of a program; also known as the program counter.

Serial transmission

The transmission of data down a channel one bit after another.

Sleepers

A term used in computer security to describe sections of code which are dormant, i.e. have no effect during the execution of a program until activated either through the passage of time or by some external stimulus.

Software engineering
A disciplined, structured approach to the design, implementation, testing and support of software-based systems.

Source code
Programs, written in a high level language, to be converted through the process of compilation into object code.

Speech output
The direct synthesis of human speech by the computer as a form of data output.

Static RAM
Semiconductor random access memory in which the storage element is a two-transistor switch circuit known as a bistable, or flip-flop.

Steerable null antenna
A radio antenna whose radiation (and hence receive sensitivity) pattern can be dynamically altered in order to reduce its sensitivity in the direction of an unwanted signal, such as a jammer.

Store-and-forward
see Message switching

Structured query language (SQL)
A standard form of query language for the manipulation of information stored in relational databases.

Synchronous transmission
A form of data transmission in which the timing of the individual data elements is governed by a clock.

Syntax
The rules of grammar of a programming language.

System dynamics
A system modelling technique which takes a cybernetic approach to the behaviour of systems.

System high
In computer security terminology, 'system high' means that the security classification of a system, which determines the degree of protection afforded, is that of the highest classification of information held by the system. The term is normally used in conjunction with an actual classification level, e.g. 'System high secret'.

TEMPEST
see Radiation security.

Token ring
A form of local area network access control protocol, where a special control data packet known as the token is passed from station to station. Only the station holding the token is permitted to initiate a transmission.

Transparency
In its general sense, the term is used to describe the situation in which a computer system can perform tasks for a user, without that user's being aware of the complex mechanisms involved in the performance of the tasks, which we describe as being 'transparent' to the user. It has a more specific meaning in the data communications field. A communications channel is said to be 'transparent' if its users can pass any arbitrary pattern of bits over the channel. A channel which is not transparent will recognise certain patterns of bits as control signals which may cause the channel to change its state in an unpredictable way, e.g. it may close itself down in the middle of a transmission.

Transputer
Derived from TRANSistor-comPUTER, this is the trademark of a family of devices manufactured by the Inmos company. A transputer is a computer on a single integrated microcircuit, consisting of processor, some high-speed main memory, and four high-speed input/output channels which can be connected directly to other transputers. The I/O channels make possible the construction of arrays of transputers, which is probably the greatest strength of the device. The computer language Occam was developed specifically for the transputer, and contains features designed to exploit the multi-processor, distributed capabilities of the device.

Trojan horse
This is a computer security term used to describe a piece of software which is imported into a system for a legitimate, innocent purpose and which contains features aimed at weakening the security protection of the system.

UNIX

A multi-user operating system, developed originally by Bell Laboratories in the USA, which is rapidly becoming the nearest thing in the computer industry to a 'standard' operating system, available on a wide range of different machines from microcomputers to large mainframe installations. Many different 'strains' of UNIX exist, but there is now a considerable weight of effort behind the definition of a widely accepted standard version. UNIX is a trademark of the AT&T corporation.

Virtual circuit

In some packet switched networks, the protocol used gives the subscribing data terminals/host computers the impression that an actual circuit exists between them, whereas data are transferred between them by means of packet switching. This apparent connection is termed a virtual circuit.

Virtual machine

The simulation in software of the features of a particular type of computer, allowing object code for that type of machine to be run on it.

Virtual memory

The use of mass storage to extend the apparent size of main memory. Calls to virtual addresses, i.e. those beyond the physical size of the main memory, will cause segments, or 'pages' of memory to be called in from disc.

Virtual terminal

The simulation of the characteristics of a given terminal type when accessing a computer system remotely over a network.

Virus

Popular term for a destructive piece of software which may be 'caught' by a system when 'infected' software is loaded. Most of the known 'strains' of virus lie dormant for a time, after which they attempt to destroy the file store of their host computer, for example, by erasing or corrupting the tables which control access to files on the disc, rendering them inaccessible. Viruses may also attach themselves to other discs which are used on the system and can thus spread from system to system rapidly. Some viruses have been discovered to be the work of mischievous programmers, whilst others have been created with deliberate, malicious intent.

Winchester disc

A hard disc unit normally with fixed, i.e. not exchangeable, discs. There is some confusion over the origin of the term, but perhaps the most plausible explanation is that this type of disc unit was first produced by the IBM company under the product number 3030—the calibre of the Winchester '73 repeating rifle.

Window

In computer display terminology, an area of screen devoted to some particular activity or application. By implication, a window-based system will allow several such areas to exist on the screen simultaneously, often with sophisticated management techniques for changing the size and position of each window, and its mode of display relative to other windows which may be 'open' at the same time.

WORM memory

Write once, read many memory, normally used for archiving purposes. Information is recorded by burning tiny pits in the surface of the recording medium with a laser beam. The pits are also read by laser scanning, but their production is irreversible, thus the data cannot be removed except by the destruction of the recording medium.

Index